AN INKLING, A BACKPACK AND ALL THE TIME IN THE WORLD....

TRAVELING ON A WHIM

Tamara K. Bryant

Published by MetaStudies Institute
Wildomar, CA 2020

Cover art by Ashley Gallagher

To my dear friend Daniella Griffay. All it took was one backpacking trip and I was hooked. Thank you! :)

UNCLE Desi, Aunt Vivian, Dad, Mom, Dex, your love and encouragement helped create this book, read at your own risk.

Escapade 1:

Take the Plunge

After a great stay in Thailand, my friends, Casey, Valerie, and I were faced with the sad reality that we only had two more days left before the fun ended and we had to board a plane for home.

It was too soon. I'd only tasted a teeny bit of Southeast Asia. I didn't want to leave yet and go back to my "real" life. But I knew I *had* to go home. My flight was booked. I had a job and family to go back to. I couldn't just stay. Or, could I? I thought, *What if I didn't go home yet? What if I explored Asia for a while?* Although I wasn't ready to leave this amazing place—not yet anyway, the thought of traveling alone without my friends, terrified me. On the other hand, would I ever get another chance to really experience Southeast Asia? Excited and scared battled it out in my brain.

My head spun for hours—I couldn't make up my mind whether to play it safe and go back with Casey and Valerie or be brave and stay for what could be the adventure of my life. *Agh!*

1

I *wanted* to remain in Asia longer, but was it something I should do? Would fear get the best of me? Could I, in good conscience let my job and responsibilities hold me back? What's a girl to do?

To help me decide, I ran down a list of the serious responsibilities I had back home. It didn't help. I went back and forth until my head hurt. In the end, my adventure self won. What a relief!

It's now or never, I thought as I emailed my boss and asked if she was okay with me staying abroad for another few weeks.

I asked Casey to stay, too. Having her with me would be the best time ever, but she'd just started a new job and didn't feel comfortable asking for more time off. I almost convinced Valerie, but she had "stuff" to do at home and decided to fly back to Los Angeles, (LA) as planned.

Ach! Responsible. Oh, well, I thought, we're all flying to Bangkok first. Maybe they'll change their minds.

When we arrived at the Bangkok airport, I connected to the Wi-Fi and silently shouted, "Yay!" My boss had emailed that she was super cool with my staying abroad for a few more weeks" and reminded me to take lots of pictures. "Yes!"

Val and Casey gave me a "look" and smiled. They knew, now, that I would not be going to LA with them.

At least we all had one more night in Bangkok before the girls took off for home. I was so excited about not having to return to Los Angeles, I immediately postponed my flight for three weeks and emailed my parents to let them know I'd be staying longer. Knowing they'd be worried, I assured them that everything was fine, and I just needed to do a little more exploring before having to come back to reality. I also told them Casey and Valerie *were* coming home as planned, so I'd be flying solo.

I wasn't sure how my parents would feel about that, but it didn't matter. My mind was made up.

Sitting in my Bangkok hotel room, I asked myself, *So, what now?* I needed to think. And think I did. I racked my brain trying to choose where to go next. I looked up flights to several neighboring countries but couldn't decide.

Thinking back, my indecision could have been because I was still a little on the fence about staying. I thought I knew what I wanted, but I guess there was still a little voice saying, "Go home." I needed to make up my mind.

I detest Bangkok. Staying there another night was not something I would do if I didn't have to. It's full of scammers. No matter how prepared I am, the con artists always seemed to be ten steps ahead of me. They always managed to rip me off. *Ugh!* It's the worst! I needed to choose where to go next. I was sure that having a destination would make it real enough for me to let go of any doubt.

I sat on my bed, absentmindedly scanning the contents of my backpack and pondering where to start my new adventure. Too many choices. I closed my eyes and blindly flipped through the pages of my travel book until it felt right to stop on a random page. When I opened my eyes, I found the answer. Ah! I'm *not* going home.

Hazard 2:

Lose My Safety Blanket and Find my Inner Wonder Woman

Just before sunrise, and only a few hours after I'd finally settled on a destination. I stood by the bed, packing my *ginormous* backpack. Lifting it, I swore it was heavier than before, even though I'd left out some things, hoping the girls would take them back for me.

I could hardly wait for Casey and Valerie to wake up so I could tell them that I was staying and would be exploring Southeast Asia on my own.

As soon as they woke up, I told them. They were thrilled and said how much they wanted to stay, too, and go on the adventure with me. But, of course, that wasn't possible for them. I thought about how lucky I was to have such supportive and loving friends.

It was weird, talking about them going home and me remaining in a strange land, all by myself. It's not that I hadn't traveled before. I had been to Thailand, but never completely on my own. I think a part of them wanted to do the same—venture out solo—but they are level-headed ladies and their obligations meant more to them than adventure. What they didn't know was how unsure I still was about my decision.

In the end, we all hugged goodbye and I was left alone, wondering if I'd made the best...or the worst...move of my life. Too late. The deed was done, and I was about to head to the airport for my first stop. Adrenaline pumping, I called for a taxi and headed to the lobby.

When I stepped through the hotel doors, the cab was already there and waiting for me. *Wow. That's service.* But then it hit me. *I'm going to be traveling in this strange country—by myself!* My nerves ratcheted to sonic level and I nearly panicked. *What am I doing? I have lost my mind. Can I change my plans back and go home? Should I?* I took a breath to calm down. Both excited and scared, I thought, *Should I run back home because I'm too wimpy to face the unknown? Or, should I put on my big-girl pants and get in that taxi?!* I set my resolve. *Do this, girl! Go for it!* Crazy? Maybe, but I lifted my chin, straightened my back and bravely climbed into the cab.

At the airport, bags in hand, I felt lost. I had no idea where to go and frantically searched for the correct check-in desk. *Where is it? Where is it? I don't see it anywhere!* As I prowled the corridors, passing plastic palm trees, ornate display-pagodas, and more, my backpack seemed to grow heavier by the minute. I vowed to get rid of more things later.

What a nightmare. Perhaps I'd wake up and find I'd been sleeping on the plane home, snoring and drooling. *No such luck. I mentally slapped myself. Stop it. You'll be fine. Just ask someone.*

Okay, nightmare burst, confidence returned. I looked around for someone to ask, but everyone seemed to be in such a hurry. After what seemed like hours, but was probably just a few minutes, I found a kind soul who directed me to the correct desk.

One hurdle down. Everything was going to be perfect from that moment on. But even as I thought that, a nagging feeling tugged at me. *I'm forgetting something. But what?* I thought over my plans and mentally retraced my morning but came up blank. Still, I couldn't shake a nagging feeling that there was something I'd forgotten. Could it be that I'd left my security blanket at the hotel—my friends from home, my *something* familiar? I was alone and a stranger in a strange world like Alice down the rabbit-hole. I pushed the feeling aside and focused on getting checked in and on the airplane.

HAZARD 3:

FORGETTING SOMETHING AND DOGGY DASTARDLY DEEDS

Relieved when I finally reached the *right* check-in counter, I gave the uniformed attendant a bright smile.

She smiled back in a professional way and ran through standard questions and instructions with practiced efficiency. "Passport?" she asked. "How many bags?" She glanced from me to my bulging backpack then back to me. "Please place your bag on the scale." Examining my passport, she asked, "Do you have a return flight booked?"

Uh-oh. I must have looked like a deer-in-the-headlights as I stared, dumbfounded. I didn't know a prearranged flight out was needed. Would she refuse to let me on the plane? "Uh. N-no but," I thought quickly, "I have a flight to the United States that leaves in three weeks." I practically shoved my proof in her face, hoping it would be enough.

Fortunately, it was, and I almost melted with relief.

She handed me my passport and boarding pass then tagged my checked bag. "Have a nice flight." She gave me a bright-eyed smile and directed me towards immigration.

After a no-drama flight, I landed at the Denpasar Airport in Bali close to midnight. Standing at baggage claim, a dreadful fact dawned on me that I'd forgotten to book a room and now had no place to stay. I hadn't thought this whole thing through enough. *Well, I can't sleep in the airport. There must be some other solution.* I'm generally positive and resourceful, so I glanced around for a likely person to help me. *Someone here speaks English and has a hotel, or something, booked. I'll just find out where they're staying. It'll be fine.*

After glancing around, I saw a likely candidate—an approachable-looking guy with blond dreadlocks, probably waiting for his surfboard—I figured *he* had somewhere to sleep tonight.

We chatted a few minutes before I confessed that I hadn't made a reservation anywhere and asked him where *he* was staying. He smiled in a way that told me he liked that I'd just shown up without a plan. Suddenly I felt better about my spur-of-the-moment decision to explore. Sometimes you just have to go with the flow, and I did.

We shared a cab to his hotel. When we arrived, I crossed my fingers that they'd have a room available. Lucky for me, there was one, but it cost a whopping 550,000 Indonesian Rupiah ($40 US) for the night. Pretty expensive for Southeast Asia and *way* out of my budget. But what choice did I have? It was there or the street, so I booked the night.

After thanking Surfer Dude for his recommendation, and for splitting the cab with me, I headed for my room. Inside, I hoisted my backpack on the bed and connected to Wi-Fi and searched for a more affordable place to stay.

Noticing a message from my parents, I stared at it a while, thinking, *Uh-oh. I'm sure Mom freaked out about my traveling alone, sometimes she still thinks I'm twelve years old.* I sucked in a breath and clicked it open. *Uh-huh.* She'd freaked, all right. I'm sure, she would have sent in the navy seals if she could.

The list of freakdom read:

> "Are you okay? Call us immediately!
> We want to hear your voice. Why did your
> friends leave? Why did you stay? When
> are you coming back? What about your
> job? Are you sure you're okay? Where are
> you now? Do you have enough money?
> Do you need help? Do we need to come
> out there?"

"Holy...." I felt bad that she was so worried, but on the other hand, isn't that what moms do? I reminded myself that her reaction was just a sign of how much she cares. Still, I thought of a lot of snarky answers I could have used but didn't. She was upset enough. My sarcasm wouldn't make things any better, so I answered all her questions straight and honestly then told her I'd call in a few days.

Dad was another story, though. I only wished I could have seen the look on his face when he got the news of my extended travel. I'm sure he had a smile as big as the moon. It seems I take after him more than Mom.

When I groaned awake the next morning, I discovered that I'd fallen asleep on my phone. I looked in a mirror and saw a big, red imprint on my face that stood out like a neon sign. *I must have been exhausted.* Rubbing my cheek, I just hoped the marks would go away before I headed outside.

Sitting up in bed, I searched the net and found a highly rated hostel/bungalow on *hostelworld.com*. I booked an affordable private room for 179,000 IDR a night ($13 US).

Later in my travels, I would realize that private rooms aren't the best way to meet people. Staying in the dorms or places that have a good common area is so much better. But, at that point, I was clueless.

Feeling good that I had solved my accommodation problem, I jumped out of bed, ready to get my first real glimpse of Bali. In the backseat of the cab the night before, most of the scenery had swished by in a blur, plus I was with Surfer Dude, so I couldn't just stare out the window. At the hotel, I was too tired to roam around and check it out. So, this was my chance.

Before leaving my room, I took a good look out of the hotel window and was struck by how beautiful the grounds looked. I was in the middle of a rainforest! No wonder the room cost so much.

I dressed and headed down to the restaurant for a good breakfast then checked out and hired a taxi to take me to my new home away from home.

The driver loaded my backpack into the trunk, and we were off. I stared out the window, taking in the scenery like a puppy on his first car trip. There were thick trees and rutted streets, ornate old temples shoulder-to-shoulder with sleek modern buildings, motorbikes, piles of trash, people walking around, and dogs— lots of dogs roaming freely through the streets. *Fantastic!* I loved it all, except for the presence of so many dogs. I didn't know it yet, but later I would have a not-so-pleasant encounter with a couple of canines.

At the Warung Coco Hostel, I checked in and was pleasantly surprised that my room was ready. Before heading to it, I glanced at some of the tours the hostel offered. A few looked interesting and I vowed to get more information later. My "room" turned out to be a little bungalow with a poolside view. *Wow! You won't get that in the US for $13.*

After settling in, I glanced at my phone. *Damn. Almost out of juice.* I searched for the charger and adapter but couldn't find them. With a sinking feeling, I thought, *That's the nagging sense I had about forgetting something.* So, my plans for the day had to change. I asked the hostel to call the same taxi driver who'd driven me there. I needed to go back to the hotel and retrieve my charger and adapter. I'd asked for *that* driver because I knew it would be the same price as before, and he knew exactly where to go. The hostel staff were as nice as could be and said they'd be happy to arrange it.

I was super annoyed with myself. It was my first day of traveling solo and I'd already messed up, costing me money I hadn't counted on spending in that way. But I never hold onto bad feelings for long and just shrugged it off, reassuring myself that I'd get the hang of things soon—at least I hoped I would.

When I returned to Warung Coco, charger and adapter in hand, I plugged in then slipped on my swimsuit to hang out by the pool. *Su-weet!*

Lots of others were also swimming. As I looked around, it dawned on me that hanging in a common area would be a great place to meet people. Like, Duh! It was. Gold star for me. I hung up my rookie badge. I had this!

I soon made new friends. I met Landin, Beverly, Cheryl, Swizz Nix, Bruce, and Alwin while lying under an umbrella scanning through my *Lonely Planet Guide to Southeast Asia.*

Landin and Cheryl, from Chicago, instantly became my friends. I loved Landin's remarkable laugh. I'll never forget it. Beverly, from the UK, was awesome. She loves practicing her American accent and even convinced another traveler that she was from the US! Swizz and Bruce, from Philadelphia, are hilarious. Swizz Nix is a rapper.

His YouTube video is hysterical "....So much paper I need a stapler...." Bruce is a musician with his own band. He also owned a gardening company—pretty much an all-around badass. Bruce was heading home because he had a show, and Swizz's next stop was the Philippines.

While poolside we all chatted as if we'd known each other for years. While we were talking, a German guy came over and introduced himself with, "Hi. I'm Alwin." We hit it off immediately and decided that we should be travel buddies.

Later that day, I threw on some shorts and a tank top and headed out with Alwin to explore Kuta. This was once a fishing village but now it's a magnet for surfers, sunbathers, and party animals. We also found a place that would take us on a trek up Mount Batur—a famous active volcano. *Maybe I shouldn't tell Mom about this one.*

We made the arrangements for the trek then had some lunch. It turned out that Alwin was obsessed with pizza so, of course, we ate at a pizza place. Pizza in Bali? Odd. Not what I'd thought my first official Indonesian meal would be. But, then, pizza is available in every country in the world, so is it really Italian? Well, of course it is, I mean, Italians invented it in the late 10th century. From there it spread to most of the rest of the world, each country putting their unique stamp on it.

After lunch we wandered around town and stumbled on a temple that was open to tourists. I had to laugh, though when I read the sign at the entrance: THOSE WHO MENSTRUATE SHALL NOT ENTER. Hah! Luckily, I wasn't on my period at the time. It seems the locals believe that the blood attracts bad spirits, or some crazy thing. To an American woman, it seemed medieval. If I had been on my period, I would have respected their rules and heeded the warning. *Don't want to take any chances!*

After wandering the town for most of the day, Alwin and I started back to the hostel. On the way, the air grew thick with the promise of rain. Just as we set foot inside, a torrential downpour fell out of the sky like an overturned bucket.

We sat on the covered patio watching raindrops splash in the pool and listened to thunder pound the sky. It was *great*, but I was glad the storm only raged for about fifteen minutes before the skies cleared, the sun shone bright, and the blanket of hot moisture filled the air again. Ever-present, stifling humidity in this amazing country is a small price to pay for the chance to experience its beauty and wonders.

That evening, Swizz and Bruce took Alwin and me to a hole-in-the-wall place for dinner, promising a tasty treat we'd never forget. It sounded good until I found that to get there, we had to walk through back alleys and corridors heavy with the nasty street-funk smell. Fortunately, I learned a while back to carry Tiger Balm. I put some under my nose to mask the smell. It worked—sort of.

When the guys finally found the "restaurant," it turned out to be a food cart in an actual hole in an actual wall. I thought about not eating after looking around and noticing how sanitary-challenged the place was.

A few kid-size tables were arranged around the cart. I thought it odd at the time but later discovered that this is common, and the teeny furniture is intended for adults.

I didn't know whether to laugh at the whole scene or just risk it and have a good time in spite of the way it looked. Swizz and Bruce said they'd eaten there before, and that it was great. "Better than it looks," they told me.

After a moment of skepticism, I was convinced enough to order. Amazing! The chicken and steak skewers were unbelievable—so good, we ordered more. Sometimes you can't go by looks.

Well as the old saying goes, "All good things must end." That was true for our trip back to the hostel. As we laughed and chatted, I felt good until we came to a gate that held back a small, mutt of a dog frantically barking at us.

We passed by but for some reason that I don't remember now, I turned around. The dog was *not* behind the gate anymore. It was charging at us. Worst gate ever!

Swizz, who walked with a slight limp, decided to be

"manly" and announced, "Fuck this dog, man. He doesn't like how I walk."

The risk of exposure to rabies in Indonesia is high and, in some places, getting to a hospital that has a vaccine is nearly impossible. I absolutely did *not want that dog to bite us.*

Someone shouted, "Run!" We dashed ahead like Olympic track runners. The dog stayed on our heels for a while, but when we turned onto a dimly lit, uneven alley, the mutt finally lost interest and turned back. No doubt, he went looking for easier prey.

I was so happy to see the doors of Coco, I almost kissed them. Although we laughed about it afterward, I still carry the memory of that chase. It creeps me out like a Steven King novel. But the good memories of how much fun it was when the four of us ran away from such a tiny dog are just as strong. Sometimes I even laugh aloud at what that must have looked like.

Escapade 4:

Trek up a Volcano and
a Thieving Monkey Attack

At 1 a.m. the next morning, Alwin and I embarked on our guided five-hour, sunrise trek up Mount Batur volcano. Before tackling the mountain, though, our first stop was a coffee farm where we sipped some amazing freshly brewed coffee, toured the farm, and listened to a presentation about how the beans are grown.

After the tour, we hung around a little while to wait for one of our other hiking companions—Chelsey, from Ireland. As soon as she arrived, we all grabbed our headlamps and flashlights and started walking to the trailhead with our guide.

Even in the pitch-dark, predawn morning, Bali's humidity makes Florida seem like an amateur. But that didn't stop us, we eagerly climbed the steep trail.

A few minutes later, hot and sweaty, I questioned why I was putting myself through this torture. I knew why, though. *To have a once-in-a lifetime experience. That's why.* As I glanced around at the others, I wondered if everyone else was also questioning whether the volcano was worth this torture. By the expressions on their sweat-soaked faces, I think they were.

Just when I'd pumped myself into being semi-okay with the steep, difficult climb in a steam bath, it got worse. With no warning, gale-like winds and buckets of heavy rain drenched us. Okay; not really a *gale* and *buckets*, but that's what it felt like.

So, we went from hot and sweaty to freezing cold and wet. Luckily, Chelsey and I were prepared. We'd brought light jackets. Poor Alwin, though, only had the shorts and T-shirt he was wearing. Hey! Who knew the weather could change that snap-quick?

After a while, the rain and wind stopped, and we pushed onward and upward. We climbed, and climbed, and climbed until we *finally* reached the top. I've never felt more out of shape, but on the bright side—what a great workout.

What was our reward for the grueling, sweaty trip, a downpour, and blasts of wind that had us chattering our teeth in the cold? *No* spectacular sunrise! Only clouds, darkness, and freezing temperatures. I grumbled to myself, *This is one of the most popular tourist destinations? Hah!* Well, at least we had the satisfaction of making it to the summit. And, I was happy to see the little snack shack with benches. We all sat down and enjoyed coffee and eggs.

As we stared into the gray clouds, I thought, *Not the sunrise I expected from the brochures, but still beautiful.*

On the trek to the crater-rim below, our descent turned into a circus. The way was through soft, slippery black sand. In some places the path was so steep, we had to slide down on our butts— not fun and sometimes painful.

Alwin had tucked his arms into his T-shirt to keep warm, so his balance wasn't the best and he slipped, tearing a massive hole in his shorts—as if he wasn't cold enough, now his clothes were air-conditioned. Cold and ragged, he pushed on with a good attitude about the whole adventure.

As the sun rose and the light increased, we had our first glimpse of the magnificent patterns left by past lava flows. The trek suddenly became well worth the effort. It was near-breathtakingly beautiful. All I could see for miles around was curvy black and red earth. It felt like I'd landed on Mars.

Weary, scratched, bruised, and worn, we rested at the rim. Ah, peace—for a few seconds. Then came the monkeys. Sensing tourists, they poured out of the crater. The guide told us that they lived *in* the crater because the escaping gases kept them warm but roamed around the rim area during the day. The guide also claimed the tourists loved it.

Huh. I was *not* amused. I'm not a fan of monkeys. They're scary and mean. They prey on tourists by following them around and stealing their stuff. One snatched Alwin's backpack and started dragging it into the crater. He chased the thieving monkey and managed to grab a hold of one end of the bag. The monkey stubbornly held on. After a short tug of war, it let go and ran off screeching what were probably monkey obscenities.

On our way back, the guide took us on a shortcut through a tiny village. Charming children waved at us as we walked by. Monkeys could learn a lot from these kids.

The landscape there was so different from where we had been on the volcano—abundant green farmland instead of a rocky steep slope with black sand.

The villagers had taken full advantage of the fertile volcanic soil. There were small lush farms everywhere. I loved being in the villages—peaceful, and everyone there seemed so happy.

In hindsight, I should have done this trek from Ubud instead of Bali, though, since we were practically knocking on Ubud's door from Mount Batur—but live and learn.

We arrived back at the hostel at 10 a.m. and were so exhausted, we slept until dinner time.

Hazard 5:

Pushed Off a Bike and Robbed

The night after our hole-in-the-wall-dog-chase adventure, I met up with Sonja and Pam from Germany, and Landin, Cheryl, and Simon from Canada for the five-level, Sky Garden Buffet— an all-you-can-eat-all-you-can drink bar/club where drinks are free until midnight.

The Sky Garden Buffet has separate rooms that each play a different genre of music. We hopped from one to the other to hear it all. My favorite was '90s pop music. I love almost everything '90s.

I was having a blast. Usually on those booze-infested nights, I outlasted most everyone else. Once I start, I can dance for hours. So, as I expected, some of our group went home before I was ready to leave. I didn't mind. Simon hung in there with me and we danced the night away.

I thought of my friend from home, Casey and how we would dance until closing time at our local pub, Gallaghers. I wished she could have been with me at Sky Garden. She's the dance master. I then thought about my best friend, Coco. When she and I were little, we danced in her living room to R&B videos, making up our own choreography. I laughed about how her older brother would ask, with a sarcastic undertone, how many more times we were going to watch the same music video and hinted about us making our own.

When Simon and I were finally partied out, we headed back to the hostel. Inside, we found Sonja and Pam in tears. What a way to get kicked right off cloud nine. Suddenly my low turned to concern. "What happened?" I asked.

Pam told me she'd taken a motorbike taxi back to the hostel, but the driver turned out to be running a scam from a fake taxi. He had driven her down a dark alley, and when another bike crossed their path, the other driver snatched her purse. Her driver then pushed her into the street while they were still moving.

I was angry at what happened and relieved she wasn't physically hurt. Sonja also had a scare. She'd walked back to the hostel alone. On the way, someone robbed her of her passport.

The girls were traumatized, so I didn't voice my question about why they hadn't come back together. "Well," I said, "the police should know about this."

Wide-eyed, they stared at me as if that hadn't occurred to them. I stared back, "Well?"

After a little eye-dabbing and clean-up, they agreed. We called a cab.

When we were all settled in the taxi and headed to the "tourist" police station, I looked forward to getting justice for the crimes committed. Foolish me. Inside the station, we soon found that justice was a joke. The police couldn't have cared less. I mean, the motto on the side of their vehicles was *not* "To serve and protect."

I don't like to generalize about the nature of other cultures, but after this I realized that the meme of Indonesia having a corrupt legal system is at least partially true. They didn't even try to hide it. The police officer interviewing us practically laughed in our faces when the girls told their stories. I considered the possibility that he was even in on it.

Advice: Don't get robbed in Bali, the police will act like it's your fault and do nothing about it.

I've always believed in the "silver lining" philosophy and this travesty also had a positive upside. It turned out that Sonja had to wait for her new passport to arrive. That meant she could stay an extra week in Bali, and Pam could go home on her originally scheduled flight—even though she was phoneless and moneyless. I was glad that at least she wasn't stranded abroad indefinitely, like in some Brokedown Palace minus the drug trafficking.

The next morning, after partying and our infuriating encounter with the corrupt police system the night before, we were all so hungover and wrung out, we just lounged around the pool, contemplating that dark spot in our pristine paradise.

For me, Pam and Sonja's scrape with the underbelly of Bali was a great reminder of how desperate people can be, and how some will stop at nothing to get what they want or need in order to survive. I really felt bad for the girls and thought of how much worse it could have been. They were lucky.

My deep musings were interrupted when two energetic guys in the pool—Russel and Chapman from London—asked me why we all looked so dead today. I told them about last night's activities. They were sympathetic, and we talked a while about crime, police, and attitudes.

Russel turned out to be one of my favorite people. He always had a smile on his face, and I fell in love with his English accent. He's just one of those people everyone adores.

For the rest of the day, I just lounged around thinking about how I was ready to move on and leave Kuta behind. But where to go? I pondered the odd mixture of heaven and hell that was Kuta. On one hand, it has great beaches, I met awesome people, and ate amazing food. On the other hand, what happened to Pam and Sonja, and my experience with the police put a smear on my rose-colored glasses. Most people, I discovered, don't spend much time in Kuta. I understood why.

Late in the day, the crew and I eventually ramped up enough energy to go for dinner, so we headed over to the Sky Garden for their 68,740 IDR ($5 US) buffet. Russel and Chapman joined us. It was good, but none of us were yet firing on all pistons, so most of the group called it an early night.

The next day Alwin and I took the bus to Ubud, about forty miles away. In Asia, the buses rarely go anywhere until they're over-filled, and they make unplanned "business" stops. So, it does no good to be in a rush. In Asia, it's wise to adopt an "I'll get there when I get there" attitude.

During our ride, we met Blair. Since Alwin and I both like experiencing unfamiliar places, we asked her where she was staying. She suggested the In da Lodge hostel. We decided to try it.

When Alwin and I arrived, we checked it out. It looked perfect—a reggae vibe, but in a tropical rainforest. The buildings are nestled among beautiful green trees. Tropical plants—and insects—are everywhere. The common area is outside, under a large canopy with plenty of built-in daybeds for lounging, free Wi-Fi, and outlets for charging devices. The bar restaurant is a stone's throw from reception, so we could order food and drinks without leaving the hostel.

The hostel was completely booked except for a two-story family house that included a private patio, bathroom, and kitchen. They offered it to us for one night at the same price as a dorm bed. The next night they could move us into the dorm. I felt like a high roller. The family house was normally expensive—68,740 IDR ($5 US) per night.

After settling in, we met with Blair and walked a short distance to the Monkey Forest. Not my choice. As I mentioned before, monkeys scare me. The idea of a forest full of them was an unpleasant thought. At the same time, I didn't want to miss any fun, either. So, I steeled myself and went with them. Visions of the Wizard of Oz flying monkeys filled my mind.

As I expected, the monkeys were aggressive and annoying. I considered turning around and leaving but didn't want to seem like a wuss, so I kept my mouth shut and my eyes open for their mischief. When we first walked in, a monkey jumped on a little girl's head and bit her on the arm. Next, a guy holding a bundle of bananas was besieged by three of the beasts. It scared him so much, he threw the bundle of fruit into the air and ran out. I admit that I found it comical to watch the demon monkeys do their thing.

The forest housing the mischief-makers, is beautiful, loaded with trees, fishponds, and a temple. I had to laugh, again, when I read the sign No MENSTRUATING WOMEN ALLOWED. Well, at least they warned us about it. Not an issue for me at that time.

I loved the labyrinth of treehouses connected by rope bridges. It had a beautiful view of Ubud. The best part though, was that there were no monkeys around. I guess they were all too busy at ground level torturing visitors.

I remembered that our hostel matron had warned us not to bring food, water, or bags inside the forest because of the monkeys' "curiosity."

As we continued exploring the forest, three monkeys greeted us. Blair and Alwin were excited to pet them. I thought, *no way am I getting that close to a monkey.* I hid behind Alwin. True to their nature, they were just being friendly while they sized us up. At some unseen signal they tried to nab Blair's purse and water bottle. She let them have the water but wasn't giving up her purse. Well, the demons weren't going to let her win. One of them jumped on her head and began screeching and chattering in monkey-speak while yanking her hair. He wanted that bag.

Fortunately, monkeys have short attention spans and as soon as the one on Blair's head saw another monkey unscrew the water bottle cap and empty its contents on the ground, Blair's tormenter hopped off and joined the water fun. Oddly, though, after pouring out the water, they put the bottle cap back on—a lot smarter than they look.

While the monkeys were preoccupied with the bottle, we snuck off.

I thought about a trip to Belize I'd taken some time before that also involved monkeys and a nature park. The creatures roughed me up, each taking turns poking me. Then, they snatched my ice cream and smeared it all over my hair and face. And when they were done, they laughed at me. I was scared to death and shaking all over, completely freaked out and terrified they would bite me. Yeah. I don't like monkeys.

Escapade 6:

A Boulder Sandwich with
Me in the Middle

Alwin and I were off to the Ayung River for our first whitewater rafting trip. We'd never been before and were so excited! Our guides picked us up from the hostel and drove us to the site where we enjoyed pastries and coffee for breakfast before heading to the path through a deep, lush rainforest.

Our group of eight hiked through the forest, carrying our paddles, for an hour to the river's edge. It was a steep descent, and I tried not to think of how painful the trip back up would be.

This forest is a textbook definition of what a tropical rainforest looks like—covered in beautiful large-canopied green trees, exotic plants, and alien-like insects. It reminded me of the forest in the movie *Fern Gully,* minus the fairies, unless you count dragonflies. They sort of look like fairies.

By the time we reached the river, everything was wet. The air was so humid it could almost be cut with a knife. We climbed aboard. When we were all settled, our guide pushed the raft into the water, and off we went.

This was both awesome and super scary, especially the massive rocks bordering the chutes and steep drops. It felt like we were going to smash into the boulders as we rafted through.

This experience was so surreal, I had to close my eyes a few times. The whitewater was filled with a lot of slopes and curves, twists and turns. One minute we would be rafting clean through, the next minute it seemed like we were on a collision course into the massive rocks then without warning we would be plunging down a steep slope.

Once, I was totally thrilled and freaked out at the same time when we'd been moving fast through smooth water and a massive boulder seemed to suddenly block our way. My heart was in my mouth. We were seconds away from smashing into it. I screamed and so did everyone else. We were so loud, I barely heard our guide telling us to stay calm.

Calm? Hah! As we tried to gain control of the raft to avoid going splat on the rock, the raft tipped, and I was on my way overboard, headfirst. Screaming at the top of my lungs, I knew this was it. I was going to die! Then Alwin grabbed me and pulled me back into the raft. All I could think of was that he was my knight in shining armor. I had swallowed a lot of water and was so terrified I just knew that any minute I'd be puking on everyone. Fortunately, that didn't happen.

After I'd calmed down a teensy bit, I saw that one of the guys had been thrown from the raft, too. The guide swam back to retrieve him. Back aboard, the guy seemed okay except for a big, ugly gash on his leg—Ouch!

A few times during our trip, we had to get out and wait on some rocks while the guide repositioned the raft to a better location. On one of these maneuvers, we had just climbed back in when we hit a huge rock and *I* was thrown overboard again. This time I found myself wedged between two boulders. I guess experience counts. Now, I was more angry than frightened. *What in hell made me do this trip? What was I thinking!* I imagined the pain I would bring my parents if I died.

I guess my guardian angel was watching because my life jacket was so thick, it stopped me from falling onto some razor-sharp rocks. I was dangling between huge boulders, waving my arms and legs, helpless and stuck.

The guide wedged the raft between some other rocks and saved my sorry ass by pulling me to safety. Oddly, after my rescue, I found the experience funny, even hilarious. I only wished that Alwin had taken a picture. Emotions. You can't trust them.

Alwin and the other rafters didn't see the humor as much as I did. They'd been scared for me. I looked at their faces. No one was smiling and laughing with me. Instead, they just stared with concern and fear on their faces. It made me feel strange. Later, I learned that I had experienced a bout of clinical hysteria. Not uncommon in these situations. I guess it's a better attitude than being totally paralyzed with fear.

When I checked my body, I was a little banged up and had hit my stomach hard on one of the rocks but, other than that I was fine. This wasn't my first rodeo with danger.

Our trip ended under a huge waterfall. Yes, *under.* The water was freezing, so of course the guide took the raft directly through it, drenching us with the icy water.

Out from under the waterfall, we all took lots of pictures then we headed toward the finish line.

Trip over, we climbed off the raft and onto dry land. It felt a little strange at first after being on the river for so long. Next, we had to hike uphill, through the dense forest to a small village. Once there, we dropped off our gear and relaxed over a buffet lunch where we chatted about the trip, telling stories, and sharing experiences.

In my travels I had discovered that small villages are often the best places to eat. This was no exception. As we munched away, I found the atmosphere peaceful and comforting after all the day's high-octane excitement.

When I looked around, "charming" seemed the perfect word to describe this tiny village. Colorful laundry hung on lines and the only sounds I heard were the rushing river and the song of the forest. No motorbikes, no horns honking, or city-din.

Back at the hostel, Alwin and I were exhausted and ready for a nap, but we had to move our gear out of the big house and into the dorm room. It didn't take long, but after we'd settled in, the exertion caught up with me and my body was tired and sore. So, instead of a nap, I decided to get a massage. When I told Alwin, he confessed he'd never had a massage, so he was in for trying it. Good choice. $12 US for a ninety-minute massage—such a deal.

Later, on the way to dinner, we were caught in a crazy rainstorm, drenching us from head to toe. And I thought, *I've had enough water for the day.*

After the rain had moved on, we had an odd urge to cross the street. No logical reason, but it was a strong feeling that we should, so we headed to the other side of the road. About fifteen seconds later, a woman lost control of her motorbike and crashed where we had been standing.

Whoa! Spooky? We started to go over and check on her, but someone else had come along to help her. She seemed okay, so we moved on, thinking about what a narrow escape that was. If we'd been there, we could have been hurt. And she might have been injured, too.

At the restaurant, I realized how hungry I was and dug into my grilled seafood, wrapped in banana leaves and special Balinese seasonings as if it would be my last meal.

After we ate until we were stuffed, we practically waddled out of the restaurant and headed to a bar where Beverly, who'd earlier arrived in Ubud, asked us to meet her. When we got there, she was behind the counter serving drinks! I had to laugh.

There's never a dull moment with Beverly.

When she spotted us, she came over and said to me, "Let's sneak away to the ladies' room for some girl talk." Inside the females-only sanctuary, Beverly eagerly told me details about a crazy rendezvous she'd had with a hot Brazilian hunk—in the bathroom at a club. Great story. She should write a book.

She also wanted to know all the juice about me and Alwin. Were we a couple, friends with "privileges," or just friends? She rolled her eyes when I told her we were just travel buds. I would have told her if something had happened.

"Whatever you say." She grinned as we went back to our table and had a few drinks with the guys. Did I say "a few?" We closed the bar. Sadly, for me, Beverly was heading to China the next day.

Alwin and I spent a few more days exploring the beautiful forest then headed for the Gilis, a group of islands off the northwestern shore of Lombok. We scheduled a 7 a.m. shuttle to pick us up and drive us to the ferry terminal. But, in Asia, for the most part, nothing is on time. By nature, I don't like being late, so I set my alarm for 6 a.m. However, being in a seven-bed dorm, I tried my best to be respectful and quiet, so I gave myself plenty of time to get ready without making noise by rushing around. Surprise! Around 6:15 a.m., Alwin came into my dorm to tell me that our shuttle had arrived.

What the hell? Usually, a 7 a.m. pick up meant 7:30 or even 8 a.m.—possibly longer. *Ugh! Why me?* I wasn't even *close* to being ready. The only choice was multitasking. I brushed my teeth with one hand and shoved stuff in my bag with the other.

I was a little more than annoyed when the guy sleeping in the bed next to mine griped, "Go in the bathroom to do that. And close the door." I was rushing because the shuttle had arrived forty-five minutes early. This guy was just an ass. I thought of telling him, "If you don't want to hear people moving about or packing in the morning, don't stay in a dorm!" The rooms are cheap for a reason. I wasn't doing anything out of the ordinary. In fact, I was one of the quieter, more considerate guests. So, I thought I could either argue with this guy or just chalk it up to him being a douche and not challenge him. I chose the he's-a-douche option, then went into the bathroom and closed the door behind me.

After finishing with my teeth-brushing, I reconsidered the decision to just let it go. I filled a cup with cold water and poured it on his face as I passed by then quickly grabbed my gear and left.

Escapade 7:

Share a Bungalow with a
Stranger on the Gili Islands

On the ferry ride to the breathtakingly beautiful Gili Trawagan (Gili T), I could already see myself lounging on a palm-fringed beach, listening to the crystal-clear blue water lapping onto the clean, powdery-white shoreline. No beach crowds, no cacophony of streets clogged with cars, incessantly honking their horns.

On Gili T, motorbikes and cars are banned. So are dogs. Only cats, bicycles, and pony-carts (cidomos) roam the streets. Much of Gili T is quiet and peaceful but a little away from the beaches, especially along the main drag, Gili T is busting at the seams with lounge bars, hipster guest houses, restaurants, shops, and diving schools.

When our boat hit the sand, we hopped out and retrieved our bags then set about finding our hostel. Alwin had made reservations, but we didn't know exactly where the place was. Although the beach was full of locals trying to rent out private bungalows to tourists, they were less than willing to help. But there was one man kind enough to give us directions. We thanked him and hoped he wasn't pranking us. Fortunately, the hostel was exactly where he said it would be.

Inside, Alwin started the check-in process. In the meantime, Simon, who had taken a different ferry, showed up. Is nothing ever easy? Of course, there was an issue with our reservation. Instead of the two dorm beds he'd booked, there was only one. Since the reservation was in Alwin's name, *I* had to find another place to stay.

I realize that mistakes happen, and I know he felt bad but I still fumed about the whole thing. In retrospect, maybe it should have been Alwin who had to scavenge elsewhere for a bed. But, alas, it was me. So, I stomped off—sort of—and sat in the common room of my "would be" hostel, mentally grumbling while searching my phone for a new accommodation.

Just like in the movies, a bad situation turned out to be a good thing. As I was sitting there with a black cloud over my head, a woman I didn't know came in, sat near me, and said, "Hi. I'm Natasha." She was also looking for somewhere else to stay. Instant kindred spirits in a pickle. As I looked at her, I instantly liked this girl with perfect, white teeth and a colorful outfit.

Later, I would discover that this interesting, outgoing woman always dressed in beautiful, bright, almost costume-like clothes, and is one of the most caring people I've ever met. But she did not pack light—five bags! I wondered at how she carried it all.

As we talked, my grumblies lightened up a bit. We quickly became friends and decided to rent a bungalow together. After a little searching, we found the perfect, affordable place, 100,000 IDR ($7.50 US) a night. Plus, it was just a couple of blocks from the backpacker hostel. *Whoop!*

After we checked in, Natasha and I headed to the beach for some girl time. By then, I'd forgiven Alwin and told him and Simon to meet us there later.

The beach was even more awe-inspiring than when I saw it from the ferry. I must have taken a hundred photos, but of course, the camera didn't do it justice. It never does. Such beauty and brilliance are hard for digital tech to capture.

After gawking at the scenery for long enough to establish myself as a first-timer tourist, I stripped down to my swimsuit and waded into the water. I had a moment of "What?" when I lifted my feet from the seafloor and floated like a beach ball. Since my college major was Marine Science, I know this part of the ocean was the most saline in the world. Experiencing it first-hand was amazing and so much fun, I stayed in the water for nearly an hour.

Lounging on the beach with Natasha, I commented that the boys were taking a long time to get there and wondered what was keeping them. She didn't seem very concerned, so I put it out of my mind. This day was too perfect to spoil by worrying.

Soon, though, Alwin and Simon arrived. I was glad to see them until Simon burst the paradise bubble by being a snot with an attitude. He whined that we were not where we said we would be and that they had to search *everywhere*. "So," he snapped, "were you trying to ditch us, or what?"

What a baby! I thought and rolled my eyes under my sunglasses. "Relax. You found us, didn't you?"

Alwin smiled and kept his mouth shut. I think he still felt guilty about the reservation mix-up. After a minute, he asked, "Did you find a place to stay?"

Feeling a bit smug, I pushed my sunglasses down my nose and peered up at him. "We did. It's a great bungalow only a couple of blocks from your hostel." I may have sounded a tad condescending. I didn't care.

His expression seemed to genuinely show that he was relieved that I wasn't having to sleep in the lobby. Now, I really forgave him.

So, snit over and chummy again, we all headed into the water and enjoyed the amazing sunset.

Later that night, we were ready for dinner. Where to go? Simon, or Alwin—I don't remember which—suggested that we just head to the street market and choose something there.

The market area is a different world—alive with people, music, vibrant colors, and smells—some nice, some not so nice. What a difference from the serene beach.

Traditional music filled the air wherever we went, and the food carts all looked and smelled mouthwatering delicious, it was tough to choose. I wanted a little of everything, but finally settled on seafood skewers, fried rice, and grilled veggies topped with a spicy sauce that set my mouth on fire—but in a good way. The meal was incredible but a bit expensive for street food ($7 US).

After dinner, we met up with some people from the Backpacker Hostel and went barhopping around the island. We played beer pong at the Jumping Spider—my team won! Yay! After that, we headed to the Beach Club and danced all night to 90s pop and hip hop—my favorite. In every bar I've been, in every country I've lived or visited, when the song *Next Episode* comes on, everyone, including me, gets excited—every time. In my opinion, it's a classic.

Good times that night proved too much for Alwin. We'd just begun the fun when he started feeling sick. He looked a bit green when he decided to give up and go back to the hostel.

I was sure he shouldn't have had tuna pizza for lunch. I mean, tuna pizza? Gross and gag! When he ordered it, I cringed but kept my opinions to myself. Not that saying something would have made any difference. I just hoped he'd learned not to eat anything like it *ever* again.

Natasha, Simon, and I *hadn't had* tuna pizza, so we partied until sunrise. We might have gone longer but the next day was Super Bowl Sunday. I wanted a short nap before heading out to one of the bars that was opening early to show the game. Yeah. Even in Bali, Super Bowl is a big thing.

Well, a short nap was the wrong thing to aim for. I was out like a candle in a hurricane. When I woke up, I groaned, "The game will be almost over!" I hurried to clean up as best I could and rushed out to the first bar I found, so I could at least catch some of the game. Barging in, I saw that the game was playing loud and clear, and I was thrilled to see that the Seahawks were about to lose. Yay team!

Later, the boys showed up at our bungalow to collect Natasha and me for lunch. No haggling this time. We all agreed to eat at a local spot around the corner and have fried eggs and fries. Not tuna pizza, but good.

That afternoon, Alwin was leaving for Thailand, so we hung out with him at the hostel, swam in the pool, and enjoyed poolside drinks. Just before he left, I handed him 30 Thai baht in coins and gave him a long hug and a kiss on the cheek. I was bummed to see my travel bud leave, but I knew we would stay connected. Neither of us could ever forget the fun we had.

After Alwin's send-off, the three of us were ready for some exploring and rode our bicycles to the quiet side of the island. I stopped to adjust my towel, waving the others on. A girl rode up and started up a conversation. Funny, her name is Tam—same as mine. She'd been riding alone and stopped to look at a nanny goat with two kids. I invited her to join our group. Her smile showed me that she was super happy to have found a new friend.

Shortly, we caught up with the others, who had stopped to take pictures of the offshore swings that are anchored to tall frames, so you can swing over the water. Too cool. Simon and Natasha took photos both from the swings and of others on them.

This side of the island was amazing and peaceful—better than a day at a spa. We swam, snorkeled, and practically had the beach to ourselves. But you can't eat sand and when we got hungry, we took off in search of food. Simon and Natasha went somewhere I wasn't interested in, so Tam and I found a nice quiet beach restaurant with sand-side food and drink service. We ate, read, then took a nap. What a perfect day.

Escapade 8:

Booze Cruise with No Beer

So much for peace and tranquility. I was ready for something wild and crazy. Good thing because the day after lounging, napping, and lazing in the sun, was Booze Cruise Day. Natasha, Simon, Tam, me, and the people from our hostel that we'd partied with before, headed for the "ship of fools" for some *insane* binge-drinking shenanigans.

Perfect weather—not a cloud in the sky and a light breeze. I barely noticed the hellish, ever-present humidity. I guess I was acclimating. Not a tenderfoot traveler anymore? It seemed like a thousand years ago that I stood, staring at my taxi wondering if I could still forget adventure and catch the plane back home.

Onboard our Booze Cruise, a 150-foot boat, we gawked at our surroundings—a pool, a bar, and a DJ. The other passengers looked like they would be fun to party with and I was ready for some action.

Soon, though we found some cracks in the veneer of drunk-monkey paradise. Not a lot of food but lots and lots of booze.

This was a six-hour cruise and I like to party as much as everyone else. These aren't called booze cruises for nothing, but getting completely trashed needs something to soak up the alcohol to keep the party from turning into a puke-and-hurl cruise. Oh, well, sacrifices must be made to the gods of carouse and whoop.

The next surprise was the pool. It was empty! We thought the crew might fill it once we left the dock but soon discovered that it would stay empty. No explanation, no reason. There was just a big hole in the boat. *Huh! But this was supposed to be a carousing celebration to make Dionysus jealous. An empty swimming pool wasn't going to stop us. What to do?* Sunbathe in it, of course.

I was surprised to see so many kindred solo travelers there. I suddenly felt like I belonged to an exclusive club—independent and unafraid to face the world by myself. It turned out that a lot of those loners were veteran explorers of Bali and gave me sage tips on awesome places to check out. Ah, if only I had years instead of weeks to really live the life.

So much for building castles in the sky. Back to the serious business of partying. Like any self-respecting woman of the world, I assessed the hotness or not-ness of my fellow cruisers. Natasha, who looks like a sporty Barbie doll, scored high. She would stand out in any crowd but here, decked out in a bright-pink two-piece swimsuit and funny heart glasses, she took the prize.

Throwing false modesty overboard, I think I was up there on the hotness scale with her. I looked awesome. Perfect RayBans and fit-just-right purple sparkly-heart swimsuit with cheeky bottoms. Yeah! We were the stars of the cruise, for sure. But as I looked around, a lot of us screamed babelicious and tasty. I was in good company.

One of the things I loved about our little group of travel buds was that we didn't think we all had to huddle together and not join the party. We just naturally spread out and mingled with the others. It's the way non-clingy people behave. Later we would regroup, share stories, and bask in the close bonds we had all formed with each other.

Pretty soon, none of us even cared that there wasn't much food. I was having a great time just being insane with friends and strangers. Nothing could ruin this good time. It was a backpackers' paradise and we were truly living our best lives, like whenever Tam and I saw each other we would yell out, "Taaaammm!"

After about two hours, tragedy struck. The boat ran out of beer! No water in the pool and starvation rations was a peanuts issue compared to this. Oh, there was plenty of overpriced liquor, of course, but *no* beer. Beer *was* the alcohol of choice because there were stories about people drinking hard liquor on these cruises and getting seriously sick, or worse—going blind. The rumor was that the drinks were adulterated with dangerous ingredients and homemade—possibly in someone's kitchen sink—or worse.

Bintang beer was the safest bet so that's what I stuck to. Fortunately, all was not lost; the Irish on board, not surprisingly, had smuggled their own booze onto the boat. Because I'd befriended them on my first day in Gili, they invited *me* to sip from their secret stash.

Soon, we anchored outside Lombok Island to take full advantage of a swim spot. Drunken passengers lined up to leap off the top of the boat into the water.

I wasn't sure if *I* was going to jump off—chicken, I guess. To cover up my cowardice, I agreed to hold some guy's phone for him while *he* jumped off. He decided to stay in the water, so I called to him, holding up my lime-green dry bag. "Your phone is in here!"

Well, I started feeling geeky and twitchy about being such a coward. *Okay,* I thought, watching the others having fun in the water. *How tough can it be? Go for it. I squared my shoulders and took a deep breath, then plunged into* the salty Indian Ocean.

"Holy Sh--! What a rush." I floated and swam and floated and swam. I could have stayed there all day, except an essential element was missing—cold beer.

As if providence itself took pity on my thirst, a few minutes later, I nudged Simon. "Look over there. People in a skiff. I wonder if *they* have beer." We waved and called them over. "Got any beer? The boat is out." They had nothing.

Disappointment crashed over me like a breakwater wave. One of the guys must have seen my expression and said they'd be happy to bring us some.

"Great!" A glimmer of hope shone through. Then it occurred to me that I was *in the ocean. My cash was on the boat. Would they wait while I climbed onboard and found my money? Probably not. I was about to say "Thanks, anyway but...," then I remembered I had a secret stash in my swimsuit top, so I reached in and pulled out a wet 100,000 IDR.* The guy in the boat smiled but didn't make any snarky comment about soggy money.

The skiff took off when the thought crossed my mind that giving him the money upfront probably wasn't the best idea. *Did I just get robbed? They might not come back with the beer.* I clearly hadn't thought this thing through and should have waited until they returned with the goods to pay them. Simon was hysterically laughing at me. I gave him the sidelong stink-eye. Okay. Dumb thing to do.

Oh well, it was done. I wasn't going to let it ruin my fun time and turned my attention back to enjoying the ocean, the music from the boat, and the fish swimming around us.

All that self-flagellation and worry was for nothing. The guys in the skiff showed up with my beer and even had the change. I was astounded and a little ashamed of myself for the things I'd been thinking about them. Not everyone was on the take. Sometimes people are great. Now, I was on cloud nine. I popped open a beer and lay back on a floaty in the middle of the Indian Ocean. Life just doesn't get any better than that.

Too soon, we were called aboard the beerless, poolless boat to head back to Gili T—but first, there was a sunset to watch. I looked for Natasha and found her napping on my dry bag. At least it was in good hands.

A little later the Brazilian guy who'd asked me to watch his phone came looking for it. I sent him to Natasha to retrieve it from the bag. Of course, it was missing. *Jeezuz Keerist.* What next? I remembered putting it in there. Why it was gone was a mystery. I made the rounds of passengers and asked if anyone had seen his phone. You've probably guessed the answer—no.

Next, I discovered that Natasha's phone was also missing. She found it, but I suspected that the person that took hers also took the Brazilian guy's phone. Natasha and I both thought we knew who it was, but without proof we couldn't accuse her. I felt bad that his disappeared, but I couldn't do anything about it. So much for a perfect day.

ESCAPADE 9:

A Full Moon Party and
A Mouth Full of Poison

Full of booze but empty of food, we were starving when the boat finally returned to shore. Soon, I headed for the nearest food place with Simon, Natasha, and my new friend from Beer Pong, Sarah, plus others from the boat.

While I stared at the menu, wondering if I could order *everything,* someone sat down next to me. Creepy-uncomfortable set in and I tried to ignore him by staring even harder at my menu, thinking, *who is this guy?* Then, I braved it and looked. It was Russel! From Warung Coco hostel in Kuta. We hadn't planned on ever meeting up again. Awesome!

He said he would join us later for dinner and the Full Moon Party. I was stoked.

That night, Russel bought the first round. The bar was out of Bintang, so we drank Heineken—a safe alternative, or so we thought. He took a sip and made a face. "This tastes weird."

I tried it, too. There was definitely something wrong. It tasted like poison to me, or who knows what. Everyone agreed not to drink it. Rumors of people dying or going blind from adulterated booze floated through my mind once again. Simon and Russel headed to the corner market for some Bintang.

While the guys were on a beer run Natasha and I headed to the bathroom, or as she would say, the washroom. The line was so long we decided to just dash for the shore and pee in the ocean. Hey, if fish can do it, why not us?

Well, I was still a bit unsteady from the cruise and stumbled after stepping into the water, soaking half my dress. Natasha thought that was the funniest thing she'd ever seen and howled with laughter. Even back at the beach bar, she giggled every time she looked at my wet dress.

After dinner, beer in hand, I wandered away from the group to a darker, less populated part of the beach to stare at the mesmerizing moon. This time, the moon seemed different, perhaps it was my drunken stupor or maybe, I thought, just maybe my dreams were coming true—dreams I hadn't even realized I had until now. My dream of travel and exploration just happened. I stretched out on the beach, beer in hand, and gazed into the sky feeling overwhelmingly happy and serene. I stared off into space for so long, that when I came back to "earth" the beach bar had closed, and the only person around was Simon. He'd passed out on the sand.

I felt awake, but my mind was elsewhere. A strange but oddly welcoming feeling. I looked around and saw that the other guys also snoozed in the sand. I nudged them awake.

As the sun rose, I was in awe as the purple sky turned to orange-red and then to yellow.

Another day in paradise.

Escapade 10:
Ride Around a Whole Island

All sobered up and ready to keep soaking up every tasty bit of Gili T I could, Natasha and I rode our bikes to the quiet side of the island. Gili T is small. It takes only about an hour to circle it on a bicycle. The day was promising to be perfect—again.

We stopped in a grass-hut eatery for lunch and gazed around. Unbelievably, we had the entire beach to ourselves. *Paradise? Hell, yes. I own this beach.*

We snorkeled with sea turtles then just blissed out and floated on the water. Sometimes talk just gets in the way of a good time. Hanging out in silence, absorbing beautiful surroundings can be the best, ever.

I was high on life. I felt completely carefree—something that hadn't happened often enough in my life. I thought about how odd it was to feel like that when there were tons of obligations, work, and stuff to worry about just waiting for me at home. I suddenly understood the saying "out of sight out of mind." I have an apartment that I have to shell out over $1000 US per month for—along with the bills that go with it. I had excused myself from work and didn't even think about when I would have to return to reality, AKA home—California.

In this moment, I honestly didn't care about any of that, I just wanted to travel, explore, eat exotic food, and make new friends. I wasn't afraid of running out of money, I was afraid of not exploring enough, not giving this adventure a chance to change my whole life-perspective. I knew I had fallen in love with exploring the world, the unknown, and the road less traveled. I had a lust for learning, adventure, and the thrill of discovery. I dove into my wanderlust like a kid with a box of candy. Responsibility could wait until I was ready to come back to it. Right then, I owned that beach!

Later that day, a couple of people from the Warung Coco crew, told me they'd decided to make their way to Australia for work. They invited me to come along. *Me? Australia?*

I loved the Gili Islands, but…Australia! I was hooked like a marlin. It'd been my lifelong dream to go Down Under. Even with all the crazy creepy crawlies, I knew in my heart it was a paradise just waiting for me.

I consider myself a responsible person, and for a split second, thought I might turn down the offer. Then reason kicked in. A chance to see Australia? Only a fool would refuse an offer like that. I thought about it for all of five seconds more before booking a one-way ticket via Sky Scanner for $80 AU ($63 US) from Denpasar. Oh, yes! I was bound for the land down under, starting with Melbourne. I was ready for a fair dinkum time, blowies, mozzies, and all.

ESCAPADE 11:

CRASH A SILENT DISCO AND GOODBYE

My last night on Gili Trawagan was more emotional than I thought it would be. I'd become attached to my travel mates and would miss them dearly.

Natasha, Simon, and I rode our bikes to a Gili resort and swam in the crystal-clear ocean until sunset. On our way back to the bungalow, we formed an ice cream crawl—stopping at every ice-cream shop between us and home. At each place, we tasted, smacked, and "mmm'd." We hotly debated which scoop place had the best ice cream as if world peace depended on it. In the end? No contest. Our third stop was voted blue-ribbon best. So good!

At the bungalow, Natasha and I cleaned up and changed clothes for a night out. We picked up Simon at his hostel and set off on our bikes. During our ride, we came across some people dancing to what looked like no music. That had to be one of the most curious sights I'd ever witnessed. When we came a little closer, though, we noticed that the dancers wore headphones and were getting down to music of their own choosing. We parked our bikes and joined the Silent Disco. It was an awesome experience. Odd, though, if one person was doing that it would have seemed so strange, but as a group, all dancing together alone, it was amazing and fun.

After about thirty minutes, we set off for dinner. *Trip Advisor* recommended a rotisserie chicken place; I don't recall the name but, it's the only one on the Island. We ordered a whole chicken to split. It came with creamy, flavorful mashed potatoes, gravy, and a fresh salad. It was nice to eat something that tasted a little more of home. Nasi goreng (Indonesian rice dish) is good but I was ready for something different.

Natasha, a vegetarian, ordered the green option which turned out to be the chicken dinner without the chicken—mashed potatoes and salad.

Now, with our stomachs filled, it was time to celebrate my last night in Indonesia. We rounded up some funsters-of-choice from Gili Backpacker and headed out. First stop, a beer pong tournament. After all, we North Americans had to show off our skills, right?

We won the first three games and would have won the whole tournament, but we'd had enough and headed for the next bar, Beach Top. It was awesome—three levels each playing a distinct genre of music. Just outside, some of my more adventurous companions drank *mushroom* shakes from a "vendor."

I've always been a square when it comes to drugs, so I passed on their offer to get me one. Besides, the day I arrived on the island, a guy had gone missing after having one of those. I was sure they weren't safe and wasn't going to take any chances, especially on the brink of my going to Australia.

The missing guy turned up dead in the water a week later, and his poor mother had to fly from Brazil to identify his body. One of the saddest stories I'd ever heard. I still shiver when I think of it.

As the night sky showed a hint of purple and orange on the horizon, I headed back to the bungalow. I had to finish packing and catch a ferry to the mainland for my flight later that evening. I gave Natasha the biggest hug and told her that I was sure we would meet again.

When I finally arrived in Ubud, hung over and glad the gut-lurching ferry ride was over, I endured another two hours on a cramped, bumpy bus ride to the airport.

I thought I was being smart to ration my money, so there wouldn't be any left over when I headed to Australia. Uh! Big mistake. I didn't know about the 275,000 IDR ($20 US) exit fee to leave the country.

Irritation doesn't come close to describing my emotions at that point. I'd paid a fee to enter and was only now told that I had to pay a fee to leave? What kind of rip-off was this? To make it worse, they only accepted cash.

I wasn't feeling great anyway but wanted to just get on with it so I could be on my way. I stomped over to the ATM and withdrew the 275,000 IDR. More grumbling when I saw that there was a $9 US ATM charge. Lucky for me, my bank reimburses me for ATM transactions. So, one bright spot in an otherwise grim experience.

Escapade 12:

A New And Awesome Continent

Around 11 p.m. my plane arrived at Tullamarine Airport, Australia. Yay! I finally made it to my dream place. A little disoriented, I missed the sign pointing to the VISA free line (a courtesy extended to only a handful of countries—US included), I somehow found myself in the regular line—a long one. It took an hour to get stamped in! *Ugh! I seriously need to pay more attention.*

Aside from that minor setback, I made it through customs unscathed and caught a bus to the CBD (city center) where the Elizabeth Street Hostel was located. Of course, because I was, by then a seasoned seat-of-the-pants traveler, I just showed up without a reservation. Luckily, they had a bed open.

Having been in Southeast Asia for so long, I'd become comfortable with the dirt-cheap costs. I caught my breath and took a moment to remind myself that I was now in a western country. Of course, it wouldn't be $7-$10 US per night. This hostel was $40 AUD ($28 US). Still, not too bad, considering that I was in the country of my dreams.

In the morning, I discovered it was the St. Kilda Beach Festival. What a way to start my Aussie adventure. I contacted Landin (from my stay at Warung Coco) to meet me at my hostel. I also found out that Pam (one of the girls robbed in Kuta) would meet us there. A mini reunion. What more could go right?

The festival was awesome—so much art, delicious food, and lots of beer. I loved shopping in all the stores, looking at art pieces, fashion designs, and, of course, I tried as much street food as I could. From the top of the Ferris wheel I could see the town—St. Kilda and the surrounding. It was beautiful.

We stayed until the last minute. Any longer and the street sweepers would have shooed us out.

We rode the metro back to the CBD then Landin went straight home to continue his job search.

I wanted to check out the nightlife, though, so I headed to the hostel's common area to scope out potential friends to hang out with. But this wasn't as easy as Southeast Asia. I didn't meet anyone who wanted to go with me for some bar shenanigans.

Disappointed, I went to the corner bar solo and ordered a beer. In less than a minute, a handsome local man approached me and asked why I was standing there, by myself, looking so awkward? His smile lit up my night when he said, "Come hang with us."

I followed him to the group of guys, introduced myself, and told them I'd just arrived and hadn't met anyone yet. They invited me to barhop with them. They were great. They even invited me to join their basketball game on Wednesday.

I had a lot of fun but didn't party too hard because I didn't really know these guys. Still, I had a blast and it seemed like they did too. They even walked me back to my hostel at the end of the night because they didn't want me to get lost.

Such gentlemen. I wondered if all Aussies were this great. Awesome night!

The next day, I went to the ultra-modern Museum of Natural History and found myself being drawn into the exhibits and learning a lot about Australia. The longer I spent there the more I realized how little I knew about the Aborigines and racism in that country.

I honestly didn't think those types of problems existed there, at least not the way they do in other countries. I learned about the famous footballer Nicky Winmar who experienced so much discrimination for being different but was so good at the game, he became one of the best players in the world.

I watched a video of the parliament apologizing to the Aboriginal people, which brought a tear to my eye. I also visited the animal and insect exhibit. I wanted to see all the spiders and creepy crawlies I might encounter during my time there. It didn't disappoint. Let's just say my visit to *that* exhibit was brief.

The Marine exhibit was my favorite as I'd read up on the Great Barrier Reef with its infamous boxed jellyfish called *Irukandji*—the kind that you can't see but can kill you in a few minutes. It's the most venomous boxed jellyfish in the world. I remember watching a documentary about it years ago. Two biologists went diving, wearing special high-tech gear to attempt to collect a sample of the invisible jelly. When they surfaced and began taking off their gear, a small tentacle from their specimen touched their skin, and they were hospitalized for six weeks. *Eeeek!*

I also checked out the mini rainforest planted as a maze. It houses exotic birds and fish. It was so refreshing to find this wonderful place in the middle of the city.

Escapade 13:

Play Dress-Up With Strangers

On my walk back to the hostel to meet Landin, I thought of Casey—the friend I'd been traveling with throughout Asia who went home. She'd spent a year in Australia, and I thought of something she'd told me about all the hot men in suits having happy hour drinks at a certain hotel. Naturally, I decided to stop by the place and poke my head in. My eyes popped. She had not exaggerated. The place was full of beautiful men with neat man-buns and sexy Aussie accents, dressed in perfectly tailored suits.

Atypically, I had nothing to say. For about a minute, I just stared like a creepy predator on the verge of drooling. Then I remembered I was on my way to meet Landin and forced myself to turn away and scuttle off.

As I passed the Elephant Bar, a tall, suited, delicious Aussie headed my way. I'm sure he noticed me gawking. He smiled. Not certain who he was smiling at, I glanced behind me. No one there but an old man with a cane. Probably not the target of his smile, unless Cane Dude was his dad.

When we passed each other, I felt compelled to turn around and look. He'd done the same. We exchanged another smile. Feeling girly, I let out a giggle. It couldn't have been a more romantic movie moment than that. It made my day!

When I arrived at the hostel, Landin had just arrived. I didn't tell him about the tall man in a suit—not that he would have cared, but somehow that was the kind of thing another girl would appreciate more than a man.

We went to a gourmet burger place that smelled amazing. I ordered a stuffed burger with bacon and avocado, and a beer. My total was $28 AUD ($22 US). Ouch! Glad I didn't order fries. Melbourne is expensive but more than worth it. I knew, however, that I wouldn't be traveling too much longer if I kept spending money like that. I vowed to economize. That meant eating Starbucks salads the rest of the week for $6 AUD.

While at the restaurant, Landin got a call about a new job. They wanted him to come in the next day for an interview. That was great news. We headed out to celebrate his potential job, stopping first at the corner liquor store to buy some iconic Australian drink—Goon wine—disgusting cheap wine in a box that had been filtered through fish eggs. I thought, *Ugh! I think they forgot to remove the fish eggs.* It was the worst swill I'd had since the funny Heineken on Gili T.

In my hostel common area, Goon in hand, we started a game of ping pong and asked if anyone wanted to play.

Two people stepped up. We played for a while and shared our Goon with them. After the game, all four of us carried the box of fish-egg-wine and some cups to a pub down Elizabeth Street but decided to finish the wine before we went in.

Our new friends from France, Sarah and Adam, told us that they planned to go into the bush for a year to work on a farm to make some money for travel. Before arriving in Australia, they'd spent six months in Southeast Asia. I thought they were an attractive couple. Sarah's curly blonde hair and freckles complimented Adam's short and straight dark hair. I was intrigued by the tattoo of barbed wire on his left wrist. I wasn't sure what it meant and didn't ask.

After we'd finished the Box of Regret, instead of going into the pub, we walked around looking for another pub, but everything was closed. Disappointed, we wandered back to Elizabeth Street.

At some point during the night—I don't remember how or when—we met a creepy, weird guy. He might have even been homeless. I don't know what his issue was, but he was definitely a sandwich short of a picnic. He decided to walk with us for a while and told us to stop when we got in front of the Goodwill store.

Someone had left boxes of clothes and shoes outside the store. In our drunken state, we all thought that it would be fun to try them on and have a fashion show. Just one example of why I *won't* be drinking Goon again. We laughed and giggled as we tried on the clothes, swapped outfits, including shoes, and had a full-on fashion show—catwalk included.

Something—I don't remember what—spooked us and we scattered. I remember the weird, homeless/crazy guy trying to come after us, but we lost him and darted back to our hostel. Sarah managed to make it back with a handful of shoes! It was all funny, but I'd really like to remember the whole story. Thanks for the dead brain cells, Goon.

HAZARD 14:

Taken and Chased

I woke around noon the next day. Fortunately, the Goon had worn off. Landin met me at Elizabeth's hostel so we could have a quick lunch and explore a different part of Melbourne.

We made a right on to Elizabeth Street, and continued past the Macca's (what Aussie's call McDonald's) and a lot of touristy shops. I was really enjoying myself until some man grabbed my arm and growled, "I've been looking for you!"

With a calm I didn't know I was capable of in a situation like this, I turned and faced him. It was the crazy, homeless dude from the night before. He carried a bag full of the Goodwill clothes under one arm.

"What the hell?" shouted Landin, looking horrified. He must have blacked out the memory of the night before because after I explained who Crazy Guy was, he said he didn't remember taking the train home or acquiring any new outfits. His memory was blank on the events that led up to our abrupt departure from the storefront.

This guy was clearly insane and said he was going to take us to a BBQ that some hookers had invited him to.

I struggled to free my arm, but he held on tighter. I tried to remain calm. We were in the middle of the city, surrounded by people. I wondered if anyone would intervene. A part of me thought this might be my last day on the planet, but another part thought, *I've sure experienced some weird stuff. Would the law consider this an attempted kidnapping?*

Landin and I began to ask Crazy Guy questions to figure out where he was taking us. I nearly fainted with relief when a friendly redheaded guy recognized our accents and asked us where were from. We told him. He said that he was from Texas and joined us on our journey to the hooker BBQ. We asked him what he was doing in Australia. He said, "Selling drugs."

Shocked, Landin and I glanced at each other. We knew then that the situation was suddenly much worse. The drug comment was music to Crazy Guy's ears. He perked up and finally loosened the grip on my arm then barraged the Texan with all kinds of questions.

I carefully removed my arm from Crazy's grip then Landin and I quietly slipped to the other side of the street. He didn't notice until we were across then yelled, "Hey! You guys trying to get away from me?"

We started speed-walking back to Elizabeth Street then ran when Crazy Guy started chasing us. We ran for at least five blocks to get away from him. When I finally looked back, he was still chasing us. *What the fuck?* We ran faster.

We eventually lost him and dashed into my hostel's movie room. We hid out there for four hours, totally freaked out by what had happened.

Ironically, the movie playing was *Wolfe Creek,* about an Australian serial killer. What are the odds? I didn't leave my hostel that evening. All night, the thought of "what if..." kept buzzing through my brain. What if the Texan hadn't shown up?

What if nut job Crazy Guy hadn't let up on his grip? Would we have just vanished never to be found? How long would it have taken for our families to notice that we were missing? I remembered how my mom was worried sick when I left the email about not returning home for three weeks. I could only imagine how she and Dad would feel if I'd been kidnapped.

Thank God we managed to sneak away from the psycho. I tossed and turned all night mentally reviewing that scenario, thinking about my trusting nature and how it has landed me in "interesting" situations. This one, though, was by far the strangest, and most disturbing. It also reinforced lessons I was taught when I was little, such as "Don't talk to strangers and don't go anywhere with someone you don't know."

As a child I often argued with my parents, saying things like, "I'll never make any friends if I don't talk to people I don't know." Mom would laugh and say that I could only talk to the strangers (children) in my class but that was it.

As I stared at the shadows forming on the ceiling from the small bit of light that penetrated the window shade, I vowed to continue making friends and having a good time. I also promised myself that I would be more critical of the company I kept and reminded myself that although most people I'd met on this trip were good and decent, not everyone's intentions were good.

Escapade 15:
Great Ocean Road, Foot-Fetish Creep and Hopes for Krakatoa

Pam invited me to spend the day with her in Torquay, a seaside resort in Victoria. It's near the Great Ocean Road. I took the train first thing in the morning. When I got off, I looked for the bus stop that Pam said would be just outside the train station. Of course, it wasn't there.

Here I was, in the middle of the burbs with no cell phone or Wi-Fi. How to find directions? The old-fashioned way. I asked people how to get to the Great Ocean Road. Even though I wasn't immediately successful, I had confidence that *someone* knew, so I kept asking. After a little while, a man, who introduced himself as Karl, told me where a bus stop was that would get me close to where I wanted to be.

We walked together to the bus, but when it was my turn to swipe my card to pay, it didn't work. Grumbling inside, I had to load more money onto it. I was so uncomfortable. It felt like the other passengers were impatiently watching me hold everything up. The "mykey" card had run out of money because I didn't know about the tap-on-tap-off system. That meant that my last trip drained the card.

Okay, settled in, I realized that I had no idea where Karl was taking me. He could be a serial killer for all I knew. *Jeez. Will I ever learn?* But I looked at him and listened to the tone of his voice. For some reason I felt safe and believed he would get me where I needed to go.

Following a stranger to somewhere I've never been and trusting him not to be a murderer or robber may sound crazy, but I really felt I was going to be okay. Still, not something my mother would approve.

I really believe there are people who genuinely want to help. Fortunately, I always find them. Well, Crazy Homeless guy aside, most people I've encountered are good and decent. Remember the guys on the skiff in the middle of the ocean? They brought my beer and *change.*

I'm sure Mom would scold, "What did I teach you about talking to strangers?" My response would be "If I did that, I would never have made any friends." All's well that ends well.

At Karl's stop, he stepped off the bus and waved me to do so, too. I looked around. We were in the middle of the suburbs. It seemed to be a quiet, clean neighborhood full of tree-lined streets, and middle-class houses with tidy, landscaped yards.

While we walked, he told me he was from Sydney, and had lived there for forty years before deciding he wanted a slower pace of life. So, he and his wife packed up and moved to Torquay.

I shared that I was on a spur-of-the-moment backpacking trip and that this was my first time in Australia. I told him how excited I was to be there. I think he was glad to have company on his routine walk to his next bus.

We'd gone about a mile when he said that he had to go a different way from where I needed to be. He told me to turn left and that I would find what I was looking for in about fifteen minutes. He waved then turned right.

I called out, "It was nice to meet you. Thank you for being so kind."

"Welcome to the Southern Hemisphere," he said, looking back over his shoulder.

Turning left, I walked for fifteen minutes and spotted the sign that read GREAT OCEAN RESORT.

After a few more blocks, I arrived at the Days Inn where Pam and I had agreed to meet.

I stepped inside and asked if I could use their Wi-Fi to contact my friend and tell her I'd arrived. They agreed and about ten minutes later Pam arrived with Sue, the five-year-old girl she was taking care of.

Pam worked as a nanny for a family who lived near the beginning of the Great Ocean Road. I was glad to see her and happy that she'd arrived safely in Australia after being robbed and pushed off a motorbike in Bali.

Pam took me to a café where we ate pastries and drank coffee. Sue was adorable and played in the sandbox while Pam and I caught up. She invited me to dinner at the house where she worked. On the way there, I noticed how adorable and quaint this small town was.

Her house was yellow with white trim, two levels, surrounded by a lawn and white fence. When I stepped in, I was greeted by an incredibly happy puppy who followed me around like I was an old friend.

Sue told me that the other family dog had died a few weeks ago and they got this one to help her feel better. This little girl was sharp. She proceeded to bring me all her books. We settled in and I read them to her.

Most of the books were by Dr. Seuss, so I had some of them memorized. *Green Eggs and Ham* has always been my favorite with a close second being *One Fish Two Fish Red Fish Blue Fish.*

While I read to her, she placed her hand on top of mine and smiled. I don't think she had ever seen anyone who looked like me. I smiled back and continued reading. One of the books dropped off the table and hit a painful spot on my ankle bone and I blurted out, "Damn!" I guess I could have used a worse word, but I chastised myself for saying it.

Well, this was a new word to her, and she kept repeating it. I was hoping she'd forget it by the time her parents and other siblings came home.

Pam was finishing dinner when the rest of the family arrived. They were all welcoming and friendly and wanted to know everything about me.

They were track athletes which I loved because I threw shot-put, discus, and hammer in college. Their oldest girl ran the 800 meters, the 4x400 meters, and the 4x100 meters. She was also a straight-A student. I was impressed.

When we sat down to eat, I felt like part of the family. The little girl invited me to her 6th birthday party. I told her how sad I was that I couldn't make it, and I was sure she would still have a wonderful time.

They offered me a room for the night, but I thanked them and declined. I had a tour of the Great Ocean Road that started the next day.

I've always felt awkward meeting new people but this time was different. I felt comfortable and welcome. What a wonderful family.

Pam and I headed to the beach early enough to explore a bit before my train arrived. We hiked the trails that ran along the coast. Amazing and so beautiful. Resting, we watched the surfers and talked about her plan to travel around Australia with her brother.

She filled me in on something I'd wondered about for a long time—what happened between her and Sonja. Their friendship was seriously strained when Sonja ditched her in Bali, and she had to find her own way back to the hostel. That's why she got on that motorbike taxi where she was robbed and thrown into the street.

Pam said she couldn't understand why Sonja thought it was okay to leave her alone like that. She said they hadn't spoken after that night and probably wouldn't for a long time, or ever.

Pam went with me to the train station. I gave her a hug and thanked her for such a wonderful day and asked that she convey my gratitude to her host family.

As I approached the last train to Melbourne that day, the doors closed right in front of me. My heart sank as I repeatedly stabbed at the "open" button. It looked like I might be stranded in the station all night or have to take Pam's host family up on their offer to stay there.

Thankfully, just when I was about to give up, the doors finally opened. "That was close," I muttered and quickly boarded.

With a last wave to Pam, I was on my way back to the CBD, Melbourne. The seats were comfy and invited a nap. The trip would take about an hour, so I set an alarm then dozed off, dreaming of the beautiful ocean-view hike along the Great Ocean Road that Pam and I took before I left.

When I woke up a strange guy was sitting next to me. *Out of all these empty seats he had to pick this one?* There was something decidedly odd about him. Uncomfortable to the max, I didn't know whether to ignore him or get up and leave. He just sat there staring at the floor. I followed his gaze and was surprised to see him ogling my sandaled feet. Really, really creepy. First Crazy Homeless guy and now this weirdo with a foot fetish. What the hell?

I wanted to change my seat but thought that might trigger something violent in him. So, first, I tried to hide my feet and turned to look out the window.

I remembered a story my friend, Jonny, told me when he was approached by a nutjob on a New York City subway. He was freaked out when the guy came right at him. So, he decided to out crazy the guy by trying to bite his ear while making loud grunting noises. I remembered Johnny telling me, "If you act crazier than the crazies, they'll leave you alone." I was psyching myself up to get weird when the guy got off the train. Well, I was almost disappointed that I didn't get to bark like a dog and bite the guy's shoulder. But mostly, I was just relieved he was gone.

That experience behind me, and safely back in my hostel bed, I went to sleep.

The next day, I woke up feeling great as I bolted out of bed, saying, "It's tour time!" After dressing in black shorts and a T-shirt, I packed my day-bag and headed to the designated meeting spot— the corner of Elizabeth Street near St. Paul Church.

I was so excited about the tour, I arrived forty-five minutes early. When it was time for the driver to pick me up, he wasn't there. I waited thirty minutes longer just in case the tour operator was running late. Nope! No one showed.

To make my day even more unsatisfying, a beggar approached me for money. I know that down and out homeless people are just a part of the ugly side of any city, but at that moment, I just wanted him to go away.

The only reason I had signed up for the Great Ocean Road tour was because I had not yet heard from the Irish guys from the Booze Cruise. They were renting a van and planned to drive the whole road. They had invited me to come along since we would be arriving in Melbourne around the same time. Now, it looked like not only was I not going to see the Great Ocean Road, I would be out a considerable chunk of traveling money.

I rushed back to my hostel and emailed the company. I had paid $89 AU for this tour and wanted a refund. They told me the driver had, in fact, been at the meeting spot and that they would not be refunding my money.

I was livid. I asked for the manager, explaining that I had waited in the said meeting spot for an hour past what the pick-up time should have been and no one showed. Could I have been in the wrong place? Perhaps but I was in the place designated in the directions I had been given.

After three emails back and forth, they still refused to refund my money. So, I FaceTimed Beverly and told her what happened. She said not to worry that she would write a letter for me.

A few hours later Beverly sent me a rebuttal to the tour company's refusal to refund my money! I read it aloud to myself before sending it.

Hello,

I understand and appreciate that your company has its policies for people attending (or missing) your tour, however, this situation is different from a simple 'no show.' I have stated and will reiterate that I was standing on the corner of Flinders and Swanston at 7:15 a.m. until I eventually decided that Melbourne's extreme weather was prohibitive of me waiting any longer (about one hour).

There is clearly a breakdown in communication between the details I received (I would be happy to show you copies) and the information I should have received outlining the exact location that you have since explained to me.

On your website you even state the pick-up details. These are the same as the directions I had been given. So, I wonder why you are now telling me that I should have been standing at St. Paul's. In case you aren't familiar with that Cathedral, it is large and a waiting passenger standing outside it, even on a specific corner, would be difficult for a driver to recognize or know who was a passenger and who wasn't.

Telling customers, after the fact, and almost $100 later, that they were wrong is hardly good customer service. Perhaps what you could do in future is mark a giant 'X' on the ground with a big flashing, pointing arrow to avoid any confusion. It is highly insulting to hear from you that I was standing in the wrong place.

Your driver claimed to have waited ten minutes for me, yet I have proof from surveillance footage and witnesses that I was standing on that corner.

If you are so adamantly trusting of your driver, could you please offer me the same courtesy and present me with physical evidence that the driver was where he or she claims? I am not inferring, your driver is lying, but by denying me a refund, you are saying that I am lying.

In addition, I do not understand how your driver could possibly search for a person he has never seen and doesn't know what he or she looks like.

Surely, any time spent looking for someone you don't know is a futile activity. It is difficult to believe that the driver looked for me at all, unless he has a sixth sense about the people attending the trip, in which case, he may have a skill set worthy of more than your terrible tour company.

I cannot fathom why your driver would even claim to have looked for me or why you are so adamantly sure I was not there, nor why you will not accept fault and refund my money.

As a reasonable person, I would have been willing to simply move the date, but unfortunately, I must be leaving Melbourne soon.

Please keep in mind that I understand you are a representative of this company and not personally responsible for the wrong done to me. This is not a personal attack on you.

I am only to blame for forgetting that we live in a world where money is the most important thing, where ensuring you have my hard-earned cash is inevitably far more important than whether I had a valuable experience or any experience at all.

I am disappointed with your company. Not only have I lost $89, but this situation has caused me great stress and anxiety.

To make things worse, because I must leave Melbourne, I have missed a vital part of the trip I was looking forward to.

I can assure you that your company's lack of cooperation, if I am still to be denied my deserved refund, will not sit lightly with me. I will pursue this further by taking to social media, trip advisor, and anywhere else I can to explain how you take fees for services, send instructions for a meeting place, not show up, then accuse them of lying, refuse to refund, and take an insulting, irritating, and sarcastic tone when you end with a "have a great day" message. This forces me, as someone only looking at what I feel is right action, to wretch at how inconsiderate, and denigrating that message is.

If your company was more customer-driven, I would have been happy to shout about how great you are. Instead, you caused me nothing but aggravation.

If you cannot help me, put me in contact with your manager. Then perhaps, he or she can give me a clear understanding about what happened and provide the proof I would like, or even better...a refund!

Sometimes being firm works. I received my refund three days later. Thanks Beverly!

After all the drama I experienced in Australia, I decided to go back to Asia. I bought a ticket to Bali and would be leaving in two days.

🐼🐼🐼

The day before I was to leave, I visited Landin on his official first evening of work and said goodbye. The place where he and I met up was interesting—a large dive-bar in New Brunswick with pool tables and darts. Landin was bummed about me leaving so soon, but I couldn't stay longer. My feelings were that something was pulling me back to Asia.

The next morning, I flew to the Denpasar Airport. It took six long hours. The inexpensive flight costs to Asia were what allowed me to make my last-minute travel plans.

I took the airport taxi to Warung Coco.

The next day I hired a driver and headed for the centuries old Tanah Lot (Water Temple) and Uluwatu. Tanah Lot, which means "in the sea," was my favorite. It sits on a large offshore outcrop that is being eroded by the sea.

In mythology, a giant snake guards this temple. For a long time, it looked like the forces of nature would crumble Tanah Lot, but the Japanese government stepped in to conserve and protect it.

Much of the outcrop now is artificial rock. I really enjoyed having to wade through water to get to the old temple.

Uluwatu was incredible, too. It was built before the 11th century on the edge of a 70-meter cliff that projects into the sea. I loved it, except for the horrid monkeys. One of the creatures followed me around as I wandered around the temple. Maybe ignoring them is the trick.

It lost interest in me when a little girl approached. The monkey stole her sandal! Perhaps this monkey had a foot fetish, like the creepy guy on the train. A woman had to give it a bag of chips before the girl could retrieve her shoe.

I continued to wander around Uluwatu with its beautiful ocean views. Usually, I like to share these kinds of trips with others, but for some reason, this time I was content to experience it solo. It was so beautiful, I got lost in the ambience.

Later that evening, I met up with Simon who had just returned from Gili T. Naturally, we went to Sky Garden for the buffet and a few drinks to celebrate his return home after seven months of travel.

Seven months? What? I'd been so wrapped up in exploring, I'd forgotten all about going home and missed my flight back to the US! Oh, well. I decided to just go with the flow.

Now that not going home until *I* wanted *had been settled— for now—I decided to visit Jakarta.* I read and heard warnings to stay away from there. Supposedly there's nothing to see and it's dangerous.

Warnings or no, Jakarta was the easiest way to get to my favorite volcano—Krakatoa. Getting there, however, proved to be a challenge. I arrived at the Jakarta airport at 5 p.m. and expected to be picked up close to that time. But, as I later discovered, Jakarta's traffic is the stuff of legends— worse than eight lanes of the 405 freeway in Los Angeles traffic during rush hour.

It should have been a twenty-minute drive to the hostel. My ride picked me up at the airport at 7:30 p.m. and had to fetch another passenger from a different terminal before we could be on our way. It took us an hour to get to the other terminal and twice that long to get to the hostel.

The other passenger, Will from Germany, was patient, though, and we spent the long ride getting to know each other. He planned to spend three weeks in Indonesia but just landed and I thought he might not have heard about Jakarta's bad reputation, so I warned him to get out as fast as he could.

We arrived at the hostel around 10 p.m.—hungry. But as we soon discovered, Jakarta is kind of scary at night, so we hit the first place we found—a Chinese restaurant that was closing in a half hour. I don't know if they were happy to see us or not but we were happy to be there.

The place was super posh, and Will and I were glaringly under dressed. I had a green tea and we split a large plate of noodles. The tea was bright green and teeth-numbing sweet. I couldn't drink it and was too cowardly to send it back, so I just left it on the table.

On our way to the hostel, we got lost. I was a bit frightened, but Will seemed unfazed by our situation, so I was grateful to be with him. Shortly, we found our way. We sat in the common area to plan our next move.

My only reason for being in Jakarta was to hike Krakatoa, so I searched for tours and the best way to get to the volcanic island chain. I told Will he might like to see Mt. Bromo and the sulfur mines, then travel to UBUD and the Gili Islands. We stayed up chatting until about 2 a.m. He alerted me to the "other" inbox on Facebook. I had no idea it existed.

I had tons of messages. Some were from an ex. I ignored them. But I was pleasantly surprised by a message from the Irish guys saying that they'd made it to Melbourne and were working on getting a van.

They asked if I still wanted to meet up to explore the Great Ocean Road. I was so disappointed! If I'd only known about this FB inbox, I would have gone with them and not had to wrestle with that horrid tour company.

Will took the first flight out at 5 a.m., three hours before I woke up, so I didn't get to say goodbye.

🐼🐼🐼

I wanted to explore and rationalized that the warnings about Jakarta were overblown. After dressing in my typical Southeast Asia outfit of a tank, shorts, and rainbow sandals, I was ready to face the humidity. Catching a bus to the nearest mall, I noticed everyone staring at me. Confused at first, I took a good look at the other passengers. It hit me that they were probably shocked by my immodest clothing. Being Muslim, they were covered from head to toe. *Sigh!* I didn't remember that this was a predominantly Muslim city and I must have looked naked to them.

I was embarrassed, but not enough to turn around and go back, so I continued to the shopping mall scantily clad. I knew not returning to change was disrespectful of their sensibilities, but that traffic was unbearable, and I just didn't want to go back.

At the mall, I had a great meal at a high-end restaurant. I ordered a chicken sandwich with coleslaw and wide noodles. Amazingly good. For dessert, I had chocolate mousse with walnut candies. Definitely a taste-gasm. I was tired of the Indonesian staple of Nasi Goreng (rice with beef), so that meal was like heaven on a plate. After stuffing my face, I spent a few hours in a bookstore to escape the heat and the loud busy-city clatter.

Later that afternoon I hung out in the Packer Lodge and met Rachel from England, Manny from Australia, Paco from Japan, and Cas from Argentina. We all got along well, and they invited me to go to dinner with them.

We went to a clean, somewhat westernized restaurant in a nice part of the city. I ordered a Kobe burger with bacon and grilled onions, fries, and a beer. *Yummmmm*. Rachel ordered steak with mac and cheese, Cas got a spinach salad, Paco wanted grilled chicken with mashed potatoes, and Manny ordered wings and fries.

I explained to Rachel about my adventure in the wrong clothes earlier. She laughed and said it happens to everyone at least once. After dinner, no one was in the mood to check out any nightclubs, especially since none of us had the proper attire, so we went back to the hostel, watched movies, and figured out a plan for sightseeing the next day.

🐼🐼🐼

Refreshed, the next morning we boarded a bus to town. Buses there have their own lane, marked by a raised concrete border, so it's much faster to travel that way than by car or taxi. Just picture five lanes on a freeway in Los Angeles, San Diego, Chicago, or New York, then picture ten lanes of cars squeezed into those five lanes. That's what traffic is like in Jakarta. And drivers there just make their own lanes, so it's completely gridlocked all day.

We took the bus for six stops and got off at the history museum exit. As we reached the entrance, we saw that it was closed for the New Year holiday, so we crossed the street and headed toward the National Monument.

On our way, it started raining and we bought ponchos from a street vendor. We checked out the monument museum and garden, but we were told that the real thrill was the view from above, so we rode the elevator to the top.

When we stepped off the elevator a security/operator charged us a fee but let the locals in for free. He claimed it was standard policy and that we had to pay extra for the view because we had the wrong ticket. Sure, we did—not.

Even though we knew it was a fleece-job, we paid the guard. It was worth it. The view was beautiful. In the South, the landscape is green and lush but there are mostly city buildings and housing complexes in the North. There's something refreshing about being up so high and looking down on the earth.

We asked someone to take our picture. It was a great photo because all our rain ponchos were different colors, so we looked like a bunch of Skittles with a killer view in the background.

There wasn't much else to do, so after leaving the monument, we wandered around for a few hours then went back to the hostel to get ready for the Chinese New Year festivities.

We headed out to the festival late enough that traffic was non-existent and walked to town square for the parade. When we arrived, the first order of business was to go into a Temple and light candles to show our respect. At the square, bands were playing, and lots of vendors and shops were open, selling all kinds of street foods and souvenirs.

I loved the live music and the dancing. We heard some awesome music coming from Café Batavia and decided to stop for food and drinks. This was a dimly lit, two-story house with old pictures on the walls.

We climbed a lovely, red staircase to the next level where the dining tables were, then up one more flight, where a band played hypnotizing music. We wanted to stay but it was full, so we had to settle for the not-so-lively 2nd floor. I loved it anyway, they served cocktails from the 1920s and delicious food. The menu was on the back of an old picture frame and the ambience was amazing. After dinner and cocktails, we went to the town square and danced, window shopped, and enjoyed the celebration. Great food, drinks, and company made that night unforgettable.

Escapade 16:
A Dream Come True

Today was my big day—the reason I came to Jakarta—Krakatoa! A car came to pick me up from the Packer Lodge at 5 a.m. and we drove three hours to Carita Beach. I had breakfast at a quaint café—fried eggs and pancakes, then met my boat mates.

As we all chatted, getting to know each other, we discovered that everyone had paid a different price. *What the...?*

I talked to the owner, who agreed to give me some of my money back. He said there was some misunderstanding. *Sure*, I thought, but I let it go without comment. Standing up for myself and asking for what I wanted felt good.

Carita is a small, sleepy beach town, and very un-touristy. I wouldn't have minded staying there for a few days, but now, my mind was on Krakatoa.

We loaded up in the van and headed for the "dock" that was just a metal post where the boat is tied. Four of us plus our captain and guide boarded and we started our journey to the Krakatoa Complex or what the locals call Krakatau.

This is my all-time favorite volcano. It's most famous for the 1883 eruption that blew the lid off the whole volcanic range—Perboewatan, Danan, and Rakata—a blast that killed thousands of people and was heard as far away as Perth, Australia. The 1927 submarine eruptions from the Krakatau Complex formed Anuk Krakatau, sometimes called the child of Krakatoa. It stands 300 meters high and is very active. As of this writing, its latest eruptions were in 2011 and 2018.

As we cruised down the Sundra Strait waiting for our first glimpse of this spectacular beauty, the clouds parted, and the sun shone bright, promising a warm, sunny day. After about one and a half hours, we got our first look at the volcano. I must have taken 100 pictures or more right then, and we were still twenty minutes away from it.

When we arrived on the island, I was mesmerized by the gorgeous black-sand beach and the lush green forest. We played around in the sand taking pictures and enjoying the view.

When another group arrived, we found out that they were there for an overnight campout. I would have loved to do that but was a bit nervous about camping on an active and currently *smoking* volcano. Kudos to them for bravery.

We hiked about twenty-five minutes to the accessible top. We couldn't hike to the actual crater because it was currently spewing out poisonous gases. But the spot where we were was still awesome, and *not poisonous*.

We checked out the hot-air vents and played with yellow balls of Sulphur. I felt like a kid exploring a new playground. Our guide showed us the lava flow from 2011, a huge lava bomb on the volcano's surface, and the seismograph. The guide pointed out that if we looked closely at the peak, we could see yellow stains that dripped down.

Krakatoa was an awesome experience, especially since there

wasn't a monkey in sight. After our descent, we sat in the forest and ate lunch. I munched on a ham sandwich and potato chips and sipped water while gazing at what was left of the original volcanic chain named Rakata.

We played on the beach after lunch. I collected some of the black glassy sand in my water bottle and we headed to our snorkel spot. As we rounded the boat to the other side of the volcano, I couldn't take my eyes off it— so incredible. My dream to see this had finally come true.

We arrived at the snorkel place. Only one guy wanted to snorkel with me, but he couldn't swim! I convinced him to put on a life vest and be my snorkel buddy. I was surprised at how shallow the water was. It seemed no more than twenty feet deep near the volcano. The water felt amazing and the fish were so colorful. I didn't want to leave.

This had been a perfect day.

I arrived back at my hostel around 8 p.m. Rachel, Manny, Paco, and Cas had flown to other destinations, so I was a lone wolf again, trying to figure out my next move. One thing I knew for sure was that I wanted to get out of Jakarta as soon as possible.

I tried to book a flight to another part of Java to meet Will and check out Mt. Bromo to see the sulfur plume and the beautiful blue gases it spews out.

There must have been a security breach or website crash with Lion Air because I tried booking multiple flights throughout Indonesia, including Sumatra, Komodo, and even back to Bali but the website kept declining my card.

I called the bank to make sure that my travel alerts were still in place and they said everything was fine and that there were no holds on my card. I was so desperate to leave the next day that I Facebook-called my friend Casey in San Diego asking her to buy me the $13 ticket to Surabaya Airport but even her card was declined.

I gave up and started looking at international flights. The only problem was I wanted to go everywhere. I finally settled on Malaysia as it was the cheapest flight out and Rachel had just arrived there, plus she knew of a great hostel. So, at 5 a.m., I headed to the airport.

Hello Malaysia! The Kuala Lumpur Airport is nice, and customs was a breeze. I rented a taxi to get to the city center and was dropped off at Reggae Hostel.

It turned out to be the wrong hostel and I ended up having to walk three long blocks to the actual Reggae Mansion, carrying my heavy backpack, and profusely sweating.

When I arrived though, I knew it had been worth it. I was greeted with ice cold cucumber-infused water—so refreshing after trudging through the extreme heat to get there. I highly recommend this hostel, it's one of *the* best—maybe even *the* best hostel of all those I'd stayed in.

It has free filtered water for refilling bottles, free breakfast, wonderful air conditioning, a rooftop bar and restaurant, a movie theater, a café, computers, comfortable capsule beds, large rooms, lockers, and awesome common areas. It's in the city center, and most importantly, it has wireless internet.

I sent Rachel a message telling her that I had arrived. She was surprised and excited because I'd told her the wrong time. We met in the café with a new travel friend, Jason, from Virginia. I loved his Southern accent, brown eyes, and dark, curly locks. We ordered a beer and I told her all about my volcano trek. After that, we headed out to look for Indian food.

I hadn't realized that Malaysia had such a heavy Indian influence. I didn't know much about Malaysia at all. I knew roughly what part of the world it was in and I'd heard it mentioned in the movie *Zoolander* (Mugatu was trying to get Derek Zoolander to kill the Malaysian Prime Minister).

I realized, then, that my time in Southeast Asia (and Australia) wasn't just about having fun. It was also about learning, embracing diverse cultures, and immersing myself in new things. Scary and completely different from my culture, I vowed to experience my time there with an open mind but without losing myself in the process. In hindsight, that was what made the whole trip, and travel in general, so wonderful.

After precise navigating via city map, Rachel successfully guided us to little India. We walked around the area for about fifteen minutes scoping out the scene and trying to make an informed decision about where our stomachs would be best taken care of.

We ended up at a buffet place. I wasn't completely convinced a buffet was the best choice but felt adventurous enough to try it without whining. Rachel's selection looked like a veggie plate and Jason's looked like mine—naan (flatbread), curry-like mystery food, some with potato and other veggies. Most dishes were spicy. After tasting the food, I had no regrets. It was delicious.

Later that night we had drinks and played cards on the rooftop bar at our hostel. I loved the beautiful view of the distant Petronas Towers. Gazing out over the city, I saw that Kuala Lumpur was filled with beautiful architecture. This was definitely a place I wanted to explore.

Rachel taught me how to play the game Irish Snap. I loved it so much, I guess I became a little obsessed with it. I'm not sure how many games we played that evening, but people kept coming to our table to see what all the fuss was about.

The next day, I got out of bed, showered, and met Rachel and Jason in the café for breakfast. I ordered fried eggs and toast with a cappuccino. Rachel chatted with some guy who didn't introduce himself, so I continued to peruse the internet until my breakfast came.

After eating, the three of us set out to see the Petronas Towers. They looked much closer than they were. We'd been walking for about forty minutes and they were still a long way off in the distance.

Luckily for us we soon stumbled on a chocolate factory—Beryl's Chocolate Kingdom. We went in relished the yummy samples, bought some chocolate—how could we not—then continued to the Petronas Towers, zigzagging through alleyways, and running into dead end streets. The more difficult it became to reach our goal, the more determined we were to conquer the mystery of the ever-distant Petronas Towers.

When we made it there, I felt like a mountain climber reaching the peak of Everest. We'd walked a long way and eyed the elevator to the observation deck but decided it was too pricey at 100 MYR ($25 US). *Yikes!*

A passerby overheard our decision not to take the elevator to the top and suggested we go to the Sky Garden rooftop bar and indoor pool. It was free. We gladly took his advice. The Sky Garden was high up and had a pleasant view as well, so we stayed, ordered food and drinks, and gawked at the amazing view. What a wonderful afternoon. We stayed until after sunset and enjoyed the beautiful night lights.

The next morning, we climbed out of bed, scrubbed up, ate, and took the train to the Batu Caves, thirteen kilometers north of

Kuala Lumpur. We accidentally ended up in a women's only car on the train. We tried to find a coed car so Jason, Rachel, and I could all ride together, but no luck. We had to split up.

When I first discovered that there was even such a thing as a "women's only" car, I thought it was sexist and belittling to women. However, after taking a moment to think about other reasons for this kind of segregation, such as sweaty funky guys who would benefit from some deodorant, or creepy men hitting on or harassing women, protection, or even religious beliefs, I became more tolerant of the idea. Besides, who am I to judge another culture's traditions?

The limestone Batu Caves are named after the neighboring village of Batu—a place of worship and one of the most popular Hindu shrines outside of India. In front of the caves is a 140-foot statue of Lord Murugan, who defeated a demon named Soorapadman.

In the open area in front of the staircase, a local man threw birdseed into the air. Pigeons raced toward Rachel and me while trying to catch the seeds. *Ughhhhhh!* Bird poop everywhere.

There are 272 steps on the staircase into the caves. I was so disappointed when I found out that the famous Dark Caves were closed, so we had to settle for the Temple Caves. These are simple and housed a small temple. Luckily, we arrived there during a performance just outside.

Am I cursed by the monkey god? I thought as the creatures from hell hopped onto the steps to mess with us. I don't care what people say. Monkeys are not cute or fun. They are infuriating.

Next, we met up with Rachel's friend Chad, from Australia. He's the guy who didn't introduce himself earlier. We all headed to the Butterfly Garden. This place, I loved. The biggest butterfly I'd ever seen landed on my back and stayed there for about five minutes. How cool is that?

After wandering for a while, I rested on a bench to reflect on the beautiful garden. A few minutes later, Chad showed up and we chatted and got to know each other. I noticed how good-looking he was—at least 6-feet 5-inches, brown shoulder-length hair, and showing a little more than a five-o'clock shadow. He'd just finished up in the Australian Navy and was traveling around the world for the next year.

It turned out that we had a lot in common—he was a sailor with a foul mouth, and I *worked* on boats with sailors with foul mouths. He seemed like a nice person. It was fun to hang out with him for the afternoon.

My favorite part about the Garden was the Bat Frog. It looked like Batman in a frog shape. If I could, I'd for sure have one as a pet. The garden is small, but it was so amazing that, for a little while, I forgot I was in the middle of a large noisy city.

For dinner, Rachel, Jason, and I treated ourselves to dinner at a fancy Chinese restaurant inside the Ritz Carlton. The prices at this Ritz were much lower than the ones in Western countries.

As a special splurge, this place was backpacker friendly with its prices. We ordered a whole duck and sides for 124 RM (Malaysian Ringgit), about $30 US. It was delicious. We all ate until we thought we would burst.

Rachel and I went home to pack for our next-day flight to Phuket. We met the boys for a nightcap at the rooftop bar.

It's funny most of the backpackers I'd met on my travels were easy to befriend and to like enough to want to travel with them. Rachel is so much fun. I adore her short red hair and her British accent. She was recovering from a breakup, so I think she was happy to have a travel buddy to keep her mind busy. I was glad she seemed to like hanging out with me as much as I liked being with her.

We met in the lobby for breakfast. Jason caught us just before we left. He'd overslept because of the partying he did the night before, plus, he also met Sandra, a girl staying in the all-female dorm with me.

I suspected that they'd gotten "friendly" but didn't comment. It was really none of my business. Still, I was happy for them if they had really hooked up.

We ran into Chad on our way to the airport. He gave me the biggest, sweetest hug and a kiss on the cheek. We exchanged info and agreed to keep in touch. You always hope that people will stay in contact, but I've learned that most guys follow the rule, "out of sight out of mind." So, I vowed not to hold my breath waiting for a message from him.

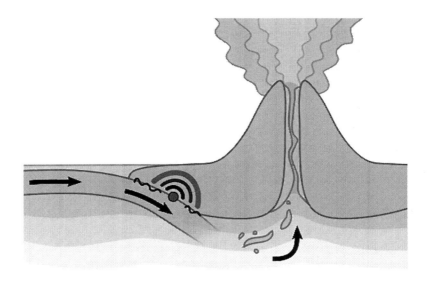

Destructive_plate_margin.png: Ævar Arnfjörð Bjarmason derivative work:

NikNaks talk - gallery - wikipedia / Public domain

Escapade 17:

Expose My Undergarments to Strangers

For the second time, I was off to Thailand. I would have loved to travel around Padang but my travel bud, Rachel was heading to the island of Koh Samui, the second largest island in the Gulf of Thailand, off the east coast of the Kra Isthmus.

Rachel and I flew through customs and had a two-hour wait for our flight. Nature called so I headed for the restroom. I love rompers, but they're such a pain having to take the whole thing off to pee. The one I wore that day had a side zipper. It slid down okay but when it was time to zip it back up, it broke. *Oh, f!@#ing great!* I fiddled with it for a few minutes before giving up. It couldn't be fixed. With my jacket in my checked bag, I had nothing to cover the gaping hole in my outfit, so I bravely marched out of the restroom and headed for Rachel in the waiting area. She didn't seem to notice, so I said nothing, thinking it wasn't really that bad. How wrong I was. Moments later, the loudest laugh came out of her mouth. "Are you trying to start a new fashion trend?" she asked between guffaws.

Never a dull moment. My gaping nakedness wasn't the only issue. When we began the boarding process, I felt like all eyes were glued on me as I fumbled around trying to pick up my boarding pass that had fallen on the ground, exposing my undergarments to the light of day. I wanted to dig a hole and crawl in. But I lifted my chin and summoned up enough courage to keep going as if nothing was out of the ordinary. *After all, I thought, on the beach or at a pool, we might as well be totally naked. Only tiny bits of postage-stamp-size cloth and a bit of string cover a miniscule portion of skin. What's the big deal? Hmmmph.*

We boarded the plane and dropped into our seats. Thankfully, before the wheels left the ground, I was sound asleep.

I woke up to the announcement, "We have now begun our taxi to the arrival gate. Please keep your seatbelt fastened and luggage stowed until the seat belt sign is turned off." Of course, people were already up, clamoring to retrieve their carry-on bags. My eyes rolled so hard I thought they might stick to my brain. *Why are people in such a rush? They can't go anywhere until the captain turns off the seatbelt sign. It's crazy.* When the seatbelt sign *was* turned off, I waited until the crowd thinned then retrieved my carry-on and slowly walked down the aisle. An impatient woman practically jumped over the seats trying to get past me. I just shook my head and took sardonic pleasure in her distress.

Being super slow departing an airplane became a ritual for me. The more frantic people were, the slower I moved. I looked around and thought, *Chill out and stop rushing for no reason. Jeez. Heart attacks just waiting to happen, people.*

Airplane chaos behind us, my mood lifted. Next stop, Phuket rainforest, a mountainous island with clear waters and a lively nightlife. It was just a short detour on our way to Koh Samui, so we took the airport shuttle to Patong Beach. Casey, Valerie, and I had just been there about six weeks prior, so I was familiar with it.

But nothing is ever straightforward and easy, so of course, our shuttle dropped us off in a very inconvenient location. The excuse was that the driver didn't want to brave the crazy traffic. I grumbled in my head about the driver but kept it to myself. After all, what could we do? Nothing. We sighed, then lugged our heavy backpacks down Bangla Road.

The best way to describe Bangla Road would be a smaller, dirtier version of the Las Vegas strip. In this town, and especially on this street, anything goes. There are no rules. It's a wonderful place to people-watch and to party.

We trekked to Patong Backpacker, dodging drunks and hookers along the way. We worried that we didn't have a reservation, but luck smiled on us. They had two beds available.

Inside, we gladly ditched our bags and headed out for dinner and to buy some food for our long bus ride the next morning. For dinner, we ended up at the three-level hookah bar/lounge, on a third-floor balcony. We all loved the perfect view of Bangla Road, so we sat back and watched the people.

Looking toward the building across the street, we could see a woman dancing in the window. It was surreal and humorous at the same time. The lounge played 90s hip-hop and pop. They had couches to recline on and watch old music videos. A lot to do there but we were not up for partying, so we ordered food and a few drinks and kept it low-key.

The next day we took a bus north to Surat Thani to catch a ferry to Koh Samui island. Again, it's never easy in this part of the world. We left at 7:30 in the morning and didn't arrive at the ferry dock until 4:30 in the afternoon. As backpackers, it's just second nature to take the cheapest, longest possible way.

But it wasn't all bad. The drive was beautiful. It took us through lush, green vegetation. I would have really loved it if we hadn't been crammed in a full van for eight hours on a winding, rugged road. Not pleasant.

By the time we reached the coast and spotted the Gulf of Thailand, I put thoughts of the rough ride out of my mind and took long, deep breaths of refreshing coastal air, heavy with briny, fishy aromas. I loved it.

When we arrived at the dock, the ferry was already there. Soon Rachel and I would be in paradise. We landed on the island around sunset. After negotiating a ride with a woman we'd met when we got off the ferry, we were on our way to the town center.

The route to town center proved interesting. The road was lined with huge trees and large, abandoned and half-finished houses but almost no people or cars in sight. I would have loved to see it during the day. We had the driver drop us off at Samui Backpacker.

Again, we didn't have a reservation and hoped our luck would hold and they would have room for us. Huh? Empty lobby. We waited a minute or two, but when we were sure no one was going to come to our aid, we connected to the Wi-Fi and searched for other hostels in the area. We'd found one and were about to head out when one of the owners of this hostel returned, looking a bit surprised to see us.

Small world, the owner was a Californian—like me. He'd moved to Thailand a few years prior and loved it so much he decided to stay and open a hostel. He didn't have citizenship, so he had to go on visa runs every ninety days.

A visa run is when you fly out of a country and fly back soon after so your allotted visa days start over. In a lot of Southeast Asian countries there isn't a set amount of time you have to remain out of the country, so people usually go to Laos or somewhere close for the weekend and then fly back to Thailand to start their visa over. Neat trick.

Jack, the owner, showed us to a twelve-bed dorm on the first floor. We changed into clean clothes and put new sheets on our beds.

Something cool we later discovered was that every evening at 8 or 9, the hostel staff gathers everyone up and shows them the best food spots, then they head to bars and clubs.

Rachel and I met everyone in the common area then headed to the night market. I love night markets and I love street food. This one was small compared to some I'd been to, but the food was great. I had a kiwi coconut smoothie, chicken skewers and Pad Thai.

After dinner, the guys took us to their favorite beach bar. It was nestled down a tiny alley behind a small bed and breakfast. It was hard to find since we didn't know what to look for. There's nothing like having drinks at a tiki bar while on a swing enjoying the ocean breeze and mellow tunes. There were small bonfires going and logs and chairs to sit on. Such a wonderful place to start off the night. I would have stayed out later, but we were tired from the long travel day, so we headed back to the hostel early.

☼ ☼ ☼

The next morning, we were ready for some serious beach time. But food, first. On the street, we found a hole-in-the-wall restaurant. It didn't look like much from the outside, and didn't even have a name, but turned out to be a terrific choice. The food was outstanding and super cheap. I ordered medium spicy seafood fried rice and a Thai iced tea. I ate every morsel.

After our stomachs were full, we roamed around and asked some locals where we could find a nice quiet beach. It turns out we were on the wrong side of the island for peace and quiet, so we hopped in a "taksi" and headed to the other side. It took about twenty minutes and the cab dropped us off somewhere, we weren't sure where. We wandered around for a bit looking for the perfect spot. This side of the island was awesome. I wished we were staying there instead of on the noisy side.

The water was clean, the shops were so cute, and it was less touristy. We spent the entire day there. We even snuck into a resort seating area and stretched out on beach chairs, ordering food and drinks like we belonged there. We swam for a while and just stared off into the horizon. No pressure. It was a beautiful day. Just a little bit before sunset we reluctantly packed our stuff and hitched a ride back to our side of the island.

image: Pixabay.com

HAZARD 18:

UNCLOG A TOILET

Back at the hostel, we all showered and met the crew in the lobby for our food run. We had a bite to eat at the big night market then headed to the Ice Bar.

Against my better judgement, I got on the back of a motorbike with Art, from London. He drove like a maniac. I thought that day would be my last. He weaved in and out of traffic and took corners way too fast.

Rachel was lucky. She got to ride with Jeff who was a cautious driver.

By the grace of God, we all arrived at the Ice Bar unscathed. I'd never been to an ice bar and was excited to see what the fuss was about. I was pleased that the place had a good-looking bartender with a sexy English accent. He introduced himself as Joe. I told him my name was Mat Backwards.

He seemed amused by that and said, "I've never met a girl named Matt before. How formal to give your first and last name." I busted out with laughter.

97

Rachel grinned and said, "Her name is Tam, you know, 'mat' spelled backwards."

He smiled. "Very clever."

I melted a little. He was a charmer, and he made a mean margarita for us—on the house. We cheered and toasted to travel and new friendships.

Joe and I stepped into our own little bubble of conversation. It felt like no one else was around. Then some girls came to the bar whining that the toilet was clogged—bubble burst. Reality closed in.

Joe told Art if he got the toilet unclogged that he would give him 100 THB ($10 US). Joe then explained that Art had come to Thailand for a vacation about a year before and fell in love with a hooker and explained, "He now lives on Koh Samui to try to win her love. He has no money, so he does small jobs to get by."

Art saluted, then headed for the bathroom, returning just a few minutes later with a wet hand and said he'd unclogged the toilet.

I screamed and said, "With your hand?"

He stared at me with wide eyes. "Yes."

Joe shook his head. "Go clean up."

I couldn't believe Art did that bare-handed. *Didn't he know that rubber gloves have been around for a long time?*

Joe took me inside the *real* Ice Bar— the super cold part. It wasn't what I'd expected. No ice blocks nor a bar made of ice, but it *was* like walking into a large freezer except it looked like any average bar. I had on a summer dress and no jacket, so I didn't stay long. I wondered, *What's the point of that? Seems sort of lame, to me.*

Rachel and I were getting ready to leave to go to the quiet tiki bar on the beach but changed our minds when three guys walked in. They were *Adonis incarnate.* I forgot all about Joe when they came through the door. *Wow.*

Rachel and I quickly ordered another round of drinks. The guys came over and started talking. Joe asked for their drink orders and gave me and Rachel a shot. He tried so hard to steal my attention back from the new heartthrobs in the room.

I'm glad he hung in there because the pretty boys turned out to be pretty but that's about it. They were bone-numbing boring. The convo wasn't really flowing and I hoped they would just leave. No luck, they seemed oblivious and hung around us like gnats on a banana.

Finally, Rachel and I excused ourselves and went outside. We decided to leave but went back in to thank Joe. He slipped me his number. I told him I didn't have a phone to call so I asked for his email address. He gave it to me without a second's hesitation.

Yes! I had delicious plans for Joe.

He kissed my cheek and gave me a hug and I was off to the Tiki Bar. Art met us there later that evening, but not because he wanted to party with us. The hooker girl he was in love with worked there. Turns out that she held several odd jobs all over the island. He just bummed around the bar while Rachel and I progressively got drunker.

We asked Art if he knew of another place for us to go because the Tiki was starting to fade out. He suggested a club a little way up the beach. "Look for the one with bright lights."

We walked about a quarter mile and came upon a fire dance. What luck. It turned out to be the beach club we'd been looking for. We hung out there for about a half hour then headed back to the Tiki to retrieve Art.

Sad-faced Art in tow, we went to a crazy club on the main street. It played techno and house music but was set up like a two-level country-western bar. The top level had no ceiling and we could look into the sky. I spent most of my time up there, getting lost in the music. For the moment, I had no cares in the world.

Rachel and I found each other when the club began to empty out. We walked back to our hostel but decided we weren't ready for bed, so we went for a swim in the gulf.

Over the next few days, we explored the island, visiting a new place every day before Rachel headed off to China. I would have gone, too if I had the visa, but I didn't so I headed to Laos. We both had to catch flights from Bangkok, so we shared one last breakfast together then went our separate ways but, of course, promised to keep in touch.

Bangkok again! I must say that BKK is one of the nicest airports in Southeast Asia. Modern and clean, it almost looks like a work of art.

If you travel through the southeast, chances are that at least once, you'll have to use one of the two Bangkok airports—Suvarnabhumi (BKK) or Don Mueang (DMK). Certain airlines fly out of one and not the other. For example, Air Asia moved from BKK to DMK.

When I booked my last-minute flight to Vientiane, I didn't check to see which airport I would be leaving from, lucky for me I ended up at BKK, the correct one for my departing flight to Laos. I could have easily ended up at the wrong airport.

I guess by then, I knew the ropes and booked the latest flight possible, just in case there were delays at the airport, something all too common in that part of the world.

Before my flight, I grabbed a bite of yellowtail sashimi, ahi, eel, and scallops. *Yummmm*. At my gate, I sat for about fifteen minutes before realizing my departure gate had changed. I hurried down ten gates, grumbling, then patiently waited to board.

While I was sitting in the waiting area, I made eye contact with a guy sitting near me. I smiled and then looked away. We made eye contact again—code for time to introduce myself. "Hello," I said.

He introduced himself as Sam. I noticed that he was dressed like Indiana Jones, including a fedora hat. I didn't see a whip, though. We started talking and I discovered that he was a geologist from Australia and was moving to Vientiane for six months to work.

My heart raced. A geologist? I lit up like Christmas. I didn't even try to hide it. I'm obsessed with geology, plate tectonics, volcanology, and more. This felt like heaven. It's not every day that I meet a geologist, and a gorgeous one at that.

I confessed my obsession, grilled him with questions, and told him how I had hiked two volcanoes and how great it would have been to climb them with a geologist. We talked all through the boarding line and ended up seated next to each other on the plane. What are the odds? We chatted the whole way to Vientiane. At the end of our flight, we exchanged email addresses and agreed to meet up the next day.

Escapade 19:

Me—an Illegal Alien in a Foreign Country and a Nasty Gash.

When Sam and I arrived in Laos and saw the sign that read WELCOME TO THE DEMOCRATIC REPUBLIC OF LAOS, we were filled with anticipation at the exciting possibilities. Our elation, however, was short-lived. The customs agent said we had to pay $35 US—in cash—for the visa. Surprise! Neither of us had known that there would be a visa charge. *Well,* I thought, *this is what I get for booking a last-minute flight and doing no research.*

Not to be discouraged, we asked where the nearest ATM could be found.

He seemed a bit annoyed as he shook his head and told us, "No ATM."

We weren't ready to give up and started talking to two others in the same boat—Stefanie and Denise. Sam and I joined forces and talked with an airport staff member. We pleaded our innocence and surprise over the charge. I was so relieved when she empathized with our situation and snuck us through customs so we could use the ATM near baggage claim.

So, for a brief time, we were technically in Laos—illegally. I thought about how this situation might have played out in the US. We would have been detained and, well, I don't even want to think about the possibilities.

After we withdrew money for the charge, our co-conspirator escorted us back to customs. We all paid the fee and entered the country legally. I always seem to get out of tight situations through serendipity.

Having gone through our little adventure together, we bonded with Denise and Stefanie, from Germany. Stefanie's English is perfect, and Denise's English is good but not as good as her Spanish. Both ladies are fit and lovely. Denise is tall and thin, and Stefanie is about my height but skinny/curvy. Denise is the more talkative one and Stefanie is more reserved.

More serendipity, they were staying at the same hostel I was. So, we split a cab. Sam tagged along but he was booked somewhere else down the street from us.

We dropped Sam at his place, then the girls and I pulled up to Dream Home hostel. I was glad I'd had the foresight to make a reservation because the place was completely full.

In the sixteen-bed dorm, I discovered that my streak of luck had worn off. The only bed left was on a top bunk. Top bunks suck. There's less storage space, most often a crappy ladder to climb, and my stuff always falls off. And in the likely case that I'd been drinking before bed, it takes extra effort to get up there. The one saving grace was that the room was cold. I sleep great in the cold. It's hot that makes me toss and turn all night.

Later, the four of us met a couple of blocks down the road for some street food. Not what I had expected from past experiences. This place was dark and smelly. As I looked around, I noticed that a lot of businesses were closed. It turned out that Laos has a curfew of 11 p.m. and it was past that hour. That was my second unexpected disappointment in this country. Not a good sign. However, as an intrepid traveler I wasn't daunted by a silly rule like that. I knew there must be an underground network of partiers somewhere, so I had a light dinner from one of the few places still open and planned to seek out the nightlife after eating.

But, intrepid traveler or not, after dinner, we discovered that we were all too tired to party, so we called it a night and went back to the hostel.

The next day, I felt full of energy and excitement about my first morning in Vientiane. At breakfast, I enjoyed a fried egg, bread, and cappuccino then headed to Denise and Stefanie's room to devise a plan for the day.

Exploring Vientiane, we discovered that most people spoke English, drove on the right side of the road, and preferred cars over motorbikes—much like in the US. We also discovered, sadly, that this was a sleepy city.

During the day, most of the people we saw on the streets were tourists. I guessed that the locals were smart enough to stay indoors during the extreme heat. I wonder if they laughed about the stupid foreigners walking around in the blazing sun and humidity while they sipped cold drinks and fanned themselves in their cool homes.

The one thing about this city that gave me the heebie jeebies were the dogs. They roamed the streets and seemed to be everywhere. They didn't really bother anyone but, being from the US, I associate free-roaming dogs with danger. I gave them a wide berth when I could.

Because of the insufferable heat, we made frequent stops at the shops to buy bottled water to stay hydrated. In one little store—typically not air-conditioned and sweltering inside—

we met the cutest petite lady, dressed in an ankle-length pink flowered skirt and long-sleeved cream top. She either worked there, or owned the shop, I wasn't sure. The woman didn't speak a lick of English but, somehow, we were able to communicate, anyway. Funny how that works most everywhere in the world. Language is not always a barrier to communication.

After I found the water I was looking for, I noticed a deck of cards laying in a stack on the counter. They were waterproof and only thirty cents, so I bought them. Now, I had something that could keep me busy on any long bus ride.

After reading up on Vientiane, we discovered that, outside of a few ancient attractions, there isn't much to do in this quiet city. We walked to the National Monument, visited The Great Sacred Stupa Pha, and spent some time in Buddha Park, which is littered with statues surrounded by beautiful green grass. We also saw the Sisaket Temple and Museum and Chao Anouvong Park, near the Mekong River.

The Mekong is a must-see. It runs through China, Burma (Myanmar), Laos, Thailand, Cambodia, and Vietnam. In some places it looks more like a muddy trickle than a river. In other places it's massive and full of rapids. A lot of people in small villages are dependent on its water to irrigate their farms, rice patties, and for the fish it provides.

After checking out some of the sites we'd had our limit of heat and decided to go to the air-conditioned mall and cool off. It's called a mall, but it's tiny by American standards—about the size of a Target. It carries a lot of goods, though, nearly everything anyone might need—groceries, fans, sporting goods, clothes, toys, and hardware.

Outside the mall was the "Outside Market." It had street food and trinkets—mostly just for tourists, such as magnets, key chains, and a bunch of cheaply made stuff from China. We weren't really interested in most of that, so we browsed for a while then scoured the area for somewhere to eat that was inside and air-conditioned. We weren't ready to brave the heat again. How hot was it? So hot, even the local wildlife stayed mostly in the shade. The average temperature in Laos is only 84°F although it can sometimes go as high as 104°F or more. It's the humidity that makes it seem so much hotter.

We found somewhere inside to eat. It had air conditioning, but the food was disappointingly mediocre. After eating, we still weren't ready to face the heat and searched for some indoor activities. Aha! An $8 full body massage, manicure, pedicure spa was just the ticket.

It was heaven, but we couldn't stay there all day so, all mani-pedied up, we headed back to the hostel for a much-needed nap.

The next day, I took my new cards to the hostel's common area, hoping to meet some new, backpackers. I found Denise, Stefanie, and Sam sitting at the wooden tables socializing with some people I didn't know, so I joined them and asked if they wanted to play a game of Irish Snap (the game Rachel taught me). Some of them gave me a blank, deer-in-the-headlights look, so I explained the rules:

All the cards are dealt face down. No one is allowed to look at their cards. The person to the left of the dealer starts the game by saying 'Ace' while flipping their top card over and placing it in the middle of the table.

The next person says 'Two' while flipping their top card over and placing it in the middle of the table. This continues with 3, 4, and 5…all the way through the deck and is repeated until the game ends.

If someone says a number, and it matches the number they flip over…for example…if someone says 'Six' and the card that they put down is a 6, everyone slaps the deck at the same time.

The first person on the pile of hands (the first one to slap) has to take the pile. The object of the game is to collect all the cards.

Also, doubles require slaps. So, if someone flips a 7 and the next person also flips a 7, that's a double, and everyone slaps the pile. The first one to slap gets the deck.

We had so much fun. I'm sure I got the girls hooked on the game. After a couple of hours of Snap and some sore hands, we'd worked up a hefty appetite. Stefanie, a food connoisseur, knew just the place—Makphet.

We weren't sure where it was but made it our mission to find it. Of course, the first place we looked was the internet. *Trip Advisor* gave this restaurant a seal of excellence. Promising.

We tucked our money bags under our clothes and headed out. Walking down the dog-filled streets, we followed the directions listed online. After passing the spa where we'd had our massages, we trekked along the Mekong River and passed a few temples, inhaling the disgusting street aroma caused by people tossing garbage into the street instead of in trash cans. *Joy.* This place was turning out to be one of my least favorite destinations. If it wasn't for the great people I'd met, I might have left for somewhere else.

After about half an hour of trekking through smelly streets, we finally reached the destination listed online. And of course, the restaurant was nowhere to be found.

Thinking it might be nearby, we headed down an alley and explored a few adjacent streets but had no luck. When all else fails, ask someone. So, we stopped a local on the street and asked if he knew where Makphet was. He was familiar with the place but told us that it had moved. He showed us where. It's a good thing he did. We would never have found it on our own.

In keeping with my luck in this part of the world so far, we arrived just as the restaurant was closing. We must have looked desperate or starving because the kind owner didn't turn us away, but we had to be out by 11:30 pm. Another near disaster helped by a kind stranger.

Well, we had to make it worth the owner's time, so we

ordered eight traditional Laos dishes and split them all family style. All the effort we made to find this place paid off. The food was amazing. I'd had no expectations about Laotian food, but *man* this was good!

One of the reasons I love to travel is because I love good food, especially food that I've never had before. The more exotic, the better.

I really enjoyed my time with Stefanie and Denise. Stefanie was on a six-week work holiday and Denise had just quit her job in South America where she worked with children and adults who had amputated limbs. One of the things she did in the past was fit people for prosthetics. What a tough yet rewarding job. She's the reason we went to the Cooperative Orthotic and Prosthetic Enterprise Center in Vientiane (COPE). It ensures that people with disabilities get education, treatment, and rehabilitation for free. Most of the people treated there had been wounded by unexploded ordinances left over from the Vietnam War.

I was surprised that people in small villages were still encountering these horrible things. Most of the victims are children. It seems that kids are the same everywhere. They like to explore. In Laos, kids discovered that they could make some money collecting these bombs. They search for them, not knowing how dangerous they can be.

The center was filled with pictures of people seriously wounded by ammunitions. We also saw some of the things people had made out of the metal from bombs—bowls, pots, pans, utensils, jewelry, furniture and more. I was fascinated by the maps of the bombed areas, and a video describing Laos' perception of the war. There was a display of a variety of prosthetics and how they've evolved from simple into high-tech.

I was amazed also, at how some people living in tiny rural villages, who'd lost limbs, had improvised, and made their own prostheses.

Another thing the COPE center does is provide education

about live ammunitions—what they look like, how to avoid them, and what to do if one is found. They also train teams to diffuse the bombs. There are teams whose sole mission is to sweep areas to find and diffuse all the unexploded ordinances from the Vietnam War.

The COPE Center receives funding and donations from countries and people all over the world.

Denise went to the prosthesis lab to work, while Stefanie and I grabbed lunch around the corner. The menu was in Laotian, so we just pointed at the pictures. The restaurant was so cute, and the people were so small, I felt like a giant sitting in my tiny plastic chair. Just picture a full-grown adult in one of those colorful kiddy chairs that you can buy in the US and probably in Europe, too.

We ordered soup. The air temperature was close to 100°F and 80 percent humidity outside and we ordered hot soup. Why? Well, as we looked around, the locals all ordered soup, so we did too. Maybe, we thought, it helped make the heat a little more tolerable. All I know is that the soup was amazing, and Stefanie and I were happy.

I love traveling with someone who likes to eat as much as I do. When we tried to stand up, the baby chairs stuck to our butts. This could have been humiliating because all the locals in the restaurant broke out in laughter, but we took it in stride and laughed, too.

On our way back to Dream Home, we stopped at several travel agencies and bus depots to find out how much it would cost to go to Vang Vieng the next day. Sometimes it's easier and cheaper to book travel arrangements through hostels, but I'd read online that the Dream House over-charged for transport and that travel agencies were a better deal. When we'd asked the hostel how much to go to Vang Vieng, it was a bit steep, so we arranged our own transport. A little research is always a good thing.

We scooped up Sam from his hotel and went to dinner at Jamil Zahid Indian and Pakistani Restaurant. We'd stumbled on this place by accident while exploring and vowed to come back and check it out.

The location couldn't be worse—down a shady-looking alley that dead ended at a dog hideout. It gave me the creeps. I relaxed a little when I found out that the dog belonged to the owner and was harmless.

Once settled in a "grown-up's" chair, I ordered samosas for an appetizer and the tikka masala with chicken and garlic naan for my main dish. When the food arrived the smell alone told me I'd made the right decision. I'll bet I couldn't have had better Indian food in India. I stuffed my face. The others had no complaints either. They "mmmed" and "oohed" while shoveling food in their mouths. After dinner we found a little ice cream spot for the perfect dessert. They didn't have many flavor options, so I stuck with a basic scoop of chocolate. Sam ordered strawberry, and Stefanie decided to go "exotic" with a chocolate/vanilla swirl.

Sam accompanied us back to our hostel but didn't stay. He had work in the morning. I gave him a big hug and said I'd meet up with him on my way back through Vientiane.

In the dorm, I packed and prepared for our trip in the morning.

The next day, I gathered all my things and headed downstairs for breakfast but sliced my foot on an open locker door. Blood gushed everywhere but the only thing I could do was continue downstairs to the lobby to get it cleaned up.

I told the hostel staff what happened. Their response was, "Wow. That has happened before, sorry."

Sorry? Were they kidding me? If this was the US, they would be rushing to come to my aid for fear of a lawsuit. Here, it was just "sorry." I held my temper and calmly told them it was in their best interest to replace those lockers—especially if that wasn't the first time someone was injured.

Denise came to my rescue with antibiotic ointment and a large Band-Aid. I had to take ibuprofen for the pain. Not the start of my day I'd been looking forward to. I gulped down my fried egg, fruit and cappuccino then literally hopped into the van with the girls. Pain or no pain I was not going to miss Vang Vieng.

The long, bumpy road was uncomfortable but so beautiful, filled with thick trees, curvy turns, meandering cliffs, and magnificent mountains. We passed by limestone caves, washes, and livestock. I was tired and needed some sleep but didn't want to miss any of the beautiful scenery. I managed to get a couple of ZZZs in, though.

When we arrived at the bus station and the van stopped, my eyes sprung open in excitement. I hadn't even realized I'd fallen asleep. The station, just a dirt field with no signs, was a short walk outside the town center. We asked the driver which way to town. He pointed in a direction and said, "Three minutes."

We grabbed our bags, thanked the driver, then trekked into town. Sweat drenched the back of my tank top in the extreme heat. The area looked abandoned, with empty roads except for the people from the bus who were looking for accommodations.

I'd heard a lot of great things about this place and was pretty excited about it, so I put the emptiness and the weird bus station out of my mind and vowed to really enjoy my stay there.

We found the hostel. Our 5th floor room was a pleasant surprise, spacious and with a balcony that overlooked the river. The bathroom had a regular toilet instead of a hole in the ground like so many other places in Southeast Asia.

Stefanie and Denise shared the queen bed and I took the twin bed next to the balcony. Exhausted after the long bus ride, we dropped into a two-hour nap while listening to the wonderful hum of the air conditioner.

We woke up famished, so we wandered around town looking for food, finally stopping at a little restaurant called the Jungle Bar. Cushions and pillows surrounded the tables, so we could lounge and relax. We ordered food and split a pitcher of beer. Stefanie and Denise invited some friends they'd met at another hostel to join us for lunch. We played Irish Snap in German so that I could learn how to count in that language. I needed more practice. Everyone was super nice, and I really enjoyed them.

Escapade 20:

Freak Out in a Narrow Cave

The Padeng caves were about a fifteen-minute bike ride from the town center. We were stoked to explore these limestone beauties, so we shopped around for reasonably priced rental bikes in good condition. The bike place the hostel recommended was close and near the river.

The local people stared at us as we passed by. I thought this might be because we all looked so different from them, and from each other. One of us, tall and skinny, another, blonde, and the third with skin of cocoa.

We walked along, noticing the local activities. Dogs played in the streets and people cooked skewers of food on tiny metal trays. A woman sat making shoes out of cowhide and restaurant owners prepared for the evening festivities.

At the rental place, I chose a blue bike with a bell and basket. Denise picked a green one, and Stefanie got red. After testing them out, we headed back down the way we came.

The wind blowing in my face felt amazing and the scenery reminded me of a 1000-piece jigsaw puzzle that I had put together when I was a kid. I remember thinking it was all so pristine. Now, however, as I look back through the photos I took, the place seems so different from the pictures in my head. It wasn't perfect or pristine. Funny how memory can distort reality.

We veered off the main road onto a dirt track and followed it through a field to a fenced area. It was a good place to leave the bikes. Locking them together, we grabbed our packs and water, then squeezed through the fence.

When we arrived at the limestone outcrop entrance, a man, who turned out to be a guide, noticed us. He collected our entrance fee of 10,000 Kp. We wanted to enter alone but he insisted that everyone needed a personal guide to get in and out. Okay, no argument.

We followed him into the cave. In the beginning, the area was wide and well-lit by the sunlight, but after about a minute or so of walking, it narrowed and grew dark. It made me uncomfortable.

We went deeper into the cave. It seemed as if with each step the walls pushed in closer. The air turned cold. I gave myself an internal pep talk. *This is creepy. I just want out. I can't be the only one feeling like this. Or am I? Stop worrying. Cowgirl-up and stop being a wuss. It will be okay.* My thoughts were suddenly interrupted when a spider slid past my face. I screamed. Everyone but the guide jumped and squealed or gasped. I guess I scared more than the spider.

At that point, I seriously considered turning around and getting the hell outta there but I steeled myself and kept walking.

The air was moist and the ground, muddy. I was ever so grateful to have the guide with us. About a mile in, Denise told me she was feeling claustrophobic. A minute later, she started to panic. I could hear her shallow breath growing more rapid by the second. I thought she was on the verge of hyperventilating.

Just when I was thinking she was about to freak out, she asked me if I could sing to help her calm down. Great idea. I began singing:

Down by the bank where the watermelons grow,
back to my home,
I dare not go, for if I do, my mother would sayyyyyyyyyyyy,
have you ever seen a bear combing his hair?
Down by the bank, down by the bank where the
watermelons grow, back to my home,
I dare not go, for if I do, my mother would sayyyyyy,
have you ever seen a frog kissin' a log down by the bank,
Down by the bank....

I kept singing until we reached the back of the cave. We had to lay on our stomachs and slide through a hole barely big enough for each of us to fit. On the other side the only thing we could see was a massive opening into darkness. It felt good to be in an open space again and out of the squeezy narrowness. I brightened my headlamp to see the amazing limestone formations. It was awesome. I felt like I was standing in outer space.

After resting and rehydrating, we made our way to the entrance by backtracking the way we came in. This time I was in the back of the line. Super freaky. I heard weird noises behind me, and I felt like something was going to sneak up and grab me. I stayed as close to Denise as possible.

We reached a broken horizontal ladder/bridge that we'd crossed on the trek in. It was still scary. On the other side, the way grew steeper and I noted that going up was a lot harder than it had been when we were climbing down. This was the most dangerous part of the cave trek. Anyone who fell through the ladder would end up in a deep hole at the bottom. At one point, we struggled to climb up and over a massive gap in the rocks. I breathed a sigh of relief after we all made it safely.

As we continued, the cave widened and the heat from outside brought the temperature up. When I saw the cave mouth, filled with light, I was so relieved. As I glanced at the others, it was clear that they were also more than happy to be out of that dark but awesome place.

Bright sunlight and hot, fresh air slammed into us. I've always been fascinated by how the cool temperature in caves never heats up. Nature's air conditioner.

I turned to Denise. She seemed to be fully recovered from the claustrophobia. She gave me a weak smile and said she was sure she'd never go into another cave again.

I wonder if she later had nightmares about it.

She told me that she'd freaked out in a cave in South America so badly they had to carry her out. I asked her why she went into this one.

She said, "I really wanted to see it, and hoped I'd have a better experience."

I thought, *Sorry Denise, phobias don't work like that. They're pretty reliable. Freak out once and you can count on it happening again.* Well, cheers to her for trying but I'd bet she'll never be joining a spelunking team.

Since we were safely out of the cave and all calmed down, the guide decided that he could squeeze a little more money out of us. He announced that the tour wasn't included in the entrance fee of 10,000 Kp and insisted we pay him another 50,000.

Sure, buster. I figured, since he hadn't told us upfront about the "tour" fee, he'd volunteered his time to take us through the cave. I'd planned on tipping him at the end of the tour but after that cheating maneuver, the tip meter went to zero.

Stefanie chickened out and paid him. He took the money and ran off. What a scam. *Ughhhhh.*

By the time we got back to our bikes, it was near sunset. The green and brown field was now mixed with orange and purple hues from the sun. We leaned on our bikes and enjoyed the view of the changing sky. It was incredibly peaceful. No one was around but us. All we could hear were insects making noises and the occasional moo from distant cows.

Hazard 21:

Watch Lanterns Float through the Sky

Later that night we ate dinner at the Kangaroo Sunset Bar, known for their tasty burgers and nice ambience. I had the Beerlao burger and enjoyed background pop music from the 90s. The three of us shared a large table with people we didn't know. We chatted for a while, sharing travel stories and tips on must-see or do activities in Vang Vieng.

Nelly's song "It's Hot in Here" came on. Talk about truth in music, the restaurant was really hot. So, what did I do? Hit the dance floor with our new friends, of course.

We sang and shook our butts, laughed and sweated to the beat as we all sang the first four lines of the verse like we were performing it on stage or for a crowd.

After leaving the Kangaroo, we wandered through the lively streets taking in the nightlife, poking our heads in a few bars, and browsing in some shops.

Even at night it was hot and humid so when we came upon an ice cream store, it was irresistible. The cold, creamy treat did the trick and we continued our exploration.

As we left the heart of town behind, the streets grew quieter and foot traffic became less and less dense. When I glanced up, I saw a lantern in the sky. "Look at that," I said and pointed at it.

Denise and Stefanie looked up. "Oooh!"

As we watched, more lanterns appeared. This was just too good to pass by, so we laid down in the middle of the dark, peaceful street and watched the night sky light up with glowing lanterns. No one passed by. No cars came. Just us, stretched out, watching the beautiful lanterns silently float by. It felt like a dream. I could have stayed there all night, but after the lantern-show was over, we stood, dusted ourselves off, and headed back to the hostel.

I climbed into bed thinking that this had been as near-perfect a night as possible. I fell asleep right away, dreaming about the beautiful warm winter night with lanterns floating across a star-studded sky.

🜨 🜨 🜨

Chirp. Chirp. Chirp.

Ugh! What time is it?" I grumbled, bleary-eyed as I slammed off my alarm and saw that I'd overslept—so did the others.

After jumping out of bed, I roused the girls. We threw on our clothes, then hurried to the corner bakery for a quick bite before heading out for our next excursion.

As usual, I ordered a fried egg with bread, and a cappuccino. But I'm not a slave to routine, so I also treated myself to a chocolate croissant for the road.

Denise said she'd go on ahead to see if our van had arrived then come back for us. That worked out perfectly. It meant I could take more time enjoying my breakfast and getting to know Stefanie better.

I mused in my head that I really enjoyed Denise and Stefanie. I've had travel experiences where that wasn't the case. Often when there are three people in the group, someone feels left out. That wasn't the case with our trio. We got along so well, I knew I'd gained two lifelong friends.

When Denise shouted from across the street, "It's time to go!" I quickly downed my coffee. Then we dashed to her through oncoming traffic.

The mornings in town were bustling with people coming and going to and from...somewhere. Midday is more peaceful and laid back. I mused that maybe it's too hot for the locals and they rest up during peak heat. Smart move. Leave the baking to the tourists.

Image: pixabay.com

Escapade 22:

Float through a Cave and Have Lunch in a Treehouse

The van dropped us off near the local water caves and we followed our guide through a field of brown and yellow grass. I noticed a nearby cow with her calves trying to prod some breakfast of their own from her udder. She didn't seem to mind.

The pastoral scenery was too amazing to just pass by. Denise and I stopped and took tons of pictures.

We continued our hike to a narrow and not-too-safe-looking bamboo bridge that I estimated to be about 120 feet long. It had large holes in the bottom and only one, broken railing. Staring at it, we voiced our doubts about walking over that death-trap but in the end, all three of us agreed that it was the only way to the caves. If we wanted to see them, and we did, then crossing was what we had to do. That settled, we decided it would be safer to cross one at a time.

I volunteered to go first, hoping that Denise would try to talk me out of it. She didn't. Smart girl. As I held my breath and carefully set one foot in front of the other on the shaky, creaky bridge, I made the mistake of looking down. My nerves shot to defcon-9 when I saw the fifteen-foot drop to a shallow, rocky creek. *EEEK!*

When I stepped off the bridge onto solid ground, I let out a long breath and motioned Denise over. She seemed a bit more confident after seeing that I'd survived the trip.

We put the thought of crossing that bridge again on the way back out of our minds and quickened our pace to a jog to catch up with the group waiting at the base of stunning rice terraces that looked like stairsteps made for giants. We walked along the edges carefully avoiding the center areas where the rice grew.

As we continued into the morning, the bright sun grew hotter, but the scenery was so awesome, I ignored the heat. As we climbed higher, the view of the terraces and river just kept growing more beautiful. I often turned and looked behind.

Crossing through a canopy of thick green trees, we finally arrived at the Schistosomiasis Cave entrance. I'm glad that, at the time, I didn't know that schistosomiasis is the name of a disease-causing parasite.

Just outside, there was a little restaurant nestled in a tree. The guide told us we could leave non-valuables there. So, we left our extra clothes and stowed valuables in our dry bags. I taped up my cut foot with bandages and duct tape.

The view from the treehouse was breathtaking. I could see a bit over the dark green canopy that surrounded the cave entrance and a small waterfall that flowed down through the bamboo passageway that we'd crossed earlier.

At the mouth of the cave, we stared into a crystal-clear pool, full of minnows and tadpoles. I didn't care. The cool water looked so inviting I just wanted to belly flop into it.

Equipped with a tube and headlamp supplied by our guide, I dipped one foot into the pool, shrieked and yanked it out. The water was icy cold! Considering the warm air temperature, I wasn't expecting freezing water. I wondered, *Should I go in or wimp out and stay on the silty shore?* I stood there for at least thirty seconds trying to coax myself into the frigid pool.

As it turned out, I didn't have to make the decision. Denise pushed me in.

After I stopped gasping, I realized that she did the right thing. I probably would have stood there forever before inching my way in. The best thing, though was as Denise stood, feet planted on the shore, gloating over her clever move, Stefanie snuck up and pushed Denise in. Laughing, she took a running leap into the water herself.

The guide pointed out a rope and told us to hold onto it while we were in the cave, so we wouldn't get lost.

We all slid onto our tubes, grabbed onto the rope, and entered the dark, eerie cave. At first, we floated along under a slightly uncomfortable low ceiling, but the deeper we traveled, the higher the ceiling became.

The humid, stale-smelling cave felt about twenty degrees cooler than the outside. The smooth gray limestone walls dripped water down on us from the ceiling. At least some of it was water. We discovered that cold drops were water. Warm drops meant that a bat had just peed on us. That's why the guide warned us to keep our mouth closed. Thankfully, I made the whole trip without being baptized by a bat.

Floating on a tube, exploring this cave was an unforgettable experience. The stalactites created stunningly surreal formations. The colors and textures were unlike anything I'd ever seen. It was almost dreamlike.

Every so often our chatter would stop, and we would listen to the haunting sounds of the cave. Moans and groans reverberated through the air. It was chilling. The movie *The Descent* came to mind. In it, explorers found an unmapped cave and discovered eyeless creatures inside that used sound to move through the darkness in search of food. Of course, true to Hollywood, they fell prey to the blind cave dwellers. Shiver and tingle time.

We reached the end of the cave too soon for me. I thought it would be deeper and longer. I wanted more time in this amazing creation of Mother Nature.

After the tour, though, we enjoyed swimming in the clear pool near the entrance. We played like kids, splashing each other while little fishy nibbles tickled our feet as they feasted on dead skin. Whoo hoo! Free spa treatment.

When I got out of the water, my wounded foot was unbandaged and bleeding. I retrieved my bag to redress the cut and worried about the bacteria my cuts might have been exposed to. Later, though, when no infection set in, I relaxed about it.

The tour had been so awesome, I guess I was expecting the food to match. Not so much. It was okay but nothing special—fried rice and vegetables with fruit for dessert. The best part of lunch, though, was the view from the treehouse.

I stared off into the canopy, entranced. It could have been the fresh mountain air that caused me to space out in some sort of dreamland because I don't have the slightest idea where my mind went. When I crashed back into the present, it was time to hike down to the bottom.

I put on my extra shorts and tank and paid a visit to the bathroom. It's hard to get used to the toilets in Southeast Asia. They are always a surprise—usually not in a good way. This one was a cobweb-covered hole in the ground, and of course, no toilet paper. It's a good thing I always carried my own. A large light blue bucket full of water with a smaller bucket floating on top sat by the "hole" to "flush." In some toilets, there was a hose to spray off your private parts instead of using paper. Some seasoned travelers call this a "Bum Gun."

Escapade 23:

Travel the Mekong

Down the mountain we went, through the lush canopy of trees and the rocky hillside, across the multileveled rice terraces, through the brown and yellow field with the cows, and over the shaky bamboo bridge above the stream.

With no casualties, we all boarded the minibus and headed to the Nam Song River. I was excited about this. Apparently, Vang Vieng was the place to be for tubing. In its heyday, people would rent inner tubes and float down the river, stopping at the many bars and restaurants along the banks. Backpackers and travelers would get wasted as they bar-hopped down the river all day and all night. In recent times, though it's less popular. Maybe because in 2011, thirty people drowned. As a result of the drop in that attraction, a lot of the bars closed.

There are still a few bars on the river and at least one of them is owned by the Vang Vieng police, which I found very interesting to say the least. Well, I wasn't going to let any tragic accident keep me from going. We just did it sensibly. We chose to kayak with guides to help us maneuver. It's not that we would be drinking ourselves senseless, but the guides knew where to go and what to do. Useful when you're a clueless tourist.

I was a little disappointed. The Nam Song River edge is rocky and shallow. The surrounding area is filled with houses and fences. Not exactly the picturesque trip to and from the cave I'd imagined. But as we continued downstream, the rocky, messy hillside gave way to grass and trees—more rural and relaxing. As usual, it was hot, with air so thick it felt like I could ball it up and make a Play Doh animal.

Denise and I shared a kayak. Stefanie shared one with the guides. Another couple joined our group with their own kayak.

At our first stop, we moored the kayaks and climbed a frayed rope to the top of the bank. There was a tiny restaurant there, so plain it was almost forgettable. The most notable thing was a nearby wide-open area with a well-kept house sitting on it. Hey, not every moment can be exciting.

It was nice, though, when they brought us ice cream and much needed chilled water. We enjoyed them in the shade of a big tree. After about thirty minutes we climbed into our kayaks and headed downstream again.

Kayaking was both mellow enjoyment and hard work. One time I scanned around and thought, *Where in hell am I? How did I get here?*

Except for occasional tubers passing us, the trip was through calm, peaceful water. I spotted a river swing and was tempted to dock and try it for a bit, but our group was cruising downriver too fast and I didn't want to be left behind.

We passed locals on the shore, fishing with nets as dogs frolicked and rolled in the mud. I wondered what it would be like to live such a simple, uncomplicated life.

Around fifteen minutes later, we heard music and spotted some tubes piled up on the shore. After climbing out of our kayaks and making our way up a wobbly wooden staircase to the top of the riverbank we were met with a strange sight—a concrete floor with basketball hoops on each end and a Christmas tree made of beer cans. On one side a group of people played beer pong. Lots of hammocks hung under trees and to top it off, there were tiki huts, too. It was awesome! *This* was the place to be.

We drank beer and lounged on the hammocks then played a few rounds of Irish Snap before napping a bit. I loved this place so much, the guides almost had to toss us out of the hammocks when it was time to leave.

There were no more stops after that, just the water and peaceful surroundings. When the guide pointed to where our tour would be ending, I handed Denise my bag, jumped into the river, and swam to shore.

Swimming here was a bit of a surprise. After spending so much time in the salty buoyant Indian Ocean, fresh water made me feel heavy. On the bright side, though, there wasn't any salt drying on my skin.

I sat on the smooth rocks and stared at the brown, murky water as my *compadres* paddled in. It was interesting to see the river from a different vantage point and I wished I hadn't given my camera to Denise.

When the kayaks arrived, I helped hold them steady, so the passengers could get out. We thanked our guide, gave him a generous tip, then headed back to our hostel for a shower and another nap. It's amazing how much the hot sun drained us. The rest of the day was quiet and peaceful.

The next day, I woke up rested and ready for more exploring. *Luang Prabang, here I come!* We ate breakfast at the corner bakery. I had my usual fried egg, bread, and a cappuccino. Stefanie ordered pancakes and fruit. Denise, who had been having stomach problems, just had fruit.

In true Southeast Asian style, our minibus was completely filled. I thought I'd enjoy the scenery along the way, but I must not have been as rested from our kayaking as I thought. After a few minutes, I was out like a light and slept the entire way.

As we neared town, Stefanie spotted our hotel and asked the driver to drop us off at the next corner. He became agitated and testy. "No. No stop for you. We stop town center." He then dismissed us and kept driving.

I didn't think our request was unreasonable and other drivers had been okay with unscheduled stops. I guessed that he wanted everyone to go to town center, so we would use his family's tuk tuk or taksi service to get back to our hotel.

At town center I negotiated a fair transit price thanks to guidance from my *Lonely Planet* and the three of us were off to drop our bags off at our hotel.

Alas, the unexpected often happens in Southeast Asia. This time, the taksi driver made a wrong turn, but instead of correcting his mistake and continuing to the hotel, he stopped, opened the doors, and got out. He then popped the trunk, took out our bags, placed them on our backs, and escorted us through an active construction site.

If I'd been a newbie traveler, I'd have been concerned, but by now I'd come to expect the absurd. It was hilarious, except that we had to maneuver a quarter-mile track of uneven dirt wearing flip flops and carrying heavy backpacks. By the time we arrived at the hotel, sweat nearly poured down my back. I couldn't wait to ditch my bag.

Stefanie had booked a bungalow for us. I was relieved to see that the hotel was really nice. We were nestled among beautiful trees with a front row view of the Mekong River.

This river seemed to keep following me. The staff greeted us with cold cucumber-infused water and fruit. *Ahhhhhh!*

They took our packs and checked us in, asking for the standard items: name, country, passport, home address and, of course, money. They then escorted us to a large, fancy bungalow.

Everything was made of bamboo and in addition to a spacious room, we had a huge bathroom with a real tub and shower. Be still my heart. I was in love. I took the smaller bed closest to the window. Stefanie and Denise would share the big one. I was glad to see the mosquito nets. I wouldn't be a blood feast for the nasty creatures while I was sleeping.

The only disappointment was that our bungalow had no air conditioning. The staff assured us that it cooled down at night and even turned cold.

Uh-huh, I thought. *We'll see.*

After indulging in showers, we took a shuttle into the town center. At the tourist information center, we explored options about what to do and when and where to do them.

The travel agent suggested Makphet for lunch. We'd eaten at another Makphet in Vientiane. It was amazingly good, so we decided to add a meal at this one to our agenda.

Luang Prabang was a much bigger place than the near ghost town, Vang Vieng. In Luang Prabang, the locals were out and about all day.

After leaving the tourist info center, we wandered around bouncing in and out of shops and travel agencies to formulate a plan for our time there. During our mini exploration, we stumbled on Makphet. "Must be a sign that it's time to eat."

Stefanie and I split a large Beerlao, buffalo bites (seasoned water buffalo), tam mak (papaya salad) and laap—a famous Laotian dish made of marinated meat or fish with vegetables and spices, plus a side of sticky rice. For dessert we ate sweet purple sticky rice. *Yum.*

Denise was still having stomach problems, so she just ate plain sticky rice. Too bad she missed out on the feast. The food was amazing.

We'd stuffed ourselves, so instead of going to our hotel for a nap, we decided to walk it off.

The tourist map marked some nearby places to visit, so our next stop was the Vat Xieng Toung Monastery. It's the oldest monastery in the area and near the Mekong River. When we entered the grounds, we found ourselves alone. This was unusual, so we roamed around, peeking through windows and doors, but there wasn't a soul in the place.

It was creepy quiet with no one else there, so we left after a few minutes to watch the sunset on the Nam Khan River. The sunset beamed bright as it cast a shadow on the neighboring rice terraces, showing its reflective face on the river's surface. When it sank low and was partially out of sight, we spotted the highly recommended restaurant, Tamarind. This is a go-to place for tasty food. It also offers cooking classes in its top-of-the-line cooking school.

We stopped in and signed up for a cooking class starting two days later then headed back to the river, beer in hand, to soak up the last few rays of the setting sun.

It was time for the night market! The girls and I walked to the tourist information building on Sisavangvong Road because that was the location of the night market.

Sisavangvong was lined in tiny white lights and vendors were set up everywhere. As we stood at the market entrance, the multicolored merchandise drew me in—handmade blankets, scarves, hats, paintings, toys, jewelry, and so much else, each with a unique design. I went to every shop, or at least looked in as I walked by.

I love bartering in the Market. When I see something I really like, and the vendor and I start our negotiations, it energizes me. Bartering is so much fun. The vendor starts with a price then I counter the offer. The vendor argues that my price is too low. I offer another price. Sometimes this is enough to make the deal. Other times we could go a couple more rounds. When a price is agreed on, we shake hands and I have my treasure.

However, in my many bartering encounters, there were times when the vendors were more stubborn and we would go for several rounds. My tactic then was, "I'll come back later." The vendor would then cut the price in half or try to offer me the item for the price I originally wanted.

Haggling is a gift and I love it. I think the shop owners enjoy it too.

Street food! *Yum*. We walked through the entire Hmong Night Market scoping out the best-looking spot. We settled on a buffet-style cart in the middle of the busy street. They offered lots of veggies, noodles, spring rolls, and meat dishes. I heaped my plate with a little of everything, had it grilled, then grabbed a Beerlao, and paid the chef the 7000 Kp I owed her.

Beer and food in hand, I sat down at a communal table filled with other tourists. Stefanie and Denise joined me a few minutes later, and we scarfed down our meal.

Refueled, we headed back to the night market to continue shopping where we left off.

Later, I wondered why I had looked at everything, but bought nothing. That wasn't like me. *Oh, well*, I thought, knowing that I'd probably make up for it later.

Hazard 24:

Get Cozy with the Bathroom Floor

About midnight I woke up with griping stomach cramps—the worst I'd ever experienced—like sharp knives tearing through me. I thought I would die right there on the bed. When I muscled up the nerve to drag myself to the bathroom, it felt like an excruciating death. The only thing I could do was curl up on the cold slate floor until the pain passed.

After about twenty minutes or so, it eased up a little and I slowly made my way back to bed, hoping the problem wouldn't resurge. But, it did. About 4 a.m. the same pain—or worse—woke me. I wasn't sure if I could make it to the toilet but rolled out of bed, tightened every muscle in my body, and crawled on hands and knees to the bathroom, hoping it would be enough to keep me from "letting loose." My time in there was shorter than the first episode, but long enough to be miserable. When I was sure it was safe, I made my way back to bed, regretting my dinner choice.

Eight in the morning rolled around faster than I wanted it to. The three of us were supposed to be on our way to Kuang Si waterfalls and Tat Kuang Si Bear Rescue Center. These were must do things here in Laos but I couldn't get out of bed.

Denise, who had only rice, felt fine, but Stefanie was sick, too. I was bummed to miss the outing, but I knew it wasn't wise to stray too far from the toilet.

After Denise left, I fell into a deep sleep and slithered out of bed around noon, dressed, then joined Stefanie on the balcony for some fresh air. Denise had told them we were sick, so the staff brought tea and soup.

I stared at the food, wondering if eating anything was a good idea. But I dared it and was fine. Feeling a bit better, I remember being glad the cooking class we'd signed up for was not that evening.

Our balcony faced a garden filled with flowers. I watched the bees feasting on sweet nectar and pollen as I drifted off to sleep.

Around 3 p.m., while Stefanie and I were reading books on the balcony, Denise, back from the bear rescue and waterfall, joined us. It was a nice peaceful afternoon and exactly what I needed for a speedy recovery.

After a while, though, I was itching to go into town. Denise suggested going to the Garavek Traditional Storytelling Theater to hear legends and folktales of Luang Prabang accompanied by ancient music played on a khene—a traditional Laotian instrument. Tickets were 50,000 Kp and all of the money went to help the company and its mission.

This sounded wonderful. After I showered and made myself look presentable, we caught the hotel shuttle into town. The storytelling would start at 6:30. We were early, so we bought tickets then went to the Vipassana Temple to kill time before the show.

I initially thought, *Sheesh, not another temple*. I'd seen so many in Cambodia, I was a bit templed-out. But this one was amazing! It's covered in gold mirrors and holds a shrine for meditation. During peak sunlight, I'm sure the temple shines like a star.

HAZARD 25:

JUMPED BY A DOG

After our visit to the temple, we grabbed a snack from a tiny market and wandered the neighborhood near the theater. This was a nice part of town, with beautiful wooden houses lining the streets that looked almost European—probably from when the French annexed it in the 1700s and made it a site for the royal residence. Or it could have been from when Vichy, France occupied it during World War II.

Around 6 p.m., we entered the little theater. It was charming with five levels of stadium seating for about thirty people. We chose the second level.

While waiting for the show to start, I glanced around. Two chairs were arranged on a small stage that had a deep-red, painted background.

At 6:30, the storyteller and the musician entered and sat on the chairs. One of the men said, "Sabaidee," which means hello. Someone in the crowd replied, "Sabaidee."

The storyteller began by telling us some of the company's history. It's a small group from Luang Prabang. Their goal is to educate people and preserve local traditions, folktales, myths, and legends of the region.

I truly enjoyed this show and recommend it to anyone interested in learning more about Laotian culture.

After the show, we left the theater and headed to the night market, already in full swing. We headed for the action, ending up at Hive Bar for a quick bite. Still unsure of what my stomach could handle, I ordered soup and sticky rice.

The market, bustling with tourists, seemed busier and livelier than my last visit. I poked around the vendors' tents, fully intending to find the best products and deals, but for some reason, nothing attracted me enough to make a purchase.

Stefanie, however, had her arms filled with stuff. As I was ooh-ing and ah-ing over *her* goodies, she tried to talk me into buying something, too. While I considered it, a white dog, that seemed to appear out of nowhere, leapt at me. I'm cautious about dogs anyway, and this freaked me out so much I screamed. His claws dug into my skin, but at the time, I was so panicked, I thought he was biting me. I shrieked louder as I tried to fend him off.

People around us stopped what they were doing and stared. I wondered why no one was helping get this creature off me.

Well, I'd panicked for nothing. Eventually, the dog backed off, wagged his tail, and showed that he just wanted to be friendly. Why he chose me, I'll never know. When I calmed down, and got over feeling foolish, I found that I liked being chosen as a doggie playmate. I pet "her" for a few minutes before the owner rushed over, apologized, and led the dog away.

After that, though, I was ready to head back, so we caught the shuttle to our bungalow.

Escapade 26:

Waterfalls and Bears

In the morning, breakfast was extra good, made even better by the awesome view of the river from the patio. Although the hotel offered a traditional Laos breakfast of soup and rice, I chose coffee, tea, boiled eggs, pancakes, cereal, muffins, and fruit. I'm sure part of the reason the meal was so good was that it was included in the price of the room.

Taking my time to eat as I gazed at the sparkling river felt like paradise.

Denise and Stefanie were headed to the Elephant Village Sanctuary. I'd been to one in Chiang Mai earlier in the year, so I opted to do my own thing for the day.

After breakfast, I wrapped a couple pieces of bread in a napkin and put them in my dry bag for later then headed for the shuttle to the town center where I hired a colorful tuk tuk to Kuang Si Falls and the Tat Kuang Si Bear Rescue Center.

The ride was beautiful. The still, cool air felt so refreshing. Later, it would heat up and the humidity would close in. But until then, I soaked in the experience and gazed at the large, thick trees and roaming cattle that sprinkled the landscape along the way.

I had considered renting a bicycle to ride through the mountains, but the heat would soon press in, and after the tuk tuk passed some brave souls struggling up the steep bike path, I changed my mind. But kudos to them for busting their asses on the eighteen-mile trek up the mountain. I imagined they were thinking that those famous waterfalls had better be worth it.

At the park entrance, I told the driver I would be back around noon. Because the sanctuary is funded through donations, souvenir sales, and the entrance fee, I was happy to pay the 20,000 Kp.

I headed into the forest, filled with large shade trees with skinny trunks and long branches. I was grateful for the protection from the increasing heat.

At the bear sanctuary, I counted seven Asiatic bears roaming around. They seemed happy and healthy and not at all concerned with people gawking at them. One bear was hanging upside down on a jungle gym. The animal-lover and biologist in me is always delighted and fascinated to see wildlife in protected, natural environments. They seem so unafraid and content.

The bears climbed the trees, frolicked about, and played with each other like little kids. I stayed quite a while, watching them with fascination.

After a while, noticing that the air temperature was ramping to uncomfortable, I decided it was time to continue my hike to the waterfalls.

When I finally reached the first set of falls, no one else was around. Arriving early had paid off. "Yess!" Beautiful trees surrounded the clear, azure and turquoise waterfall. It was too inviting to ignore. I kicked off my sandals and plunged my feet into the water then sucked in a breath. "Ooh!" glacier-cold! I shivered as the iciness crept up my spine. Oddly, it felt both painful and wonderful at the same time.

Slipping my sandals back on, I continued up the path to the next set of falls. These were even more incredible than the first. Instead of going into the water, though, I decided to see all the falls first then pick the best pool to swim in.

I'd never seen such pristine, magnificent waterfalls. I must have taken a thousand photos. When I reached the top, the sight of the huge fall slamming into a pool below took my breath away with its magnificent beauty. I stood on the bridge, gaping in awe. The roar of the falls was so therapeutic, I could have spent the whole day in that spot.

After a while, I finished crossing the bridge and followed a path that led to steps going up to the top of the waterfall. The way proved to be treacherous, with uneven slick rocks and loose boulders. I almost fell to my death a couple of times, but I didn't—obviously—and made it to the top unscathed.

Even though I couldn't see the waterfall, the view of the forest was awesome—definitely worth that dangerous hike.

The steep path down was just as dangerous as the way up, but I managed to make it with only a few scratches and bruises.

Some people claim the pools have healing properties, so I decided to test that theory. I waded in to one of them. Refreshed, I gazed into the pool, amused at the fish nibbling at the skin on my legs. It was a weird tickling sensation.

After about an hour in the pool, at least thirty people showed up and climbed in with me.

Disappointing. I was a bit grumpy about it and took their presence as my cue to exit.

Grateful for the alone time I'd had in that magnificent place, I sat on a wooden bench and dried off then headed to the nearby restaurant for a fresh mango juice.

The others in the pool just watched. Maybe they were thinking I was anti-social. I didn't care. I'd had my moment.

Since I'd originally gone in the water to test the healing claims, I examined my cut foot. There didn't seem to be any difference. So, theory busted. I wanted to get back in the water, and I found a less crowded pool to enjoy.

Around 11:30 I left paradise behind and started down the trail, back through the bear sanctuary, and out of the park. On the way to town, I noticed how rejuvenated I felt and thought that maybe the water was healing after all.

ESCAPADE 27:

COOK LIKE I'VE
NEVER COOKED BEFORE

Today was cooking school! The shuttle dropped us off on Sisavanvong Street—about ten minutes from the Tamarind Restaurant. Denise, Stefanie, and I checked in with the staff and piled into an over-crowded tuk tuk, heading to the cooking school.

The bumpy and uncomfortable ride contrasted sharply with the picturesque scenery of tiny villages on a lush hillside. The tuk tuk pulled up in front of a well-manicured house and indicated that we had arrived. I was surprised at how modern the school was. I don't know what I'd expected, open fire and a clay oven or something?

As we walked in, on our right I saw long, covered tables that would seat about forty people. We headed down some stairs to a room with sinks for hand washing on the left, and cooking stations set for twelve people. Behind the cooking stations stood a large counter with all the food and ingredients we would be needing for the course. We went down yet another set of stairs to a dining area that overlooked a cliff with a view of Luang Prabang.

The chef introduced herself and told us about her cooking history. She gave some information about Tamarind then asked us to introduce ourselves.

It turned out that eight of the twelve people taking the course were from the United States. I was surprised but pleased. I'd never met so many Americans abroad, and was happy to see more of us venturing out to explore the world.

Back to the room with cooking stations, Karen, our instructor, asked us to wash our hands, then laid out the itinerary. We started by preparing salads. I chose to make papaya salad—my favorite.

We ground garlic and chilis together in a mortar and pestle, then chopped the papaya, lemon grass, and cherry tomatoes.

After that, we made laap (minced meat salad). Next, we prepared the mok pa (steamed fish in banana leaves).

I was happy to discover that the produce used for this class was the best of the best. The tomatoes were bright red and blemish-free. The lemon grass had a strong, crisp aroma, and the chilis were a perfect, textbook shape and spicy.

I lightly sautéed my buffalo meat with salt and fish sauce. Fish sauce smells awful, but it sure makes things taste good. When the meat was cooked, I added the minced garlic, green onion, chopped cilantro, lemon grass stalk, chilis, and lime juice. It was heaven.

I admit my mouth watered in anticipation as I mixed everything together then placed the salad on top of lettuce and sticky rice.

We made a paste of the veggies we'd chopped by grinding them with the mortar and pestle. Then we warmed banana leaves and placed the fish and paste inside.

To make the "lunch box," we folded each filled leaf into the shape of a cube and tied them with thin bamboo strips. Lastly, we steamed them.

146

For the main course we sliced lemon grass, creating cylindrical slits around the entire stalk, but careful not to cut through to the opposite side of the stalk. I found this tedious and difficult. It took a delicate, artist's touch.

We blended ground chicken, onions, chilis, garlic, fish sauce, and spices then stuffed it into the sliced lemon grass stalks. This caused them to bulge with yummy goodness at the base. Next, the whole thing was dipped in beaten egg and fried in hot oil.

For dessert, I chose to make purple sticky rice with coconut and fruit.

We also made our own dipping sauces.

The whole meal consisted of a variety of meat and veggie dishes to please just about anyone.

The built-up anticipation of having to wait to eat until all of it was prepared kept my taste buds on edge. When everything was ready, we carried our dishes to the dining table overlooking the cliff and dug in. My dishes turned out so good, I practically licked each of the plates. The mixture of fresh veggies and Laotian spices hit my palette just right. I was in foodie heaven.

Our knowledgeable instructor did a wonderful job. When dinner was over, we received our cookbooks and practically waddled back to town. We got there just in time to catch the last shuttle to our hotel.

At our bungalow, I had some decisions to make. The girls wanted to stay in the area a little longer than we'd planned so they could go north and check out a massive treehouse. It sounded interesting, but I felt ready to make my way south to explore the 4000 Islands.

Another thing I couldn't ignore was that soon I would need to go to Bangkok to catch my flight to the Philippines. I went back and forth, trying to find a way to do the treehouse and the 4000 Islands, and make it to Bangkok for my flight. No decision came, and I fell asleep thinking the answer would magically appear in the morning.

Escapade 28:

Work on an Old-School Rice Farm

The next morning, Stefanie, Denise, and I had our usual delicious and large breakfast on the patio overlooking the river. It was so serene with birds flying overhead and small vessels floating along. I enjoyed catching a glimpse of the locals' daily routines.

After breakfast, we talked a while about the activity of the day. *And now, for something completely different.* We were going to a living farm to work in the rice fields. Our transport arrived while we were still lingering at the table, so we snagged the extra pieces of bread and rolled them in napkins for later then grabbed our gear and boarded the bus, where four other staunch volunteers sat, looking as eager as we were.

At the farm, the owner and developer of the Living Farm Project, Mr. Laut Lee, gave us a cheery greeting. I could tell right from the start that he was proud of his farm. And why wouldn't he be? His program benefits the whole community.

Laut Lee shows travelers how rice is produced in the age-old way, with no modern machinery. His farm uses sustainable organic ways to plow, plant, harvest, and process the rice. And, it's not simple. He taught us that there are fourteen steps to growing rice. I don't remember all of them, but I do remember having a wonderful time. I was so stoked to be a part of living history.

Laut showed us how to use traditional tools for rice farming—from baskets to thrashers and more. We enthusiastically tested them out. He then asked us to take off our shoes and socks, gave us hats, and sent us to work with his assistant, Bam.

Our first task was plowing. Plowing in a rice paddy is now done mechanically, but for nearly 8,000 years, a water buffalo and a wooden plow guided by a human was the way it was done.

So, there I stood, bravely about to be holding a primitive wooden plow hitched to a water buffalo named Suzuki (yes, like the car and nearly as large) while wading through knee-high thick, gloppy mud. Staying upright would be the first order of business.

Suzuki was huge, with massive horns and dark-gray skin. Some in the group were a little afraid but I thought he was cute and gave him a pet.

Bam showed me how to hold the plow and guide the water buffalo. I guess I wasn't the best student, though. I had a hard time keeping my mind off the vastness of the farm and thoughts about this ancient way of life. Suzuki must have had enough of my mental wandering. He decided to bring my attention back to business by licking my leg with his big rough tongue. What a hoot. I grinned and kissed him back—right on his gigantic head.

More focused, I set my resolve to be the best plower in the history of…plowing. "Okay," I said. "I'm ready." I grasped the handles and followed and plodded through thick mud, guiding the big, adorable beast up and down the field. It wasn't as hard as I thought it would be. Suzuki knew his business.

The thick, squishy mud felt cool against my bare feet. I loved it. I remembered that Bam had said there were a few eels and who knows what else in the soupy mud. I thought, *Should I have asked more about the "who knows what else?* As I was thinking that over, something brushed across my leg. *Eek!* My whole body tensed up. *Was that an eel?* It felt big and sliced through mud pretty fast. At first, I had a shot of fear but then thought, *As long as whatever that thing was doesn't bite. I think I'll be okay.* I felt better, but on hindsight, I was partly whistling in the dark. Still, I did my best to put it out of my mind and keep plowing.

Each of us took turns working Suzuki-the-plow. When one of us tired, the next person took over. In the end we were all caked with gray mud-clay from knees to toes and other places, too. As usual, the sun was blazing hot, but the mud cooled us off a bit. *Maybe I should just wallow in it like a water buffalo.* Tempting, but I didn't.

Something else I found interesting while plowing were the dozens of tiny translucent eggs in the mud, each with a black dot inside. I thought they might be frog or toad eggs, so I was careful not to disturb them.

With plowing the massive field done, our next task was planting. After a little instruction, we grabbed as many rice seedlings as we could carry and began planting them in the muddy soil about four to six inches apart.

This was back-breaking work and I wouldn't want to do it every day but being a volunteer and a part of this living history made it enjoyable. My mind turned to how much fun I'd had as a child while playing in the mud and making mud pies with my brother. Sometimes, after a rainstorm, we would have mud fights in our back yard.

Planting completed, we happily headed to a terrace where the rice was ready to be harvested. Bam showed us how the rice was watered. Terrace farming is the most practical way to grow rice. Once the top terrace has used the water, it is released into the terrace below. This kind of farming can be traced back more than 13,500 years.

After we'd harvested the rice by cutting it, we learned how to gather it and brought it back in fifty-pound baskets we carried on our heads. This was a task none of us seemed to be able to master. I made a lot of attempts but just couldn't do it. I think Bam was used to this. He didn't seem overly disappointed.

The farm also uses ancient husking mortars instead of chemical fertilizers to remove the colored shell (husk) that encases the rice kernel. There is also a bran layer that must be removed to produce white rice. The bran is left on for brown rice.

To de-husk, the rice is placed in special handmade, shallow baskets and shaken by hand. This is harder than it sounds, requiring a special technique. We learned that Laotian women didn't get married until they mastered rice husking.

We all practiced really hard. We shook and flipped the rice to remove the husk while trying not to spill it all over the ground. What a sight we must have been. At least we entertained the farmer.

Surprisingly, we all passed with flying colors and were now eligible for marriage according to Laotian custom.

The farm also makes rice powder and flour. The mill is a wooden contraption that holds two large stone discs—one on top of the other. The top one has a long wooden lever-handle sticking out horizontally. There is an opening in the center of the stones to pour in the husk-free rice and an opening for the flour to pour out into a container.

We each had a turn grinding the flour by pushing the lever to turn the top stone so that it would grind around the lower stone, producing the flour. It was harder than I thought it would be. I remember thinking what a great whole-body workout I was getting.

Around and around we went, grating the stones against each other, crushing the grains of rice between them to produce a fine-grained flour. We worked until all the rice we'd collected was ground into fine flour.

Our last fun task of the day was to extract juice from a sugar cane. This turned out to be harder than grinding rice and required two people to do the job.

The farmer inserted a couple of stalks of sugarcane into the mill. I took one end of the lever-handle and Denise took the other. We ran around and around, pushing the lever so the two large millstones could crush the sugarcane and release their juice.

The ancient juicer took some force but once the stone was moving it was easier to keep it going than to stop and restart. There were a lot of freshly cut sugar canes, so we all took a turn until we processed them all.

He then poured the juice into small cups for us to taste. It was extremely sweet, of course, because it was pure, liquid sugar.

The sugarcane activity ended our workday on the farm and the payment and reward for our hard labor was sampling all the rice and sugar cane products produced by the farm and knowing that the Living Farm helped the people of Laos.

After we cleaned ourselves up, we gathered on the second floor of the farmhouse for a picnic-style banquet. The feast was arranged on a large table in a sumptuous display.

The farmer seemed proud of his food as he explained what everything was—rice cakes, a pancake made of rice flour, plain sticky rice, sweet sticky rice, rice chips, rice noodles, rice wine, dried and flavored water buffalo and a variety of sauces. I tried the rice wine. It was too strong for me and I didn't like the smell, so not a fan.

He had mentioned earlier in the day that Suzuki's mother died earlier in the week. I wondered if some of her was here on the table.

Before we left for the day, the farm women showed us how they made the carrying baskets. When I tried it, I discovered that basket weaving is harder than it looks. Mine fell apart faster than I could weave the bamboo together.

Basket weaving aside, I had a wonderful, fun experience and I met some really nice people and we exchanged email addresses.

As soon as we got back to the hotel, I told the ladies I wouldn't be staying any extra days and needed to get my ticket to Vientiane at the airport because it would be cheaper than online. I took the next shuttle into town and hired a tuk tuk to drive me to the airport.

I didn't really want my time with the girls to end, but they would be heading north, and I needed to go in a different direction. I really enjoyed my time with them. It was great to have travel buddies like Stefanie and Denise—adventurous, like-minded, and ready for just about any situation. No-fear girls. Well, at least we had a little time left before going our separate ways.

At the hotel, a picnic was going on in the garden in honor of International Women's Day. Stefanie and Denise were already there and called me over to join them. I looked at the sumptuous spread with anticipation—chicken, noodles, salad, fruit, rice, and more, all spread out on multicolored blankets.

The hotel owner was in a great mood and kept filling our cups with either Beerlao or Lao whiskey (lau khao). Even if our cup was three-quarters full she would grab it, fill it up, raise it to the sky, and say "*Nuk nuk.*" I thought cheers was *khob chai,* so I don't know what she was saying. Perhaps *nuk nuk* means 'drink up.'

After the festivities, we headed for the night market. This was my last opportunity to buy a souvenir from this area and I wanted to get something special.

The next morning, I lingered over my last breakfast at the hotel with Denise and Stefanie, then, with mixed feelings, checked out. The girls checked out too and accompanied me into town where they moved into a more affordable place for two people.

Fortunately, their hotel allowed me to leave my bag there until my flight.

We had some time to kill so we headed to the Royal Palace Museum. I fed the fish in the koi pond and walked around the grounds. After exploring the garden, I discovered a garage with classic cars on display that had been gifts from other world leaders. Very cool.

This large museum houses entire rooms that the royal family had used and displays some of their most treasured items. The royal clothes were elaborate and heavy-looking. They were beautiful, but I don't understand how anyone could wear those in such a hot and humid climate.

After our palace visit, we stopped at a nearby restaurant for a quick meal before I left for the airport. I ordered fried water buffalo and a lemongrass vegetable dish. We finished just in time to hustle back to the new hotel to retrieve my bag and call a cab. When it arrived, I gave Denise and Stefanie big hugs, thanked them for their friendship, and wished them well, then I was off to the capital.

Leaving them gave me such a rush of sadness. But I turned my attention to the next adventure and making new friends.

Escapade 29:
Dorm Screamer and
Dropped off in the Middle of Nowhere

I checked into the same hostel I'd stayed at when first arriving in Laos—Dream Home—and went straight to my room to settle in and claim a bed. As I walked into the dorm, three travelers were already there.

One of them asked me if I was from California or Colorado.

I answered, "California. Where are you guys from?"

"We're from Colorado. I'm Shawn." He turned to a blond beauty with a bright, vibrant smile. "This is Sage." He pointed to the third traveler, who had curly hair, brown eyes, and a mustache that connected to his beard. "That's Branden."

Shawn towered over the two at over six feet tall and Branden charmed with his British accent.

I introduced myself and shook their hands then asked what *their* plans were and said, "I'm hoping to go to the Kong Lo Caves and the 4000 Islands."

They told me they'd arrived earlier but found that Vientiane didn't have much going on, so they'd also like to see the caves.

"That's great. We can all go together," I said. We discussed plans to leave the next night.

After a quiet evening, I went to bed, hoping for a good night's sleep. But around 3 a.m. some woman jolted me awake with loud bitching in the dark about how frigid the room was. She was right. It was *really* cold, but why wake everyone else? I tried to ignore her and go back to sleep but she kept going on about it, ramping up her volume into a full-on screaming tantrum about the room temperature.

Pillow over my head, I was really annoyed. Then, at the peak of her rant, there was a loud *thump* then silence. I bolted upright. *Did she fall off the top bunk?* I was about to check when I heard her storm out, slamming the door behind her.

Most everyone laughed.

I thought, *Oh, well, when sharing a room with strangers, some will be "stranger" than others. All I can say about that event is, #dormlife!* I went back to sleep.

Branden, Shawn, and Sage joined me for breakfast. After that, we bicycled into town and rode to the capital building then cruised around the city to see the sites.

I feel so carefree when I'm riding a bike it's like being a kid all over again.

Branden needed a new charger for his camera so finding one was a part of our mission for the day.

Along the way, a corner stand caught my eye with its neatly stacked mangos, oranges, peaches, apples, kiwis, and melons all arranged in a translucent case. The mouthwatering fruity aroma was irresistible. I motioned to the guys to let them know I was stopping then ordered a mango, peach smoothie with no sweetened condensed milk. Sweetened condensed milk is heavenly, and I like it in other things but in my shakes, I prefer the natural flavor of the fruit.

Later that afternoon we worked up a big appetite. I asked if they liked Indian food, and if so, I knew the perfect place. I was happy to hear that they were all in for Indian food, so I took them to Jamil Zahid Indian and Pakistani Restaurant, the same one that Sam, Denise, Stefanie, and I had gone to during our first full day in Vientiane. They loved it.

On our way back to the hostel, we stopped at a bus station to buy tickets to Tham Kong Lo Caves. Our bus was scheduled to leave at 8 p.m. and would arrive at 6 or 7 the next morning.

Back at our hostel, one of the staff at the front desk asked what our plans were for the evening. We told them we'd bought a night bus ticket to Tham Kong Lo Caves. They tried to convince us that we'd made a bad choice and should change our plans and take the day bus. But we were eager to get out of Vientiane as soon as possible. They kept insisting but we held fast to our decision.

That evening, after checking out, we headed for the local station. Soon we were on board our bus to the caves. Branden sat next to me and offered a Valium, so I could get some rest. I gladly accepted and went straight to sleep then woke about two hours later when the driver stopped for our routine bathroom and food break. It was mandatory for everyone to leave the bus or I would have stayed there and continued to sleep.

Our meal was included in the ticket, so we ate. I felt a bit loopy from the Valium—super happy and giggly. Branden, Sage, and Shawn talked about how excited they were about the caves. When we were allowed back on the bus, I went right to sleep.

I abruptly woke up when Branden nudged my shoulder. I was so groggy, I wasn't sure what was happening. Why had the driver stopped the bus and motioned for us to get off? There was no explanation, but we didn't argue. We just grabbed our belongings and exited.

It was 1 a.m. and there we were standing on a dark street in a tiny town in the middle of nowhere. Okay, so much for arriving at 6 or 7 a.m. We weren't sure what to do, so we just shouldered our bags and started down the street, exhausted and laughing at our predicament.

We were in the middle of a debate on whether or not to camp outside when someone in a van pulled up beside us. Hanging his head out the window, he asked, "Do you need a ride to the caves?"

Perfect timing, I thought, believing he meant to take us there right then. Disappointment set in when he nodded, smiled, and said, "Good. I'll find you in the morning." With that, he drove off, leaving us alone in the middle of nowhere.

We just looked at each other in disbelief then laughed. For a little while, we stood in the darkness taking in the beautiful stars and the quiet surroundings. A few minutes later, we shouldered our bags and continued walking down the dark, empty street, hoping for a miracle. We weren't disappointed. As we neared a modest-looking house, a man stepped out of the front door. "Do you all need a room for the night?"

"We sure do," said Branden. The man motioned to us and we gladly followed him inside. The home was a welcome refuge to my tired, sleepy self. Without hesitation, he showed us two rooms. "Will these do?" he asked. Was he kidding? I was ready to sleep on a bench that night. We all answered, "Yes. Thank you," and paid him on the spot.

As I watched our host walk away, I reflected on my luck. Whenever I find myself in a sticky situation, something always happens to make it okay.

Branden and I shared one room and Sage and Shawn shared the other. Although I was really tired, and the room was fairly comfortable and clean, I had trouble falling asleep. I thought it might be a side-effect of the Valium, but Branden was also wide awake, so we played Rummy until we got sleepy enough to go back to our beds.

In the morning, refreshed, we gathered our gear, thanked our host and headed down the street to find a breakfast spot.

I looked around at this cute, remote village, located far south of Vientiane in the Phu Hin Bun wilderness. I was sure the place had a name, but I didn't see it posted anywhere.

Fortunately, we found a restaurant close by. It had a few tables on what looked like a person's front porch. We sat down and waited for someone, anyone, to show up and feed us. A moment or two later, that someone approached and asked what we wanted to eat. I ordered my usual fried egg, bread, and a cappuccino.

We weren't sure when, or if the man in the van would show up, so we passed the time by playing Irish Snap and Rummy. After breakfast, Shawn busted out a frisbee and we tossed it around in the street. There wasn't much to do in this sleepy village. After looking around, we were sure that we'd eaten at the only "restaurant" in town.

I took a stroll down the only street and saw a couple of children playing. I was reminded, looking around, of an old Western movie set. All it needed was tumbleweed and a cowboy.

When the van showed up, the driver hopped out and opened the doors. "Ready for Kong Lo Caves?" I thought, *No wonder he said he'd find us. There wasn't much territory to search.*

It took around two hours to get to the caves, but I didn't mind. It was a beautiful drive through lush green trees with limestone mountains in the background. We saw farms, horses, water buffalo, chickens, and dogs. It was magnificent.

During the drive we passed quaint little houses, miles apart from each other. We also noticed structures that looked like they'd burned down.

The drive through the Laos backwater made me want to spend more time in the villages and country. It was all so breathtaking.

We arrived at a small town and found a sign that read, THAM KONG LO. *We made it yeahhhh!* The driver dropped us off at the cave gate. After thanking and paying him, we hoisted our bags and went through, walked past the park office and bathroom, and headed to the cliff.

At the cliff, I couldn't believe my eyes. I gazed at a beautiful blue-turquoise lake with a footbridge going across and a dark shadow at the base of the huge limestone wall. The shadow turned out to be a deep crevice next to a massive granite boulder that served as a diving board to the center of the lake.

The water was so pristine I could see the translucent fish swimming. Trees flanked the lake and ranged along the top of limestone walls. *This must be what heaven looks like*, I thought. The lake wasn't easy to get to, but we made it without a scratch on us. Once there, I was happy to see that we mostly had the place to ourselves. The only other people were two girls sitting on the large granite rock.

After changing into our swimsuits, we walked to the Kong Lo village-office and asked to rent a boat. The attendant informed us that only four people would fit in the boat and one of those spots was for the guide. I told my travel buds to go ahead and that I would get my own, but they didn't want to split up, so we decided that the best solution would be to wait for more people to show up and share the cost with them. Clever.

While waiting we dove into the amazing, blue lake, swam, and frolicked with the fish. An hour later, another group arrived and agreed to share boats with us. Perfect!

We carefully boarded tiny wooden boats that looked like they were on their last voyage. No one else seemed to be concerned, so I just shrugged it off to enjoy the ride. In a few minutes, we were swallowed up by the big crevice—the mouth of the cave.

Inside, the cavern grew wider. With its magnificent and eerily beautiful stalactites and stalagmites, I felt like I was on another planet. Some sunlight filtered in near the entrance, so we could clearly see the formations. I marveled at how the water had carved out the limestone to make such beauty.

As we moved deeper into the cave, the sunlight left us behind and we were shrouded in darkness with only our headlamps to see by.

It was all so surreal.

The guides docked the boats on an inside shore and said we were free to roam around for a while. Some of the formations looked like melted wax on a candle and others like ripples in a ravine but most of the formations were indescribable. This was one of the most beautiful places I'd ever seen.

After we explored this dead-end section, we went back to the boats and continued the tour down the river. We stopped at another spot. This time the guides said they would take the boats ahead while we took the footpath. They left us on our own and disappeared into the darkness. I was a little uneasy about that but shook it off. *After, all,* I thought, *they wouldn't just abandon us. That would be bad for business.*

We explored by following a rope that guided us through the crevices. The cave opened into a chamber that glimmered like a starry night. I didn't want to leave but I also didn't want to be left behind so I kept with the group and explored, admiring the water-carved limestone until we spotted our boats about a half-mile in.

Climbing in, we drifted along the river, our headlamps shining in the pitch-black fairyland.

The boats floated into the sunlight and the cave journey was over. After adjusting to the brightness, I saw yet another amazing landscape—dense stands of tropical trees hugged the riverbank, reminding me of an Amazon jungle cruise.

We docked downriver at a small village. I was happy to be out of the boat and we all headed to a place for snacks. Afterward, we explored a bit. Branden climbed one of the large trees on the riverbank and jumped into the water. He did this a few times, attracting the attention of some local children who thought he was great entertainment. They studied his every move then gleefully began mimicking his actions. It was adorable to watch.

When town-time was over, we climbed into our rickety wooden boats, again, and headed back through the cave to the turquoise lake with the granite boulder in it.

This was one of my most memorable days.

After the tour ended, we changed clothes, retrieved our bags, and headed to the nearest village, a couple of minutes up the road. It was a simple place with chickens running around and dogs roaming free. We passed two cows enclosed by a small wooden fence. They paid little or no attention to us as they grazed on the bright-green grass that covered the entire landscape.

We stopped at the first guesthouse we saw and asked the price for two rooms. After agreeing that the rates were reasonable, the owner showed us our quarters on the second (top) level. I was at first startled that their family dog took a liking to me (just trying to avoid rabies). He followed me everywhere but was friendly and didn't try to jump on me or bite.

This town was a tad larger than the one where the bus had dropped us off but otherwise it looked nearly identical. We ordered dinner at our guesthouse, expecting it to be really good. Usually the food is excellent in the obscure places but not there. It was plain and uninteresting.

After eating, we wanted to devise a plan to get out of town, so we walked to the restaurant next door because they claimed to have Wi-Fi. Even in the middle of nowhere, there is usually internet—of a sort, maybe snail-driven. After a frustrating try to get the Wi-Fi to work, we gave up and enjoyed a few beers and played cards.

After the sun set, the Milky Way shone like a diamond bracelet in the inky black sky. I stretched out on the grass and watched it. Soon, the others joined me in silence for a while, then we went back to our rooms.

Before turning in for the night, we asked the guesthouse owner how we could get to the 4000 Islands. He said we needed to go to Savannakhet, which is a larger city—like Vientiane. He was good enough to arrange a minibus to take us there the next morning.

ESCAPADE 30:

SUDDEN CHANGE OF PLANS AND

LEAVING FRIENDS BEHIND

It took us about three hours to get to Savannakhet. When I looked around, it was obvious that this was not a popular tourist destination, especially since we had to walk for about twenty minutes to the nearest hotel. Shawn asked the staff where to find food and what there was to do while in town. They were helpful, but there was little or nothing to do.

In the lobby, Branden said he was starving and ordered a snack while I freshened up in the bathroom. After having a small bite to stave off stomach growls, we hoisted our bags and went in search of a full meal. On the way, we stopped for a water and a rest and I was wishing my pack wasn't so heavy from the statues I'd bought for my dad.

Sweat drenched my clothes and I was glad to take off my backpack and sit for a while, nearly gulping down two bottles of cool water. While resting and rehydrating, the group from Kong Lo Caves came in. It was good to see them. We chatted, and they joined us for lunch.

They had been there for half a day and agreed that there was even less to do in Savannakhet than in Vientiane and suggested we head down to the 4000 Islands that night. The plan sounded good to me.

At the restaurant, they only offered soup with noodles so that's what we all ordered. Fortunately for our hungry group, it was tasty and filling.

After lunch we bid the cave friends farewell and headed back to the bus station. The thirty-minute walk with my heavy bag had me thinking about ditching some things but I quickly nixed the idea.

Sage suggested we stop at the nearby ATM because she'd heard rumors there weren't any on the islands and debit and credit cards were not accepted. I had some cash but withdrew $100 US just to be safe.

At the station, I scanned the schedule. There was a bus going to Thailand in 35 minutes. Without even thinking it over, I decided that I wanted to go there instead of heading to the 4000 Islands with Branden, Sage, and Shawn. They were great, but something just pulled me to Thailand. And, I only had three days left until my flight to the Philippines and it might be too hard to get to Bangkok from the islands.

I bought some snacks from the little shop. It was Shawn's birthday, so I treated him to a beer and thanked my travel buds for letting me join their group. I hugged them and got on the bus to Thailand then had my usual moment of sadness at leaving such great friends behind.

The bus pulled away about five minutes after I boarded. Oddly, after being crammed in so many buses butt-to-cheek with the other passengers, I was the only rider on this one.

About a half hour later, we came to the land border between Laos and Thailand. When we stopped, I retrieved my bag and took it to the customs agent who put it through the X-ray machine. He stamped me out of Laos and I re-boarded. Easy. A few minutes later we were at the Thailand border and I had to do the same thing. This time, though, I got stamped-in instead of out.

Hazard 31:

Wrong Currency and
a Stubborn Tree

I was excited when the bus pulled into a station around 6 p.m. because it meant I could catch the last bus to Bangkok at 7 p.m. and wouldn't need to spend the night in town.

I thanked the driver and went to the counter to buy my ticket. So much for plans. It turned out that the bus was full and the next one wasn't until 7 a.m. and there were only two seats left. That meant an overnight in whatever town I was in.

Okay then. I asked for a ticket on that bus. I tried to pay with Laotian kipp because usually border towns accepted both currencies but of course, this one didn't. I told her to hold the ticket and asked where I could find an ATM.

She directed me to the nearest one. I rushed over and inserted my card. No luck, it spit it right back out because it only accepted cards with chips—mine, of course, didn't have one. What the hell? I tried another machine. The same thing

169

happened. By now, my stress level was at Defcon 9. I knew the woman wouldn't hold the seat for much longer.

I went back to her and asked where the bank was because my card wasn't working. Her face screwed up and in a pretty nasty tone she said, "No money. No ticket!" I wanted to slap her. I wasn't asking for a free ticket. I had money; I just couldn't get it out of my account.

The bus driver who'd let me off saw what was happening and came over to help. I told him that I only had kipp and needed to exchange it to Thai baht. He was an angel and we traded kipp for baht. I thanked him profusely then bought my ticket.

Crisis over. All was well again.

I'd spotted a guesthouse next to the bus station. There, I asked for a room. When I tried to use kipp to pay, the woman in charge looked at me like I was crazy. She told me there was a bank at the mall nearby where I could exchange it.

Of course, the bank was closed. I wouldn't be doing any exchanging that night. I couldn't figure out what was going on. One obstacle after another. As I stood there, wondering what to do, I spotted the bank's ATM and was relieved when it accepted my chipless debit card. Money in hand, I let out a breath of relief that I wouldn't be sleeping under the stars that night.

I went back to the hotel and paid the owner. She showed me to my room. It was huge, with a king-sized bed, a shower, a western toilet, cable, and air conditioning, all for $7 US per night.

After I showered and cleaned up a bit, I walked to a restaurant across the street that looked busy and sat at a table towards the front, so I could people-watch.

I ordered Pad Thai and a Singha beer. The food was great. I'd brought my Lonely Planet guide with me so I could see where I was, figure out a plan, and book a hostel for the two nights I'd be staying in Bangkok.

I read that Laotian kipp isn't supposed to be taken out of the country and most places won't accept it or had never even seen it. Good to know. I should have read that part before I left Laos. Oh, well, live and learn.

I checked out the border map and thought I was in a town called Mukdahan, but I wasn't entirely sure. I connected to the Wi-Fi to see what hostels were available for two nights in Bangkok. Bodega was the first one that popped up and had great reviews. I booked it and started my search for hostels in Manila.

Even though spontaneous is more fun, my time in Indonesia had taught me the merits of planning ahead.

The next morning, I was the first one in line to board the bus to Bangkok. We had assigned seating and mine was the first seat on the second level. This gave me a view out the front window. I was excited to start my next adventure and looking forward to whatever experiences awaited me.

After the bus was underway, the food attendant brought me breakfast, which was included in the ticket price. I received a bottle of water, some sort of guava juice, fruit, and yogurt. After breakfast I fell asleep. About an hour later I was awakened to what sounded like thunder and heavy rain on the windshield. I loved it and dozed off again to the chatter of precipitation on the windows. The bus swerved and screeched to a halt, jolting me awake.

I stood to better see what was happening and saw that a huge fallen tree blocked the road. A group of people were already on the scene trying to clear it away. I didn't know how they planned to accomplish what looked to me to be an impossible task, but I had a front row seat to the fascinating drama.

I watched as ten people tried to push the tree. It wouldn't budge. I laughed as someone drove up, attached a rope from a branch to his car, then sped off. He got away with a branch. The tree trunk stayed where it was. Another guy drove up with his car thinking that he could slowly accelerate into the tree to push it. This was the best idea so far. He managed to move it slightly before crunching the front of his bumper. The damage wasn't too bad, so everyone had a good laugh. Somehow, I was confident a solution would present itself. In the meantime, I enjoyed the show.

After a while of watching one failed solution after another, I closed my eyes and drifted off. The movement of the bus woke me up. I looked out the window and saw that the tree had miraculously been cleared away. I was a bit sorry to have slept through the best part of the show.

Hazard 32:

Special Candy Gift

The bus continued our wet and rainy journey south on the one-lane road, passing through tiny villages and open country. After a couple of hours, the driver made an announcement in Thai that I couldn't understand.

Twenty minutes later, we stopped. Everyone got off, so I followed. Assuming this was a rest break, I made a beeline to the bathroom. It was more like an outhouse and I cringed at the sight of the small, crooked wooden shack surrounded with high grass.

Inside the dim structure I looked for a light switch. Nope. Lit by mother nature from a small window, I sighed as I looked around. A cement slab with a hole in the middle sat on the floor. Cobwebs covered the corners, and water dripped from the roof. A bucket of water for flushing sat next to the "toilet." The movie *Texas Chainsaw Massacre* reeled through my head. A shiver ran up my spine. I've never peed so fast in my life.

When I entered the restaurant, I must have looked confused or lost because a kind-looking man approached and told me it would be a thirty-minute stop for lunch, and to show my ticket at the register so I wouldn't have to pay because it was included in the ticket price. I thanked him and walked around a bit to wait for lunch to be served.

I got my food and headed for a table. A fellow traveler invited me to sit with him. I accepted his invitation. He introduced himself as Sal. He'd been visiting his family in Northwest Thailand and was now on his way to a town just north of Bangkok.

I briefly gave him my story but was more interested in learning about him. He said it was the first time he'd been able to see his family in five years. He owns a shop in the northern region of Bangkok and has no one to run it while he's gone so he doesn't leave very often. He said, "I learned English in California when I was young. I would like to return someday… maybe…if I sell my shop."

We chatted a while then I noticed it was close to time to get back on the bus. We went our separate ways. I bought some snacks, boarded, then settled into my seat and waited for the trip to resume. Sal came over and gave me a bag of Thai candy. "Only the locals know about this candy," he said. "I thought you would like it."

I was touched. Like many people I'd met along the way in Indonesia, he was a genuinely nice and caring person. I also know that there are plenty of awful people in the world, but in my experience, the good ones outnumber the bad.

When the bus arrived at Sal's stop, he said goodbye and wished me well then reminded me to get off on the next stop, in thirty minutes or so. I thanked him for his kindness and waved goodbye.

HAZARD 33:
WILL I NEVER LEARN ABOUT BANGKOK?

After fourteen long hours, we finally arrived in the Bangkok city center bus depot. I was exhausted and in dire need of a shower. It felt great to step off the bus and stretch my legs. I hurried to the luggage compartment, claimed my bag, and headed to the taxi counter. I asked for a metered taxi and withdrew cash from the ATM. I was so tired, all I could think of was getting clean and resting up.

The cab driver offered to carry my bag and stash it in the trunk. I gave him the address and name of the hostel then climbed in. After a minute or so, I noticed that there was no meter. "Excuse me. I ordered a taxi with a meter. Please stop the cab."

He didn't, of course and argued that his flat rate was cheaper than the meter because of traffic. "And the hostel is forty minutes away from the bus station." He kept blabbering, "Too far to walk… no other cab…" Blah, blah, blah. I gave up but inside I was livid.

This kind of bait and switch is one of the many reasons I don't like Bangkok. These guys always get you when you're overly tired and off your game.

About seven minutes—yep, seven minutes later—not forty—we arrived at the hostel. He boldly said, "300 baht." That's roughly $10 US. Way too much for that short ride and the swindle of meter/no meter.

I quietly stepped out of the vehicle, retrieved my bag, and handed him 100 baht. Without a word, I turned and walked away. He said nothing. I'm sure it was because he knew he was a scammer.

Before going inside, though, I glanced back and smiled. "Thanks for the ride." Still fuming, I thought that even 100 baht was too much for a seven-minute taxi ride. After all, my fourteen-hour bus ride from the Laos Border was only about 200 baht. I hate getting ripped off. The no meter thing wouldn't have been such an issue if he'd charged a fair price. These guys really go out of their way to rip off tourists.

As I stood there, I grudgingly admitted, though, that it was partially my fault. I'd let my guard down. Maybe because I was so tired, I didn't follow my own rules to always check the hotel instructions before a trip because they might provide free pick up, or the hostel might be within walking distance of the airport, bus, or train station. I vowed to be more on the alert for the rest of my stay there.

After checking in and cleaning up, I thought about my travels so far. I'd been gone for months with no plans of going back to the US. My flight home had been pushed to the back of my mind. I just didn't think about it. Oddly, I didn't care. I was living carefree and just wanted to let the good times roll. I'd get home eventually...maybe.

But I wasn't a fool. I Skyped Mom and made arrangements for her and Casey to continue sending off my rent checks until I could get someone to sublet my apartment.

She told me how much she missed me but was happy that I was having so much fun. I told her that I missed her too, but this trip was just something I had to do.

I took care of necessary business, though. I had my cellphone turned off, my gym membership paused, and stopped payments on every bill I could.

I emailed Casey and asked if she could find someone looking to sublet my apartment short term, so I could travel for a few more months.

I emailed my boss to let her know that I was alive and well but didn't know when I would be back. At the same time, I wondered whether I still had a job or not since I hadn't originally said anything about staying away so long, I just didn't go back.

I took stock of my situation and was satisfied that all responsibilities were covered. I had a minimum amount of money coming out of my account to cover health insurance and rent. But as soon as I found someone to sublet, I would be golden.

In Indonesia, I spent around $10 a night for a dorm—roughly, $300 a month. With someone renting my US apartment, I would save $800 a month. Yep, I had it all figured out. There was no need to hurry home.

Escapade 34:

Trade Books with a Stranger

The Bodega Hostel was a pleasant surprise. Just inside, I saw a spacious courtyard with tables, chairs, and a beer pong table. A large doorway on the left led to a covered lobby and bar area. When I scanned the bar, I saw that all five stools were occupied and there was no shortage of liquor on display.

The whole atmosphere felt friendly and inviting.

Even before I'd checked in, a staff member greeted me and offered a welcome drink. I cheerfully accepted then glanced around the lobby. There were two desks—one for check-in and the other for check-out. I was glad to see two shelves full of books.

The hostel operated on a tab system. That meant I could eat and drink anything I wanted and pay at the end of my stay. As insurance, I had to give them my passport to hold while I was in residence.

Turning my attention back to the bar, I smiled. On the wall was a tally written in blue chalk of the highest tabs ever racked up from alcohol related purchases. The top number was $1,500

US, roughly 50,000 baht. That's a fortune in Southeast Asia. To spend that much money on alcohol at a hostel is incredible. The average beer price is only 60 baht ($1.80 US) so that's a lotta beer. *Well,* I thought. *Cheers to Big Flashpacker.*

After checking in, I followed the staff person back through the courtyard down the alley to a door with an access code. Max, a staff member, typed it in and I followed him up the stairs. He led me into a twenty-bed dorm with crisp air conditioning blowing. I was glad to see a large, indoor bathroom.

A German guy resting on his bunk said hello then introduced himself as Christian then asked if I had any books in English that I wanted to trade so he could practice.

Perfect timing. I had just finished reading *The Beach*, about an American Naval Captain stationed in Melbourne, Australia after a 3rd World War.

He had just finished "Hotel K" which was about the corrupt Balinese prison Kerobokan. We swapped books. He headed down to the common area and asked me to join him.

I said I would after I settled in. Bangkok or not, I thought this stay might turn out to be better than it started.

Escapade 35:

Fake Sky Bar and
Crooked Taxi Drivers

I put fresh sheets on my bed, unpacked, showered, and made my way to the common area to meet Christian. There was an opening at the bar, so I sat down, ordered a drink, and put it on my tab. The man seated next to me introduced himself. "Hi. I'm Harry, from the US." I liked his vibe, and he had an interesting face with a mole on the left side and a small patch of beard under his chin. We started an easy conversation. He was finishing up a three-month Southeast Asia loop. Shortly, we were chatting with other backpackers there and found out that we were all going to head out for The Sky Bar.

I glanced around for Christian but didn't see him anywhere, so I hurried upstairs to get some baht then met Harry on the street. He hailed a cab, but the driver said he didn't want to use his meter, so we moved on to the next cab. Same thing. We'd asked about four more cabs to turn on their meters. They all declined. So, we gave in and negotiated a price with the next driver to take us to The Sky Bar. Of course, he insisted that it was far away from Bodega Hostel and gave us what I thought was an inflated price, but I wanted to be on my way.

Fifteen minutes later we arrived at The Sky Bar and paid the driver. We all knew we were being ripped off, but we'd already negotiated the price, so we forked over the baht.

I didn't leave the cab quietly, though. I turned to the driver and said, "I know what you're up to and it isn't nice to cheat people." He just laughed and said I was funny then slowly drove off.

Harry and I climbed the black metal steps to the second floor then found the elevator to the rooftop. When the doors opened, we were stunned. The cab driver hadn't taken us to Sky Bar, but to Heaven Bar. *What the hell! That guy doubly ripped us off!*

After a moment of frustration, I remembered that holding on to indignant anger was pointless and let it go. Harry had the same epiphany. We looked at each other and laughed.

Likely, our hostel mates ended up at the real Sky Bar and were wondering what happened to us! Ah, the curse of Bangkok struck again! Oh, well. Heaven Bar looked good, so we stayed instead of trying to find Sky Bar. We had drinks and food. Later, I enjoyed the dance floor while Harry held down the table and watched our drinks.

I realized that fake-Sky Bar was cool. I imagined the prices were a bit more reasonable, too.

After a while, I was ready to go back and climb into bed. We headed to the hostel and agreed to meet downstairs for breakfast in the morning.

Escapade 36:
Ghost Tower Bribe

The breakfast bar at our hostel served BLTs (bacon, lettuce, and tomato sandwiches) and Bloody Marys, so I broke with my usual breakfast fare tradition and ordered that and a cappuccino.

After a few minutes Harry joined me. He brought another man and introduced him as Vincent, someone he'd met in his dorm.

As we ate breakfast and chatted, Harry and I talked about what to do for the day. We weren't sure. Vincent suggested that we go to the Ghost Tower. This sounded intriguing, so I asked what it was.

"The Ghost Tower," he said, "is a forty-nine-floor, unfinished and abandoned high-rise condominium complex in the middle of Bangkok."

He held my attention as he further explained that public access to the building is forbidden, but if we paid the guard 200 baht, he would unlock the gate and let us in.

I smiled to myself and thought, *Bribery can get us nearly anything. Hmm.*

We all took a tram to Sky Bridge, a few blocks from the tower. The dirty and dilapidated, tall building was easy to see from the bridge. Wow. I couldn't wait to get inside.

We stopped at a 7-Eleven store for water, beer, and snacks and headed for the Ghost Tower. When we arrived at the gate, just like Vincent had told us, we paid the guard 200 baht and he let us in with the warning, "Be down before 8 p.m. That's when I close up for the night."

The first floor we explored was all walls. It reminded me of a parking lot without lines. We continued up to the next floor which looked much like the first.

After climbing a few more flights, we came to a hallway with doorways but no doors. All the walls were white, and construction debris was everywhere. Some of the floors were concrete slabs, others were wood.

I went into a corner room at the end of the hall. It was a spacious suite with three bedrooms and a balcony. If this building had been completed, it would have been super posh.

We explored all the rooms on that floor, but none were as big as the suite at the end. Some of the walls were covered in graffiti and broken glass from shattered windows blanketed a lot of floor space. One of the strangest things, though, were the toilets. Someone had gone through all the trouble to move them from the bathrooms only to place them in what seemed to be random spots throughout the building. Quite a few were filled with debris, trash, and mystery-junk. *Squatters? Why?*

We continued climbing toward the top, checking floor after floor and encountering much of the same—graffiti, construction debris, random furniture, and trash.

As we climbed higher, we found levels with some missing, or no, outer walls. A few rooms had interior walls and an open space where an outer wall should be. The street view from these rooms was spectacular, and the higher we went, the better the view. On each floor, we carefully stood as close as we could to the edge of where an outer wall should be in order to catch a bird's-eye view of the ground. Not being the bravest (or most foolish) of the bunch, I held on to the adjacent wall the entire time. At even higher levels we found rooms with finished balconies and floors. From the balconied rooms, we could see all of Bangkok and the surrounding areas.

Elevators had never been installed. We couldn't resist poking our heads into the empty shaft to peer down. Just for fun, we sometimes dropped rocks down to see if we could hear them land. Now that I think of it, though—what were rocks doing there in the first place?

This building was creepy and dangerous. I loved it. At the top of the building we struck the jackpot. A Greek-style circle of pillars filled with multi-colored graffiti stood in the center of the roof. Ten other people were there, enjoying the view. Six of them were having a picnic but others were solo.

After exploring a little more, we sat on the edge of the roof, cracked open our beers and enjoyed the view. It was worth the forty-nine flights of stairs. Everything was so quiet from that high up.

Our way down was quick because we didn't stop to explore. At the bottom, the guard unlocked the gate and let us out. We thanked him and headed back to the Sky Bridge to catch the tram.

Before going back to Bodega, Harry and I stopped at Terminal 21 shopping mall. He collected pens and wanted to see if they had any specialty pens before he left the country.

Awesome! Not only was it air-conditioned, each floor had a different theme. When we first went in, I spotted the double decker bus with the British flag and a red phone booth showing that this was the London level. Another level had replicas of the Golden Gate Bridge and the Ghirardelli Chocolate factory. Obviously, this was the San Francisco level. Other themes were Paris, Rome, Tokyo, Istanbul, and Hollywood. We visited all the cities in search of a special pen for Harry, but no luck. We left pen-less.

Escapade 37:

Proper Send-Off

For my last night in town, my hostel mates decided to take me out to the famous Khao San Road. I'd heard about this place but never made the time to go. It was my last chance, so after finishing our beer pong tournament, we were off to the famous "Road."

All of us squished into three cabs and were on our way. Arriving, we poured out of the cabs and I looked around. This place was nuts. What seemed like a bazillion food places and bars were all crammed on one street. It reminded me of a smaller Patong Beach. A bit classier, but still raunchy—in a good way. Colorful lights and clever signs hung at the bars, each trying to lure tourists in for cheap drinks and a good time.

Most of the prices and drinks were the same at each bar so we searched for a spot that had a good vibe and a big, empty table. When we chose one, the first order of business was to order three towers of beer. Hey, there were a lot of us in the group.

I hadn't eaten much that day, so I left for a minute to buy chicken skewers and fried rice at a nearby food cart manned by a vendor who looked clean then took it back to the bar. The food was awesome.

I had a flashback to the food cart upchuck incident in Luang Prabang and hoped I wouldn't be seeing any remnants of my meal selection the next day.

That night we celebrated with a lot of dancing, drinking, and bar hopping. We didn't crawl into our hostel until about 3 a.m. The only reason I knew the time was because earlier I'd arranged to have a taxi waiting to take me to the airport at 3 a.m.

I stumbled to my room grabbed my backpack and dragged it down the stairs and all the way to the cab. I paid my tab, a task I don't remember doing. I only knew I had done this because I had my passport with me. Head spinning from such a fun night, I headed for the airport.

When I woke up, I was on a plane heading to the Philippines, I didn't remember the ride to BKK, going through customs, or even getting on the plane.

I had a layover at Kuala Lumpur that had escaped my memory as well. So, waking up on a plane bound for Manila was a pleasant surprise. Some part of my brain had been working all that time. I thought, *My autopilot is a champ.*

We landed in Manila. I was slightly hungover, annoyed and again, amused by the impatient people practically jumping over seats to get off before the seatbelt sign was even switched off. I patiently waited my turn. Backpack and my dad's statutes from Bali in hand, I departed the plane in peace.

Customs was a breeze. I received my entry stamp and headed to baggage claim. My big green bag, large enough to hold a small child, was circling around and around on the conveyer belt all by itself. I pulled it off and dragged it over to the currency exchange line and tried to exchange the equivalent of $80 US in the Laos kipp that I still had. The woman behind the counter laughed and wouldn't accept the kipp but gave me a fairly decent exchange rate for the Thai baht, so I didn't need to stop by an ATM.

I'd learned my lesson about not reading the hostel tips prior to arrival and found that Cozey Monkey Backpackers picked up travelers from the airport who made arrangements in advance. Luckily, I had done that and the driver for the Backpacker was waiting for me with a sign that had my name on it. I didn't have to worry about explaining to a cab driver where the hostel was or wonder whether or not he was running up the meter.

Because of the awful traffic it took twenty minutes to get to the hostel that was just around the corner from the airport. I liked that it was in a gated community with a 24-hour guard. We entered with ease, passing by large houses with children running around. Some of the homes were well-kept up and nice to look at, but others were a bit run down. This seemed like a peaceful and safe area.

The driver pulled up to a three-story gated house. He kindly took my baggage inside and showed me to the front desk.

The house was huge. Just inside, I spotted a 50-inch flat screen TV on the wall, lots of movies and video games, board games, books, and bean bag chairs. Near the check-in desk I saw two staircases leading into a dining room with two large tables that connected to a spacious kitchen with an island and a six-person well-oiled wooden table. I felt like I was at someone's house, and it gave me a feeling of cozy friendliness.

The pleasant owner checked me in. She asked if I was hungry and if I would like to try chicken adobo. I remembered trying it a long time ago at a high school friend's house and liked it, so I said sure. She then told the cook to make a fresh batch.

Next, she led me through the dining area and kitchen to a staircase that took us to a large, open room with a creaky, wooden floor. There was a table topped with beautiful flowers.

This floor held five rooms. A couple were dorms and a couple were private rooms. Mine was a six-bed dorm. Luckily, I was the first arrival, so I had my choice of the bottom bunks.

I collected my toiletries and headed for the bathroom, conveniently located inside the dorm. The large bathroom included a tub and shower. I thought the tub was odd because I don't think anyone would dare use a dorm bathtub. Gross! Pink tile covered the walls and there were shelves to hold toiletries. I slipped-on my shower shoes and bathed.

Feeling clean and refreshed, I headed to the common area with my *Lonely Planet* guide to devise a plan for my time in Manila and future travel throughout the Philippines.

My food wasn't quite ready yet, but I didn't mind. It smelled terrific. I sat at a table with two other people and introduced myself as Mat Backwards. The guy and girl laughed and said "Tam," then introduced themselves as Charles and Martha from England. They were staying in a private room on my floor. I asked them about their time in Manila and what there was to do. They had just arrived a few hours before I did and had no plans but were trying to figure something out, too.

We came to a mutual conclusion that Manila was dangerous and we didn't want to go anywhere at night. I picked their brains about places they had gone in the Philippines and heeded their tips on hostels and accommodations. Martha insisted that I visit Palawan Island, specifically, El Nido, Northern Luzon, and especially Batad, which was the home of the original ancient rice terraces.

I noted these places in my book. She also mentioned a small colonial town with beautiful Spanish houses in the northwest corner of the island. I was stoked that there were so many amazing places to see.

The chicken adobo was beyond delicious. I saw that its aroma convinced some of the other backpackers to order some.

After dinner, Charles and Martha went to freshen up then met us downstairs later for some card games. Meanwhile I connected to the Wi-Fi to give my family and friends an update. The first non-spam email that popped up was from my mom.

> Hi Tamara. Where are you now? When are you coming home? I hope you're having fun, but I miss you. Dad says hi. Love, Mom.

I replied:

> Hey Mom, I just arrived in Manila. I'm staying at Cozy Monkey Backpacker and will be here for a few days. I don't know when I'm coming home. I miss you too. Tell Dad hi. Love, Tamara.

Next, I went on Facebook Messenger and read a message from Natasha, my roommate for seven days on the Gili Islands. It had been five or six weeks since we'd seen each other, but we kept in touch. She said:

> Hey Tam, I'm flying to Cebu in two days please meet me there, let's explore. Love, Nat.

I replied:

> Yes, of course. See ya in a few days. I'll give you hostel details later. Cheers.

I perused some websites looking for reviews on hostels and things to do in Cebu.

My *Lonely Planet* was the best tool for this kind of thing and seemed to be spot on, although it was good to use the internet, too. I found a flight to Cebu via Air Asia and booked it for two days out then made a three-night reservation at Le Village Guesthouse Bar and Hostel. I relayed the new plan to my mom and Nat then continued searching for things to do around Manila. Seeing the beautiful volcanic Taal Lake was my first choice. I am fascinated with volcanoes.

Martha and Charles were on board to trek to the lake with me, especially after I gushed about how I had wanted to be a volcanologist when I was growing up. It was exciting to have travel buddies. I really enjoyed getting to know them and I especially loved their English accents.

We gathered a group of five people to play Irish Snap. Who knew that calling numbers and slapping cards would draw such a crowd? The next thing I knew, there were ten of us playing and we had to add another deck to the game. We played until quiet hours began then headed off to sleep, promising to meet each other in the morning to catch a bus to the lake.

Escapade 38:
Ride in a Jeepney and
Reconnect with a Friend

After breakfast with Martha and Charles, I asked someone at the front desk about transportation to the volcanic lake. She told us the earliest bus going there would be the next day. I was so disappointed. I already had my flight to Cebu scheduled, and Martha and Charles would be going back home. It looked like I wouldn't get to see the volcanic lake after all but considered that there might be time on my way back through Manila. "Okay, then, what can we do today?"

Adam, from Canada, overheard our dilemma and mentioned that he was on his way to the Mall of Asia, and if we were looking for something to do, we could join him there. We all agreed that it sounded like fun.

He gave us detailed directions to walk down the street, past the airport gate, and look for a Jeepney going to the Mall of Asia. *What's a Jeepney?* I had no idea but didn't ask. Later, I found out that Jeepneys are World War II U.S. military Jeeps and Humvees left in the Philippines when the Americans pulled out of the area. The Filipinos lengthened them to serve as public transport—like a bus. Just picture a rundown, stretched Humvee limo painted with bright colors, decorations, photos, and designs. They don't leave for a destination until the vehicle is full of passengers so we knew this would be a crowded ride.

Okay, we were off to find a Jeepney to take us to the Mall of Asia. It wasn't difficult. They were just where Adam said they would be.

Climbing into one of the more colorful ones, we waited until all the seats filled and there was no standing room left. The driver shouted a few words that I assumed was something like, "Pay now." The cost of the trip was 7 pesos (13 cents US). With so many people standing in the aisle, I couldn't walk to the driver with the fare, so I handed the money to a passenger in front of me, he passed it on, and so forth until it reached the driver. I had learned that it's a good idea to carry small bills and coins for situations like this and had the exact fare. Expecting strangers to pass change back could be a problem.

All paid, we were off to the mall. The Jeepney was like a steam oven with twenty-five bodies crammed inside a metal box with no air conditioning. The outside temperature was 90° Fahrenheit and felt like 100 percent humidity. I can only imagine how much hotter it was in the vehicle. I thought, *This mall had better be spectacular.*

Although the Mall of Asia wasn't far, about an hour later we were still stuck in traffic. I'm sure that if any of us knew how to get there on foot, we would have abandoned the Jeepney and hoofed it to the Mall.

In this part of the world, traffic made going anywhere feel like swimming through quicksand. A lot of the cars, taxis, and motorbikes created their own lanes. I saw four marked lanes and ten 'unofficial' ones. What chaos!

We finally made it to the *first* Jeepney stop. Some people got off and others got on. It took about ten minutes before the vehicle filled and we were on the road again. Five minutes later, we arrived at the mall.

One of the best lessons I learned during my travels was to never be in a hurry. I was there to experience another culture and learn new things. Waiting was just a part of it.

Standing in line to get through a metal detector before entering the mall was a surprise. I'd never experienced this at home or in any other country I'd visited, either. But I shrugged it off and glanced around. Wow! It looked like Fast Food City. There was McDonald's, Starbucks, KFC, Shakey's Pizza, and more. I could have been in the US. I never realized that the Philippines had so much fast food. This was culture shock of a different kind.

Inside the massive mall there was a bowling alley and a movie theater. My favorite, though, was the huge ice rink. I stood and watched people skate while the others went to scope out some lunch choices.

As I watched, I spotted some skaters who looked like pros, executing near-perfect turns and twirls with finesse. They were beautiful to watch.

After a few minutes, I joined my friends and explored the mall, walking around and poking our heads in and out of shops. We found an ice cream store and each of us ordered double scoops, then took our cones outside to a lookout point where we could see the Pacific Ocean. The cool breeze was nice, but it couldn't compete with the hot, muggy air. To our right was a small amusement park with a Ferris wheel. We talked about the possibility of coming back to visit later that evening.

Ice cream gone, we roamed around the mall for a few hours before heading back to the hostel. Taal Lake popped into my mind. I really wanted to see it and again hoped I would have the opportunity on my way back through Manila.

The day had been fun but now it was time to prepare for my morning flight to Cebu. Getting to the airport was problem free but there was a two-hour delay at the gate. When I finally boarded, though, I was relieved. When the plane touched down. I collected my belongings from baggage claim and did exactly what the staff at Le Village had instructed before I checked out. I walked outside the airport, made a right at the baggage ramp, and found the taxi stand located at the corner. According to the Le Village staff, the drivers in that area were cheaper and more honest than the others.

I was handed a small ticket for taxi number 732 and joined the line of waiting people. When the little white cab arrived about fifteen minutes later, I handed the driver the ticket, loaded my bag into the trunk, got in, showed him the hostel address, and made sure he knew where it was. He turned on the meter and we were off.

Because of my flight delay, I arrived at the height of heavy traffic. I wish I could say that it was stop and go, but we were mostly stopped. The drive to the hostel took three hours. The fare was only 350 pesos ($7.50 US), not bad for such a long ride.

Inside Le Village guesthouse, bar, and hostel, I looked around, pleasantly surprised. One of the first things I noticed was the huge bar on a large patio with plenty of adult-sized chairs and tables. I was glad to see the guest house furnished with comfortable bean bag chairs, books, a flat screen TV, and plenty of movies to choose from. I noticed a small kitchen area along one wall and admired the photos of various Philippine regions taken by guests who had visited them.

Everyone on the staff was polite and friendly. As I checked in, they explained where everything was and helped me gather information on nearby places to visit.

After check-in, I went to my six-bed room, called the Green Dorm because of its wall color. Inside, I saw a handsome guy sitting on a top bunk, reading. I introduced myself as Mat

Backwards. He chuckled and asked, "Tam?"

I smiled and nodded. He told me his name was Sean, and that he was from Brazil. We chatted for a bit. I asked how long he'd been traveling, and where he was heading next.

As we talked, the room began to heat up. That's when I realized there was no air conditioning in the dorm. This was a big-time problem for me, so I trudged downstairs, bag in hand, and asked for a room with air conditioning. I'd half-expected this to be an issue, but surprisingly, it wasn't. They were nice about it and moved me to the Blue Dorm—again, called that because of the wall color. Happy, now, I settled in then went out to wait for Natasha.

When her cab arrived, I smiled in amusement as I watched the driver pull out ten bags and pile them up in the hostel driveway. Natasha doesn't travel light. I ran out to her, and she ran to me. We wrapped each other in a huge hug.

I helped lug her bags into the common area and waited while she checked in, thinking about how Nat is a bubbly and enthusiastic person who always tries to make sure everyone feels welcome.

She dropped her luggage off in the Blue Room and the two of us headed to the mall for food and to catch up. We ordered wraps at a Greek restaurant and later stopped in a nearby sports bar for a few drinks. Nat told me that she planned to join a travel group in a few days but was having second thoughts.

Escapade 39:
Blue Dorm Surprise and Beach Disappointment

When we arrived back at the hostel, the staff told us that no one else would be staying in the Blue Dorm that evening. That was music to my ears because we could get comfortable and spread out our stuff.

Nat was wearing only her undergarments while sorting laundry. I was spread across my bed in a sports bra and night shorts, reading *Hotel K*, when a man with an eye patch walked in.

Nat gave a little squeal. I pulled the blanket over me, both surprised and annoyed because the staff didn't give us a heads-up about another guest. "Give us a minute?" I asked.

He looked surprised, apologized, and nearly sprinted out of the room.

After we put on more clothes, Natasha opened the door and let him in.

He apologized, again, for barging in on us.

"It's okay," we explained. "Not your fault. The staff told us there wouldn't be anyone else staying here tonight."

He relaxed and introduced himself—Frances, a native Californian, but currently living in Wyoming.

I guessed that he was about 6-feet tall and probably in his mid-forties. I was close. We later learned he was 6-feet 2-inches and forty-seven.

We introduced ourselves and were soon chatting away about Asia, our travels, and adventures. When we asked him why he was in the Philippines, he confessed that he was looking for love.

I wasn't sure how to react. Was he joking? I didn't think so. It was certainly straight up, so we just let it slide as if it wasn't an unusually soul-baring confession.

I told him that Nat and I had originally met in Bali and that she'd just arrived yesterday for a quick reunion before meeting up with her travel group.

Frances turned out to be a great guy and I was glad that he'd been brave enough to stay in a dorm with us girls. When he stepped out to use the bathroom, Natasha and I busted into laughter and I don't think we really knew why—maybe stress release because of how matter of fact his "looking for love" statement was.

When he re-entered the room, Nat just blurted out, "Why do you have that eye patch? Were you injured in combat?"

I don't think he was expecting the question and stumbled over his words a bit when he told us that it happened when he was hang gliding. All he remembered was that he woke up in a hospital bed without use of his eye.

The next day, Nat and I explored Cebu City. It wasn't what I'd expected. When I'd first heard about it, beautiful beaches with golden sand came to mind. But no. We spent most of the morning looking for a beach. There were none. Anything remotely close to one was filled with boats, and the water was covered with an oil sheen. Natasha and I finally broke down and paid to enter a resort. We swam in the pool most of the day. For lunch, we had a Filipino delicacy—haluhalo or halo-halo. I'd heard of it before but didn't know what it was.

The server arrived with a massive bowl of colorful food. I took a bite but wasn't sure what I was tasting, so I asked the waiter what was in it. He looked a bit amused when he handed us a list of ingredients: shaved ice, sweetened condensed milk, boiled sweetened kidney beans, coconut, plantains, sugar, sugar palm fruit, sweet potato, jack fruit, flan, cheese, corn flakes, and rice.

I liked some of it but wasn't a fan of the rest. I knew there were variations of it, and might try it again elsewhere, but at that moment, halo-halo was on my not-a-tasty-treat list.

We headed back to the hostel disappointed that there had been no decent beaches but happy about our day at the spa. As we walked up the driveway, we spotted Frances sitting outside, chatting with Sean, the guy from Brazil I'd met in the Green Dorm.

I said hello and joined them. Nat went on to our room.

Sean asked me why I'd left the dorm the day before. He was worried that he'd done something to offend me.

It struck me that rushing away with no explanation had been inconsiderate. That's not usually like me. "It wasn't you," I said, "I was starting to sweat after being there for only five minutes and had to change rooms to one with air conditioning. Sorry for barging out like that. I should have said something."

He seemed relieved that it was nothing he'd said or done and told me it was too hot for him, too but didn't think about changing rooms.

When I asked Frances about his day, he said there hadn't been much to do in the city, so he just hung out at the hostel.

Not the most stimulating conversation and I needed to pack my day-bag to prepare for our 3am departure for Oslob. I excused myself and joined Nat in the dorm.

Escapade 40:

Swim with Whale Sharks

At 3:30 a.m., Nat and I were out the door and in a taxi that would take us to the bus station. When we arrived ten minutes later, we found ourselves in a big, busy, and chaotic place. Locating the bus to Oslob was a challenge, but we persisted until we found it then bought our tickets from the driver.

Natasha stayed on board while I raided the little shop for snacks to take with us. When we were finally on our way, I slept for the first three hours, waking up just in time to see turquoise water and adorable beach homes on the outskirts of Oslob. *Paradise.*

The bus dropped us off in the middle of the street—not an official, marked stop. Not unusual, everyone seemed to get on and off buses in Cebu at random.

We walked across the street and followed a sign with an arrow that read WHALE SHARK TOURS. The snorkel office was attached to a quaint, gray stone hotel overlooking the coast. Inside, the manager greeted us and asked if we were there to snorkel with the whale sharks.

203

We said yes, and he told us the fare—900 pesos ($17.86 US). I was relieved when he charged a fair price, the one I'd read in my book. But then, he asked for an extra 200 pesos ($3.96 US) and my "rip-off" radar kicked in. He claimed it was the "environmental fee." *Hah!* It sounded like a scam to me and I grilled him on it. "So," I asked, "what is this fee used for and how often is it imposed?"

He held his ground and stated that everyone had to pay it and it was used to help keep pollutants out of the water.

I was still skeptical, but this was Nat's birthday, and we were going to swim with the whale sharks if I had to pay three times that.

Nat and I locked up our dry articles and headed to the dock where a narrow, blue boat with room for five people was moored. Our guide helped us board then steered over to the viewing area. We put on our snorkels and jumped in.

The water was amazingly beautiful and clear. We spotted seven whale sharks, including one baby. These speckled creatures are massive and unbelievably docile. I couldn't believe I was swimming around with them.

I wondered how they got them to stay in this area, but when I saw a nearby boat feeding them, my question was answered. The whale sharks were so beautiful with their gray-black skin covered in white and gray speckles that seemed to change colors to blue, green, and purple as they zipped through the water. I watched their massive mouths open and scoop in the chopped fish from the feeding boat.

Images of being swallowed by this huge, gaping mouth ran through my mind and I tried to stay at least ten feet away.

Although a part of me thought it was a shame that these magnificent animals had been tamed by being fed instead of their natural way of eating in the wild, it was an amazing experience to be so near and watch them swim and maneuver their long powerful bodies.

Being so close strengthened my already fiery passion to preserve and protect natural resources.

Nat and I swam around trying to visit all the whale sharks. Of course, we loved seeing the baby. It was tiny in comparison to the adults, but it was still large and could easily swallow a human if it had a mind to do so. I felt such a rush sharing the water with these gentle giants, but it was also humbling.

Later in the day, we walked around the small town in search of lunch and found a spot nearby that had little huts and an ocean view. We checked their menu to see if they had veggie options. They did, so we knew this was the right place for us to eat. The huts have pointy roofs covered in long brown grass. They have no walls, only support beams to keep the roof in place. Inside, there are benches and a large table.

Our next bus back to Cebu city was scheduled to arrive around one o'clock, so we had plenty of time and settled in to wait. I read *Hotel K* and enjoyed a beer and seafood fried rice. Nat ordered a fruity drink and lumpia then stretched out on the seawall edge to soak up some sun.

Since the hut was next to steps that led to the water, we agreed that more swimming would be in our day's activities. After eating, we headed for the ocean. With few people around, we enjoyed a serene and peaceful swim, checked out the colorful fish and the tidepool communities.

After swimming, I dried off and went back to the hut for some water and shade then glanced at my watch. "What?" We were about to miss our ride. I yelled down to Natasha. "The bus is about to arrive. Get up here, fast!" She came running.

We packed our gear, paid the restaurant, and dashed to the street only to arrive just as the bus was leaving. I jumped up and down, waved my hand in the air, and yelled, but it kept going. So much for the perfect birthday.

The woman who ran the restaurant came over and asked where we were going. "Cebu City."

She smiled and said, "It's okay. That bus wasn't for you. The next one comes in ten minutes. That one will take you to Cebu City."

I nearly fell over in relief. Nat said nothing, but I know she was glad we didn't have to walk back or spend the night there. We stood, planted to the spot, and waited. Sure enough, a bus came, but drove right past us! We freaked and ran after it. It finally stopped just when I thought I would burst a lung. It turned out that the reason it didn't stop was that we were *not* standing at a marked official bus stop.

I thought we could get on the bus anywhere. After all, that's what everyone else did. At least it worked out. Go figure, we had to have the only bus driver in Cebu who followed the official rules.

When we arrived at the hostel, the owner was giving a huge 1st birthday party for her nephew. Everyone from the hostel was invited to eat the catered food and join in the festivities. There was an open bar, and karaoke headlined the agenda.

Nat got up and sang. She was a natural—not a nervous bone in her body, or she was good at hiding it. She sang Aretha Franklin's *Respect,* Shania Twain's *That Don't Impress Me Much*, and would have stayed up there all night if there hadn't been a list of people waiting to sing.

We drank and celebrated with our hostel mates. I'm not sure what time we went to bed, but we'd had a lot of fun, so it didn't matter.

Since Cebu City was such a sleepy town, with not much to lure me into staying longer, I thought about my next move. Natasha would be going to the hotel where her travel group was staying. She invited me to come along and swim in the pool. I agreed— as long as there was Wi-Fi so I could make arrangements to get out of Cebu the next day.

At breakfast I spotted May, from Canada, and her boyfriend. They had stayed with me at the Cozy Monkey in Manila. When

I approached them, I saw that they were having balut—a boiled, partially developed duck embryo. Although I had heard about it, I had never seen it. They were eating it with vinegar and said it was wonderful. When they offered me one, I suppressed a gag and politely declined. Now I think, *What a coward I was. I should have tried it.*

I scarfed down my "normal" breakfast then caught a cab with Nat. We headed to her new digs. When we arrived, I connected to the Wi-Fi then went straight to the pool to research my next move.

Seeing the tiny, dirty pool, I decided not to swim. Instead, I sat in a lawn chair and got to work debating on whether to go to Malapascua and the Chocolate Hills or not. The photos looked stunning, but I'd read they were hard to get to. I realized that it would have been an easier trip from Oslob, so I decided to fly to Palawan instead. I booked my flight to Puerto Princesa for the following day and reserved two nights at Sheebang Hostel.

Booking travel accommodations can be tedious and difficult, especially if flights don't work out or hostels are full. Sometimes things happen exactly how I want them to and sometimes they don't. It's all a part of the fun of long-term, solo travel.

Nat's group went out to dinner, but she and I did our own thing and said we'd join them later in Mango Square, where all the bars and clubs were located.

After dinner, we joined the group. They were all friendly and we drank, and danced, and danced, and drank. It was a fun night and a great send-off for Nat and me.

I was feeling a little too good and gave Nat a big hug goodbye and wished her safe, happy travels then I hailed a cab to Le Village Hostel.

I hit the bed and went right to sleep.

Escapade 41:
The Most Beautiful Place in the World

I picked the worst flight. It didn't get me to Puerto Princesa until the following morning around 2 a.m. Off the plane, I forgot how awful the trip was as I looked around and saw how gorgeous Palawan was—even at the airport. I especially liked the beautiful dark-green trees lining the perimeter fence.

Normally, I'm like a zombie in the wee hours of the morning, but this time I was fueled by my passion to explore a new place.

As I thought about how to get to where I would stay that night, I met some people who were going to the same hostel I was, so we shared a tricycle transport—colorful three-wheeled vehicles with a driver peddling and a passenger compartment behind, or sometimes in front.

Our tricycle was open with only a windshield for the driver, making this a welcoming cool and breezy ride. The crisp air blowing in my face and through my hair was a nice change from the hot humid atmosphere I'd experienced throughout most of Southeast Asia.

At the hostel, the front desk person was sleeping in a hammock. I was tired and wanted to drop my bags and get some shuteye, myself so I reluctantly woke him.

Thankfully, he was pleasant about having his slumber interrupted, checked me in, and showed me to my room. It was a sixteen-bed dorm but only had seven people in it. Lucky me. I snagged a lower bunk then fell asleep within minutes.

I woke up starving, so I quickly showered, dressed, then headed to the bar and ordered breakfast—a fried egg, toast, bacon, and a cappuccino.

While eating, I glanced around. The common area was like a botanical garden with bees and hummingbirds hovering over a multitude of flowers. There was a canopy with hammocks, beautiful mahogany tables, trees, and plants everywhere. The bar area was in the middle of this serene setting.

I met two girls from England heading back to Manila who said they'd had a blast on Palawan Island but advised me to leave Puerto Princesa as soon as possible because it was pretty dull.

They suggested I head to El Nido and stay at OMP hostel and said to book a room right away because it fills up fast. They had camped at Port Barton, near an underground river and cave system and said it would be worth the stop, but there were better caves in Vietnam.

Stoked about that, I decided to take their advice. Another girl sitting at the bar near me introduced herself as Allison, from Canada. We started talking and I asked her what her plans were and if she might be interested in traveling to El Nido with me.

"You bet," she said, and we rushed to the front desk to book transport and accommodation. Our hostel set up a minibus to pick us up first thing in the morning for the five-hour journey to El Nido at the northern tip of Palawan Island.

Allison is fair-skinned, petite, and blond. I felt like Gigantor next to her with my 5-foot, 7-inch, athletic, curvy frame. But she didn't seem to notice and acted like we were already best friends.

This is one of the many reasons why I like staying at hostels. I had known Ally for all of thirty seconds before we decided that we liked each other enough to be travel buds.

When I returned to the bar to finish my breakfast, one of the English girls asked if I had any books that I wanted to trade.

I had just finished *Hotel K* at the airport the day before, so this was a serendipitous stroke of luck. She handed me her book and I scurried to my dorm room to fetch mine to give her.

I had the thought that it would be cool to start writing my name, date, and country on the inside of each book I read while traveling. That way I, and those I traded with, could track how many different places these books had been to.

I had received *Hotel K* in Thailand and now it was being handed off in the Philippines. Cool.

In the dorm, I packed and left for the city center. I soon realized that the British girls were correct in saying that there wasn't much to do in Puerto Princesa. *Yawn.*

Ally and I wandered down various streets looking at houses and observing local activities. We also paid a visit to the waterfront which had carnival rides but looked like they hadn't been used in a long time and thought it might be off season.

The waterfront was nothing to write home about, but it still made for a nice stroll. We came to one of the only restaurants in the area and stopped for a late lunch.

I ordered shrimp adobo and drank two servings of freshly squeezed mango juice. I never get tired of fresh fruit juice. After lunch we walked around, enjoyed watching the people, and browsed some of the local shops.

We got back to the hostel just before sunset and found the

common area packed. When I dropped my bag off in the dorm, all the beds were "tagged" with personal items. I was glad I'd checked in early enough to claim a bottom bunk.

More people meant more fun. I played ping pong then danced a while but went to bed early. I needed to repack my bag and prepare for the morning bus ride to El Nido. I said good night to Ally and we agreed to meet for breakfast first thing in the morning.

The minibus arrived promptly at 7:30 a.m. Ally and I were excited and ready for our new adventure. El Nido isn't far from Puerto Princesa. The trip takes so long because of the unpaved and barely maintained road that meanders along the ever-changing landscape.

The road could safely fit only one car, so we were continually jerked around by sudden stops or swerves to turnouts to avoid oncoming vehicles. The drive was bumpy, wild, and jarring, but the massive green rolling hills, dense forests, and terraced mountainsides, carved perfectly to preserve the natural contour of the land made it all worthwhile.

I was glad we'd nabbed front seats. I'm sure I would have been puking all over the floor if I'd had to ride in back.

Escapade 42:

Zipline to an Uninhabited Island

After arriving at the El Nido bus station, we asked around to find out if anyone else was heading to OMP Hostel. One person was, so we split the tricycle fare. I was grateful the road to town had been recently paved, so minimal bumps.

We passed through a cute little downtown area and a market I decided to check out later. So far, El Nido was what I'd expected—not very touristy and kind of quiet.

At OMP hostel, I looked around to size it up. It was great. A bit rustic and laid back but clean, and lots of potential new friends.

Ally and I had the whole day, so we headed out to do some exploring. The hostel staff suggested we take a tricycle to the closest beach and arranged a ride for us.

Our driver was awesome and showed us a quiet place where we could zipline to a small uninhabited island and have the beach to ourselves.

Ally and I were stoked when we saw it. We hiked along a moist dirt path through the beautiful, forested wilderness area and up a steep hill to a treehouse with multiple levels offering views in all directions.

As we approached, a man waved from the top of the house then came down to greet us. We told him we wanted to zipline to the other island. He nodded and motioned for us to follow him up the stairs to the center level.

Ally and I were fitted into our harnesses and stood looking down at the other island treehouse, 750 meters across the water.

The guy behind us seemed impatient for us to get going and take the plunge, so I took a deep breath. *Here goes.* I placed the SLR around my neck, hit record, took a running start, and jumped off the platform. I dropped a bit then the cable yanked me back up then off I went. What a rush! I screamed the whole way across. Not because I was scared but because it was so awesome. After a bird's-eye view of the beach below with its little restaurants and huts, out over the water I zipped. From the spectacular panorama, I looked down at the shallow, clear, turquoise sea.

The small, rocky island covered with trees loomed closer as I zipped toward it and I wondered how this tiny lump in the ocean had formed. Had it been a part of the large island at some point and water eroded the land away? Or, did the island flood, submerging some of it? I could have used Sam, my geology friend from my trip to Laos, to help figure this out.

Flying through the air felt like a dream. I can't even begin to describe the beauty that surrounded me. The brown sandy beach, encircled by long skinny palm trees, looked unreal from there. Then, suddenly snatched out of my beautiful dream, I landed.

Turning to gaze at where I'd been, I thought, *Beautiful, but nothing compared to the view from the zipline.*

Ally came next. She ran off the platform with a loud scream. As she approached, all I remember seeing were teeth because she was smiling so wide. Before landing, she spun around a couple of times then hit the platform with full force. It sounded painful, but she said she was fine.

Adrenaline still rushing, we gushed about how awesome it was. At first, we thought we wanted to do the zip again, but when we calmed down a bit, decided not to.

Now for the trek down the steep slope to the beach. It was a bit rough, especially since we wore sandals. The sharp and unforgiving limestone made walking tough, especially in the slippery wet places. At one point I took off my flip flops to gain better traction, but the rocks were too sharp to walk on. It felt like stepping on a pile of Legos.

We eventually made it to the beach with minimal scratches. Ally and I took lots of photos, but as always, they couldn't capture the full-blown beauty of the place.

We spotted a little beach bar on the main island, so we waded through the shallow, rocky clear water to get to it. The bar was cabana style with no real walls. We sat at one of the little tiki tables with brown grass on its edges. I ordered seafood noodles and a mango juice minus the sweetened condensed milk. Ally ordered a coconut.

We were delighted when a young man actually climbed a tree and cut one down for her. Talk about fresh food! Watching someone plucking your coconut from a tree is priceless, and I think if Ally had had a choice, she would have taken the coconut *and* the man who got it for her.

The rest of the afternoon we hung out at the bar. Just after sunset, but before the last light left the sky, it was time to start our trek back up the mountain to where we'd asked the tricycle driver to wait.

We were sure he would have left, but to our surprise, he'd waited for us all that time. The drive back was wonderful. The stars weren't quite visible yet, but cool night air refreshed us as we passed through the adorable little town.

When we entered the OMP, there were a lot more people there than when we'd left that morning. It had filled with backpackers, so I knew it was going to be a good night.

We headed for the dorm to shower and change. The bunks were three beds high and I had the unfortunate luck of having to take a top bunk. A guy laying in the second bed of my three-bed tower said, "Hi," and introduced himself as Mark, from Canada. He was just starting a year-plus trip around Southeast Asia and asked how long I'd been traveling.

I told him, "About four months," and talked about not being sure when I'd be going back home. It all depended on how long I could make my money last.

After showering and changing into fresh clothes, Ally and I joined Mark in the common area. He introduced us to the two girls sitting with him—Courtney and Alissa, from Norway. They were also our dorm mates.

I pulled out my cards and asked if they wanted to play Irish Snap and was delighted when they said yes. I taught them how and we were at it for a good hour.

The longer we played, the harder it was to be quiet. After a while, we were attracting others with our rowdy laughter and banter. Soon there were seven people playing with a few waiting to join the next game. But the party really started when someone brought a handle of vodka and passed it around.

Quiet hours came too soon, and we had to stop the game. We didn't mind so much when someone suggested we all head to the Reggae Bar on the beach—about a five-minute walk. The party continued.

The bar was super beachy, with a grass-covered pointy roof and just enough wall to keep the place from crumbling into a pile of rubble. A band played to a packed dance floor. I ordered a San Miguel Pale Pilsen and joined Courtney, Alissa, Ally, and Mark on the dance floor. It was a fun crowd and when I looked around, I saw that a lot of others from our hostel were there, too.

When a song started that I wasn't really into I excused myself and went outside to sit near the water. I'm always drawn to the ocean and feel great when I'm near it. I love the briny smell and the soothing sound it makes.

I pulled a beach towel from the chair and spread it out to lie down so I could do some stargazing. Lately, I'd found myself looking into the night sky a lot, wondering what's out there but not really wanting to know. I guess I'm secretly terrified. Too many sci-fi movies, perhaps.

After a while, I sat up and gazed at the ocean, fascinated by the bioluminescent plankton on the beach, I hadn't noticed it at first because—too busy looking at the stars. I glanced around but no one else seemed to notice it. Or maybe they just didn't care. *Oh, well, their loss.* I sighed. "What a beautiful place."

Soon, I was ready to head back and told my new friends that I was leaving and would see them tomorrow. When I arrived, there was a message from Chad (we'd met in Malaysia), asking me to meet him in Chiang Mai for the water festival happening in three weeks.

I hadn't expected to hear from him again and this gave me a huge smile. But after thinking it through, I wasn't sure if I could work my travel schedule to be there. Bummed, I simply replied, "Thanks. Sounds great but I'm not sure I can make it. I'll let you know."

The next day, Ally and I took a trip to the beach we'd seen from the zipline. We bought snacks from a little market for a picnic then just relaxed and read all day.

My book, *The Little Boy Under the Cupboard*, was depressing and horrifying. Some parts actually made me sick to my stomach. I hadn't read the back cover first because it ruins my excitement of the unknown. Often, I prefer to jump in without clues or expectations. Maybe this time should have been an exception.

As gruesome as the story was, I forced myself to keep reading, hoping there would be a happy ending. I took some breaks and waded in the surf to clear away the horrific images in my head from the book. The water was a little colder than I'd expected, but still comfortable and it helped me feel better.

Ally was searching her *Lonely Planet* trying to get some ideas for what we should do next. I was sure she'd come up with something good. I put my book aside and took a nap.

When I woke up, I went for a swim to cool off. After a couple of minutes, I heard people making a commotion and saw them pointing. When I turned to my left, I saw a gigantic jellyfish too near for comfort. Yikes! I dashed out of the water as fast as my legs could carry me.

At first, the jelly looked like a massive gray blob, but when I looked closer, it appeared pink. Pink jellies, sometimes called "Pink Meanies," aren't as big as the gray ones, but can be three feet across and have seventy-foot tentacles! After calming down, I saw Ally laughing hysterically at my frantic sprint.

From the beach, I watched until I was sure the jelly had gone. Stings from this creature are painful. If it had stung me, not only would it have been excruciating, I thought I would have had to endure the indignity of needing to pee on myself or ask someone else to do it to counteract the poison.

Later, I discovered that peeing on a jellyfish sting only makes it worse because it ignites the venomous cells from the jelly's tentacles that embed in the skin. Vinegar is a better first-aid. Medical treatment is the best choice.

After our day on the beach, my mind turned to what Ally and I could experience next. We bounced a few ideas around. A few minutes later, I told her about a camping trip I'd read about. It included a visit to uninhabited islands of the Bacuit Archipelago. The trip also included two guides, a boat, booze, food, and camping gear, plus a full tour.

After researching it more and looking at all the pictures, I was determined to make it happen.

Ally agreed.

I left a message with the hostel to tell anyone who was interested in joining us on the camping trip to email me.

Later, Ally and I searched for a good place to have dinner. We found a rotisserie chicken cart one street over from the hostel. It looked good, especially since we were both a bit tired of Filipino food. Something different was more than inviting. We ordered fries with homemade aioli sauce and a half chicken to split. The owner smiled and said he'd have a fresh chicken ready for us in about twenty minutes.

Since there were lots of chickens freely roaming about, we half wondered if "fresh" meant the cook would just go out in the street and catch one.

Since we had a little time to wait for our dinner, we decided to explore the dimly lit town and walked down the main street. Outside the tourist area, children ran around playing, and adults stood in groups, socializing and enjoying each other's company.

I think the locals weren't used to outsiders roaming their turf because they stared with surprise and curiosity as we strolled past them. A Filipino couple came up to us and complimented Ally on her "yellow hair" and me for my "soft brown skin." They even gently caressed my arm and stroked Ally's hair. It was such a nice experience. These people accepted us even though we looked vastly different from them.

We made a loop and headed back into the busy part of town, passing a school where a night basketball match was in full swing. While we watched the game, a local woman whispered to us that this was an important game and that basketball was a serious sport around there. The players and the spectators *did* look intense. She told us that the winner would advance to the finals, then the winner of the final round would be accepted into an international tournament. I guessed that a tournament victory would be a serious achievement for them.

Back at the restaurant, we picked up our rotisserie chicken to take back to OMP. It smelled so good, we had a taste on the way. It was amazing, and the aioli sauce, mouthwatering. We were tempted to turn around and order more sauce and fries but didn't.

When we walked in, the aroma of the chicken attracted attention from our hostel mates. They ask where we bought it. I told them, "Just walk outside the hostel, make a left, and when you reach the next corner, make a right. The cart should be on your left."

Later, Ally and I did go back to thank the cart owner for the incredible meal and told him he would be seeing us again for dinner real soon.

He was tickled that we liked it so much.

Escapade 43:

Camp on Uninhabited Islands.

Shortly after Ally and I had arrived at our hostel with the chicken, Mark came in with Courtney and Alissa. He said they'd seen my message about the camping and wanted to join us, and that he'd found a good deal for the trip, but we'd have to leave the next day.

Always open for a deal, I said "Sure. No problem." So, the five of us marched down to the travel agency.

The owner explained the options and packages, described the food we would have, and what was included in the deal price. I thought it a little steep, but with five people, affordable.

I told the group I was in for sure. Three of the others said they were too. Ally was undecided and asked if she could let the agent know in the morning. He agreed. We each put in a small deposit then went back to OMP to prepare.

My bag included clothing, toiletries, beach towel, book, dry bag, camera, and my trusty waterproof playing cards. When everything was packed, I headed to the common area to socialize.

A couple on spring break from Stanford University was playing Rummy. I joined them for a while but went to bed early, excited about our camping trip in the morning.

In the dorm, I thought about how Courtney and Alissa are a lot like Ally and me—physically polar opposites but spiritual soul sisters. Courtney is tall and thin with beautiful curly hair and similar milk chocolate skin like mine. Alissa is short with golden skin and fair hair like Ally. Courtney and Alissa had been friends since childhood when Courtney's family moved from East Africa to Norway. They were traveling for a few months before going back to school in the fall.

In the morning, I drank a fruit smoothie and grabbed some fresh bread then headed for the travel agency, stopping at an ATM for some cash. On the way, I ran into Mark, who had already paid. He told me the captain wanted to leave in forty-five minutes.

I paid my part of the fee at the agency and made sure to get a receipt. When I arrived back at OMP, Courtney and Alissa were heading out to pay. Ally had decided to go so she was scrambling around to get her things together.

The hostel said we could store our bags there while we were camping, and that everything was all set. I packed a few snacks for the trip and met our group at the agency. While waiting, I connected to Wi-Fi and let my parents know where I was headed then did a quick Facebook check. Chad had written back saying that I should really try to make it to Songkran and asked what my travel plans were *after* the Philippines. Was he hinting at something? I told him I wasn't certain what my plans were, but I was thinking of going to Nepal and perhaps meeting up with a friend in India (Casey's old boss and friend Kevin). Burma was on my list too. I was pretty sure I wasn't going to the water festival but told him I'd think about it.

The agency owner walked us to the boat and introduced us to our guides, Jon and Cary. They took our bags, helped us aboard, and handed us life jackets.

The boat didn't look like much, but I'd been on worse, so I wasn't too worried. They decided to take us on the "C" tour today because there would be fewer people on that loop. The captain started the engine and we were off.

As we cruised out of the bay, the water became clearer and cleaner. There wasn't a piece of trash in sight. I have seen some beautiful places but El Nido and the Bacuit Archipelago take the cake. We passed by limestone karsts covered with greenery that left me speechless. Fish swam around the boat, jumping into the air as we cruised by. It was beyond perfect.

Our first stop was Hidden Beach. It's called that because it's surrounded by massive limestone walls that, from a distance, make it look inaccessible. We arrived just as the day tours were leaving, so we had the beach all to ourselves.

I was so eager to explore this pristine wonderland, I practically leapt off the boat before it docked. The others did the same. We had just started our trip and I thought, *It doesn't get any better than this.* We all swam around and stretched out on the beach while the guides prepared our lunch of grilled squid and some sort of white fish with what I like to call a garlic onion tomato-less salsa, and white rice. The food was great and so was the company. After lunch we took another swim and then climbed on board to cruise to our next destination—Dilumacad Island. It's called "Helicopter Island" because it's shaped like a helicopter. I would have loved to see it from above because just circling around it in the boat didn't reveal much about its resemblance to a helicopter.

The next activity would be snorkeling in an incredible spot. We were completely sheltered from the waves, so it was wonderful to just float and watch the fish. We swam through a small opening in the limestone walls and ended up in a secret lagoon that we had to ourselves. The tall limestone walls limited sun exposure, so it was a bit cold but cozy. I thought it could have been a fairy tale movie set. This was the most beautiful place I'd ever seen. We stayed quite a while, snorkeling and enjoying our surroundings. I don't think any of us could believe how amazing it was. We were in the water so long, one of the guides swam in to retrieve us. It seems that we needed to get to the campsite before sunset so they wouldn't have to set up everything in the dark. Reluctantly, we took our last photos and swam to the boat.

The secluded campsite was hidden by a massive wall of limestone. When the boat turned the corner to show us a glimpse of our home-for-a-while, I was blown away and couldn't wait to explore the island. I spotted a guard shack on the far right and close to a limestone formation and wondered why we needed a guard. I would soon find out that this place had a secret.

When I set foot on the powder-soft sand, a super friendly dog ran up, tail wagging. I stooped down to pet him. He seemed more than delighted at the attention. I thought the dog must belong to the guard. I played fetch with him for a while then left to retrieve my belongings from the boat. The dog followed me, but at the water line, he started barking and growling at something. I turned to see what he was so upset by and cringed when I spotted a pink jellyfish flattened on the sand. Stingy beast or no, I wanted to help it, so I found some rocks and pushed it into the water. The dog stopped barking, so I guess he was happy that the island was now safe from the big bad jelly. It really made me wonder if he'd had a past encounter with a sting or if he just sensed the toxin it carried and knew it was harmful.

Captain Jon explained that the dog was trained to help protect the island and the tourists. Mark chimed in and asked what type of danger was out here.

Jon replied, "Pirates."

Well, that was unnerving. *Pirates? Really?* Something I would never have thought about. *So that's why there's a guard and a dog.* I was suddenly grateful to have protection. Later, I mused that the danger might also explain why there was a navy ship not too far offshore.

I was in awe of the white sandy beach. Tiny palm trees in picturesque groupings dotted the island. The only word for this place is 'paradise.' I noticed a large log with baby palms behind it in the middle of the beach and headed there. After climbing over the log, I found the small wall enclosure for the tents.

Ally and I chose a tent close to the water, so we could have an unobstructed view of the sunrise. I was secretly freaked out that we might be taken by the pirates. But knowing the dog would warn us of danger helped.

At dinner, I dug into fresh fish, scallops, crab, rice, and tomato-less salsa. The food was plentiful and so very good.

Captain Jon lit a fire and we played games while enjoying rum and beer. Our guides showed us a Filipino card game where the loser of the hand received marks on their face by everyone playing. By the end of the night we all looked like we were covered in war paint. Ally looked like a zebra which showed that she lost the most.

Later that night, as I stared into the deep, cloudless, sky, I drew imaginary lines between the stars with my finger. The Milky Way gave us a dazzling show.

Escapade 44:
Bioluminescence and
Spear Fishing

Every night we would put on our snorkels and masks and flutter around in the sea, kicking up the bioluminescent plankton that lit up the water in a flash. The glow lingered for a second then faded away.

I love walking along a shore at night and seeing the outline of my feet glow in the dark and watching the illuminated waves break on the shore.

Every morning we woke up to the aroma of coffee and the sizzle of frying eggs then feasted on a full breakfast of eggs, fruit, bread, and coffee before sailing out to the next remote, uninhabited island. Each one turned out to be even more beautiful than the last.

From the boat, we spotted sea turtles surfacing for air and fish jumping like children in a playground. I couldn't wait to put on my mask and snorkel and join them.

We had every island all to ourselves, like explorers of old, discovering new lands. Snorkeling among the healthy coral and fish was a favorite activity of mine on each island we visited—especially Seven Soldiers Beach. Although not as pristine as the others, with overt trappings of the tourist trade such as hammocks and a volleyball net, it was still breathtaking with its silky white sand and glacier-colored water that mirrored the bright-blue sky. We drank from coconuts and swung on the rope swing. We shared hammocks and read books. This was the best camping trip I had ever been on.

One night while we were swimming through the illuminated sea, we spotted Jon and Cary holding spears and wading through the water. They were going fishing and invited us to join them. Cool. A new experience.

I soon discovered that the age-old art of spear fishing is hard work and not as easy as I'd imagined. Because of the way water bends light, the fish aren't exactly where you see them, and they are pretty savvy about a spear coming at them from above.

Alissa caught a fish on her first try. But after an hour, the rest of us, except the guides, were still empty-handed. If Captain Jon and Cary hadn't speared some squid, we would all be extremely hungry and sharing Alissa's only fish.

On our last day, the guides took us to Miniloc where we explored an abandoned church sitting on its own side of the island, cut off from the other side by huge jagged-edged limestone walls. The building had a dormitory, perhaps for orphans or for the sick. The grounds looked like they had been hit by several storms.

We climbed to the highest point of the rough limestone for an aerial view of the church and the reef where we were about to snorkel. What a great spot!

Later, when I was swimming, enjoying the fish and feeling at one with nature, oblivious to anything else, I heard Mark yell at the top of his lungs, "Shaaark!"

My mind went to *Shark?! Jaws?* Was he alerting me to get

out of the water—fast, or telling me, "Come and look at this shark?" I decided the safest option would be to get out of the water as fast as I could but when I looked around, my fellow snorkelers had disappeared. Where was everyone? Were they on the boat? Did they get eaten? I tried to stay calm, but panic took hold and the movie *Open Water* flashed through my mind. I snorkeled toward the boat as fast as I could. When I turned the corner (which seemed to be the longest corner, ever), I saw the others on the deck checking out a blacktip reef shark. Relief rushed through me. Thank God! When someone yells "Shark!" I always think 'great white,' even if I'm nowhere near an ocean. Phew!

As hot and humid as the Philippines are, nights can be chilly, and I was grateful for the two excellent fire-starters with us and for our guides, Jon and Cary. Like my travel buds, I hadn't brought many warm clothes, so there on Miniloc Island, as the cold crept in, we huddled around the fire until we were warm from the rum.

We told stories and played cards and I wished we had a way to make s'mores. But the scrumptious combination of melted marshmallows and chocolate sandwiched between Graham crackers are a North American thing. When I mentioned them, Mark and Ally agreed right away, but Alissa and Courtney didn't have a clue what they were. I promised to make them when they visited me in America.

After the many amazing beaches I'd visited, I would have thought that beach fatigue would have set in. But it didn't. Each one was so unique that I never grew tired of them. One stands out as exceptionally special because of the baby goats. I'm not sure where mama was but they were so adorable.

As soon as the boat grounded on the sand, the kids moved away. Ally and I slowly followed to see if we could get close enough to pet them. We tracked them through palm trees, but the vegetation became extremely dense. We were afraid we'd get lost, so we turned back, leaving the kids to their tropical forest.

We headed to the coastline, stripped to swimsuits, and jumped into the water. Some of the others were enjoying the nearby reef.

When it was time to end our paradise adventure in the Bacuit Archipelago, the boat headed back to Palawan. Once there, we were ready for a night on the town.

At the hostel, some people we'd just met invited us to join them for dinner at a restaurant overlooking the water. Cool. There were eight of us, so the night proved to be a lot of fun. I especially remember Andre from Amsterdam. He sat next to me and must have asked a thousand questions about our archipelago camping trip. He was good-looking with his dark-brown hair, inviting light-brown eyes, and tan skin. I was ecstatic that he sat next to me and was willing to talk about *anything*. I didn't want to let on how attracted I was, though, so I intentionally put on my best poker face while we talked. But who was I kidding? I have the worst poker face, *ever,* so he probably wasn't fooled for a second.

I had my camera with me and Andre asked if he could look at some of my pictures to get ideas of where he wanted to go. When we were talking, it felt like we were in our own little bubble. I was only vaguely aware of other people in the restaurant and don't remember talking to anyone else.

ESCAPADE 45:

UNOFFICIAL FIRST DATE

After dinner, we meandered back to the hostel. Once there, Mark brought out all the beer and alcohol left from our camping trip and passed around bottles of San Miguel Pale Pilsen. After a few rounds we were ready to go out and party.

Ally, Courtney, Alissa, and I headed to the reggae bar and danced to a live band. I really liked that place. It was filled with locals who didn't mind sharing their bar with foreigners.

Other backpackers eventually rolled in from late dinners or other bars along the beach. Alissa met a local named Tuni and they danced the night away. I think Ally felt obligated to dance with Tuni's friend, Tom, but she didn't show it. She looked like she was having a great time.

It was obvious that I was the fifth wheel, so I made my way to the bar for a beer with hopes of bumping into someone from OMP or a local I might like. Almost as soon as I sat down, Simon, a creepy guy from our hostel approached me. He was seriously weird. I remember thinking, *Why do I always attract the 'off' ones*? But I didn't want to cause a scene, so I sat there for the ten or so minutes while I waited. Things went from mildly strange to really twisted when he typed a message on his phone's notepad and showed it to me, "You have nice lips, can I touch them?"

My head exploded. *WTF!!*

When the bartender finally returned with my beer, I tried to make the transaction as lengthy as possible, so I could ditch the creeper. No luck, he just stood there waiting for a response to his seriously freaky message. It crossed my mind that he might have found that pick-up line on some sicko porn site.

I completely ignored the issue and said something about heading for the bathroom then walked away as quickly as possible. My spine shivered when I noticed him following.

Andre came to my rescue by coming over and talking to me. Maybe he had seen what was going on. I turned my full attention to Andre as we chatted, hoping Stage Five Clinger would just give up and leave. No such luck.

After a few minutes, he chimed in with, "Didn't you have to go to the restroom?"

I'd been so focused on Andre, I'd nearly forgotten Creepy, now Stalker Guy. He was still there, so I did the only thing I could think of in the moment. I introduced Andre to Simon then left as quickly as I could. I found Ally and danced with her. When I looked around, I didn't see my stalker anywhere and hoped he'd taken the hint.

After a while, I was fading, so I told Ally I was going back to the hostel and danced toward the door, ready to call it a night. I was nearly there when Andre showed up again. Suddenly, I wasn't so tired. I couldn't hide the smile on my face. Ally must have picked up on our vibe and gave me a wink. I grinned.

Andre and I talked about everything. I'm pretty sure we told each other our life stories that night. He and I talked about our wildest dreams and biggest fears. He shared life events with me like we'd known each other forever. It felt that way, too.

I was so focused on Andre, I had no idea how long we'd been talking, but when I finally looked up, the bar was empty. We were the only two left in the place. I snapped out of the daze I'd been in and told him I was ready to head back to OMP. He came with me, holding my hand. We stopped a couple of times to gaze at the water and admire how peaceful the streets were without the hustle and bustle of daily life.

When we arrived at OMP, Andre walked me to my door. I gushed about what a wonderful time I'd had and that I hoped to see him tomorrow. He said that he'd also had a great time and was happy to meet me. Then he leaned in to give me a kiss. I was so ready I felt tingly. But the bliss bubble shattered and crashed when a drunken girl in a shower cap and little else staggered down the hallway with her naked, bouncing *ta-tas* hanging out. The magic melted like chocolate on a hot sidewalk and the kiss never happened. Just like in the movies, I laughed about the odd interruption and ducked into my dorm before things got awkward.

My time with Andre felt like a first date. I was totally smitten. I had to tell *someone*, so I connected to Wi-Fi and sent Casey a long, chatty email about Andre and the almost kiss.

The next morning, I was back to reality and thinking about where to go next. Plans needed to be made and flights had to be booked. I asked Ally what her future travel plans were and if she wanted to go somewhere with me or meet up in the future. I had to smile when she said she would consult her pendulum and get back to me by day's end. I thought she was joking about using a new-age oracle tool to make decisions and I laughed. She wasn't offended, though, and confessed that, by nature, she was indecisive, and the pendulum helped.

Oh well, I thought, *people must do what works for them. Who am I to judge?* So, I said okay and went to the coffee shop to connect to Wi-Fi and search for flights to Boracay—my chosen next destination. I found a steal from Puerto Princesa to Kalibo with a connection in Cebu for $26 US then emailed the Frendz hostel that had been recommended by others, to see if they had any bed cancellations. Plans made, I hustled back to OMP for a beach date with my camping buds.

Escapade 46:
Local Tour Guide,
Not-a-Snake, Secret Cave

Tuni, the guy Alissa had met the night before at the reggae bar said he would drive us to a nearby beach. Cool. His tricycle only had room for three people, so we squeezed in to fit a fourth.

On the way, he stopped to show us a secret cave that he said the tourists didn't know about. "Secret" was right. It was so hidden, anyone who didn't already know it was there could never find it.

We trudged through thick brush with no defined trail, wondering if Tuni was playing a practical joke on us. When we entered a stand of trees, I heard something moving in the vegetation and stopped to look more closely. Sure enough, about ten feet away, a snake slithered across my line of sight. "Snake," I whispered. We all stopped to look, but by then it had disappeared. Tuni just flatly said, "No snakes in this area." *Pretty matter of fact*, I thought and felt a bit dismissed. *I know what I saw.* Maybe he just didn't want us to be frightened.

He led us to a narrow crevice in the limestone wall. Although I had initial doubts about some of us fitting, we all managed to squeeze through without getting stuck.

The pitch-black cave, lit only by our puny headlamps, was tiny and cramped. *I hope it gets better than this,* I thought as we kept moving deeper into the cave. I did my best to ignore the near-claustrophobic feelings that threatened to make me turn around and get the hell out of there.

The stuffy, stale air rang with squeaks from bats perched somewhere above us. I cringed. Bats poop and pee a lot. I suddenly regretted not wearing a hat.

After what seemed like an eternity, we finally reached a large chamber and I was glad I hadn't turned back. It was remarkable. Our headlamps illuminated strikingly beautiful stalactites and stalagmites that draped the gray and green walls in what looked like intricate clay sculptures. I never thought water stains on a surface could look so amazing—until now.

I had to walk carefully. The ground, a mixture of damp soil and slick limestone, was a bit slippery. It didn't matter. This cave was out-of-this-world breathtaking.

Awestruck by what I was seeing, I soaked in the eerie beauty around me—almost in a trance in that alien world. Then, something dripped on my head, crashing me back to earth. *Bats giving me a yucky gift or just water?* I tried to ignore it and go back to gawking. Then it happened again. I gave up and paid attention to whatever was pelting my head. Was it warm or cold? Cold meant water. Not an issue. But warm would be bat urine. *Arrrgh.* I pleaded to the imaginary patron saint of spelunkers for it to be water and attempted again to determine cold or warm. *Damn.* I couldn't tell and decided to deal with it later. Water—no harm. Bat pee—clean up later. I did remind myself not to look up with an open mouth, though.

When we started back, I felt both glad and sad to leave that wonderland.

Outside, we adjusted to the bright light again and continued our trek to the tricycle through the thick brush. In the stand of trees, regardless of what Tuni had said, I was on the alert for snakes.

When we arrived at the ledge above the beach, Tuni invited us to have dinner with him and Tom. He would pick us up from the beach after sunset. That sounded great. He waved then turned toward his home.

We happily padded down to the white sandy beach and settled at the edge of a palm tree forest to spend the day leisurely reading, enjoying the view, and periodically cooling off in the water.

At sunset, I was once again treated to an awe-inspiring view as mother nature painted the sky. I mused that each sunset I had watched on this journey was more spectacular than the last. That night, the show looked like molten fire resting above a purple sea.

At twilight, we gathered our gear and climbed the path to the ledge where Tuni waited. Happily piling into the tricycle, we were off.

Arriving at Tuni's house, I heard music and saw some tables and chairs set up on the patio for us to have dinner. I liked his home. It was comfortable and modern—unlike other houses in the area. I was especially grateful for the western toilets and indoor plumbing.

We girls lounged around while Tuni (he looked like a Filipino Steve Segel) and Tom went fishing for our dinner. Talk about fresh seafood. It doesn't get any better than right out of the ocean.

Not long after, they came back with their catch of squid, fish, crab, and fresh veggies they'd purchased from the local market. We offered to help them cook but they refused. We were guests in their home, they insisted, and it was only right that we relax and enjoy ourselves.

Okay, then. I pulled out my cards and Tom poured drinks. When dinner was ready the guys carried the food out to the patio. It smelled amazing and tasted even better. The grilled seafood was beyond delicious and seasoned with exotic spices I'd never tasted before. The chopped veggie salad was cool and crisp bursting with flavor. For dessert we had sweet, fresh mango and juicy pineapple.

After our little party, we reluctantly headed to the hostel. On our way, we stopped at the local recreation center and played a few games of pool. I especially liked this part of town—mostly locals, quiet—not bombarded with tourists, resorts, and pushy vendors hawking their stuff in my face. The people we met were friendly and eager to hear about us. Some wanted to practice their English. Immersing myself in their culture felt good and I realized that one of the things I like best about traveling is getting to know the people and experiencing their way of life.

I put my musings aside when Mark said that someone mentioned a beach party nearby and invited us to come along.

Like...of course! I wouldn't miss it.

When we arrived, though, it turned out to be on a cliff overlooking the beach rather than at the shore itself. Even better! I remember thinking that if it hadn't been so dark, we would have had a spectacular ocean view.

Although the party was fun, after a little while, I realized that I'd rather have gone back to the reggae bar again. I saw Andre as I was leaving and told him that the music at this party wasn't my thing. I wasn't feeling the vibe and would be heading out. He seemed disappointed but understood.

I found Ally, who also wasn't really feeling it. We left with every intention of going back to the reggae bar but quickly reconsidered. I had a five-hour bus ride to Puerto Princesa the following morning and didn't want to stumble around in the wee hours trying to pack. Ally agreed so we went back to the hostel.

It didn't take me long to get ready for the next day's bus ride, so we decided to hit the reggae bar for a few drinks before calling it a night.

Early the next morning I looked around the hostel, sighed and fondly thought, *Aah. On to another adventure.*

After saying goodbye to my hostel mates, I thought about how hard it was to leave people who had quickly become cherished friends—even though we all knew it was only for a short time. I hugged Alissa and Courtney, who would be heading out on their own adventure. Ally planned to stay in El Nido a little longer, so I told her to let me know her plans. Of course, we all vowed to keep in touch.

As I walked out the door, my heart reached out to Ally. She looked as if she was about to cry. I felt sad, but somehow, I knew we'd see each other again. *After all,* I told myself, *we both live on the same continent.*

The tricycle driver lifted my backpack and drove me to the bus station. On the way I asked him to make a stop at the local veggie stand so I could buy some fresh fruit for the trip.

At the market, a darling, black lab puppy started following me around. I picked him up and hugged him. I sat on the curb and we played a bit. Soon more puppies showed up and surrounded me with love. This felt so amazing, I didn't want to leave, but I had to go. I managed to break away from them and hop on the tricycle.

When we took off, I glanced back. The puppies ran after us for a few seconds before something distracted them and they rushed toward their next bit of fun.

The bus ride was so uneventful, I slept through most of it. When we reached Puerto Princesa, I hitched a ride with some tourists heading to Sheebang Hostel. There, I was surprised to see Mark sitting at a table, working on his next travel move. He looked up and grinned. I said "Hi," and told him I'd check in then join him after getting my bed situated.

Sitting with Mark, we chatted about our plans. He was going to fly to Cebu the next day, so I gave him tips on where to stay and what to do, remembering to tell him that Cebu City wasn't worth spending much time in because it's a pretty quiet place and there are no beaches. The outlying places, however, were magnificent—Oslob, and the Chocolate Hills.

When we compared schedules, it turned out that Mark and I would be on the same flight. Cebu was my stopover. I'd be catching a connecting flight from there for Kalibo and Borocay. That meant we could share a tricycle to the plane.

He gave me travel tips and recommended a great place to stay the next time I passed through Manila—Pink Manila hostel. We spent the afternoon researching and planning our travels. Mark was always good company.

Later, I received an email that Frendz hostel in Borocay had an opening for six nights and asked if I still wanted to book it. I replied yes, and that I'd be there the next evening. That turned out to be fortuitous since I'd found out that all other accommodations were completely booked.

The next morning, Mark and I had breakfast together and met Justin, who also needed to get to the airport for a 1 p.m. flight, so he joined us.

I thought Justin looked like Leonardo DiCaprio. Of course, I was immediately smitten and made sure to sit next to him in the tricycle. He was heading to Manila and from there to Vietnam.

We arrived at the airport around noon. Justin checked in first and was in for a shocker. His flight had been scheduled to leave at 11:30, not 1:00. The flight attendant told him she would see if the plane was still around and would try to get him on it.

A couple of nail-biting minutes later she returned, smiling. The plane was still there, and he could board immediately.

Sometimes Southeast Asia's leisurely tradition of not paying too much attention to schedules is a good thing.

He waved bye to us as he dashed off. I'd so wanted to get his picture. *Darn!* Mark must have read my mind because he was laughing.

Mark and I checked in then sat in the waiting area. Someone came up to us and said Hi. I didn't recognize him, but Mark did—they had recently stayed at the same hostel. He was also booked on our plane, so we all sat together.

The short flight was just long enough for a good chat. After landing, ladies with "Welcome to Cebu" gifts greeted the disembarking passengers. It was awesome! They gave us goody bags and placed beads around our necks.

At the gate, I gave Mark a huge hug and wished him safe travels then rushed off to my connecting flight to Kalibo that, go figure, as I suspected, would not be departing on time. So, I had an hour to wait and reflect on my trip and all the wonderful people I'd met.

Hazard 47:

Real-Life Crucifixion and Puka-Beach Killer Wave

Just after sunset I finally arrived in Kalibo. And, as I'd been warned, was bombarded by people trying to give me over-priced rides. I scrutinized the hucksters, looking for the recommended shuttle to the ferry terminal I'd read about in the hostel instructions. When I spotted it, I pushed through the sea of people shouting their sales pitches at me and boarded, glad to be out of the maelstrom.

This was going to be about an hour and a half ride, so I settled back and waited for the shuttle to fill so we could be on our way.

Soon, we were off. I gazed out at the roads, surprised at the thick crowds. When I asked the woman next to me if she knew what that was all about, she said it was spring break and that Sunday was Easter. *Wow! Easter? Already? That really snuck up on me. No wonder the hostels were all booked.*

As we rode deeper into Kalibo, I looked closer at the people congregated in the streets. They were watching a Christian ceremony—Stations of the Cross. I was fascinated at the intensity of the participants. Some were shirtless and whipping themselves with flails. Blood and sweat sprayed around them. Others reenacted the crucifixion itself. Some, less dramatic players somberly carried pictures, statues, Bibles, flowers, and crucifixes.

Young and old watched the spectacle, most of them dressed in nice "Sunday" clothes. I saw young women holding crying babies, old people looking somber. Some with physical handicaps leaned on canes or were helped by what looked like family or loved ones. Many wept or showed expressions ranging from pained sadness to ecstatic bliss.

This was unlike anything I'd ever seen. In my Catholic-school years, we had to act out the Stations of the Cross, but this was a powerful and dramatic event. I was fascinated.

The procession slowed us down and I was a little concerned I might miss the last ferry to the island, but the driver assured us that lots of ferries leave late during the Easter season and that the last one left at midnight. That was a relief.

At the terminal, I found out that the two women sitting next to me in the shuttle, Thea and Emily, were staying at Frendz hostel, so we boarded the ferry together. After a ten-minute ride, we arrived in Boracay and split a tricycle fare into town.

On the way I mentally groused at having to pay another environmental fee when I purchased my ferry ticket. This fee bugged me. I was sure it didn't go towards protecting the environment. It reeked of "huge scam" fattening the pockets of politicians or officials. Then I reminded myself, I was there to enjoy the trip, not stew in issues I could do nothing about.

For the rest of the twelve-minute ride from the terminal, I luxuriated in the cool night air gently blowing through my clothes and hair. It was amazingly refreshing, especially after being cooped up in a fifteen-passenger mini-bus for a while.

The tricycle dropped us off in front of a dry-cleaner's shop and told us the hostel was around the corner. We headed in the direction he'd pointed but soon discovered that the hostel had moved two blocks down the road. *But, hey,* I thought, *it's Asia.* We just shrugged and strolled down the road.

Frendz hostel is like a mini resort. Everything is made with bamboo, tiki hut style. Cute. Alex, at the check-in counter, dutifully asked all the usual questions such as my name, where I was coming from, how long I was planning to stay, and so forth. I handed him my passport and said I'd booked six nights and would let him know if I wanted to stay longer.

Obviously proud of his place of employment, Alex described its amenities and showed me to my room.

The other girls checked in after me and we made plans to meet at the hostel bar for food and drinks in an hour.

I unlocked the dorm door and walked down a long hallway to a medium-sized room with four beds lined up parallel to each other with about a four-foot gap between them. I claimed an empty bed near the hallway by placing my stuff on it.

It had been a long, sweaty day, so I freshened up with a shower in a bathroom so small I could barely turn around. The water felt great until I saw it backing up from the drain so fast, I was afraid it would top my shower shoes. That would be bad. Hostels often have faulty plumbing, but this was the worst, yet. In record time, I scrambled out of there then scrubbed my feet in the sink.

I recalled dropping my washcloth in another communal shower some time back. When I'd picked it up, it had been coated with a nasty white film, so I cringed and trashed it.

Back in the dorm, refreshed and glad I'd escaped the possible stew of bacteria rising from the shower drain, I saw a tall, athletic looking girl with brown hair and tan skin rummaging through her bag. I introduced myself.

She said her name was Madeline, from London, and had been there two days. She invited me to join her and the other dorm mates on a trip to Puka Shell Beach the next day. I happily accepted and remembered reading that puka shells were all the rage with 1960s American surfers and surfer wannabes.

That night, Madeline and I took the one-minute walk to White Beach. It was lined with posh resorts, hotels, bars, clubs, and filled with loads of people. Even with all that, it was still beautiful.

We took a quick, evening stroll around, squeezing through the crowds of tourists and locals. I was told it normally wasn't this packed, but because of Easter weekend, everyone and their mom were on holiday and, it seemed, spending their free time on White Beach.

We made our way down to the water to check out the bioluminescence, but it was a little difficult to see because of the light pollution from town. I kicked off my sandals and waded into the sea. Even a hundred feet out, the water was still only calf deep. I couldn't wait to see this place in daylight.

Shortly, we headed to a bar for some eats and drinks. Inside, I spotted Thea and Emily, having a beer. After introducing them, I scanned the menu and ordered pizza and a local beer, San Miguel Pale Pilsen—local beers are always the least expensive. I invited Thea and Emily to come with us to Puka Shell Beach the next day, but they had their hearts set on parasailing, so we made plans to meet up after.

The bar was full of partying travelers obviously preparing for a crazy night out on White Beach. Normally I would have joined them, but after such a long day, I was tired and decided to go to bed early. I finished my food and returned to the hostel.

🏨🏨🏨

Loud construction noises jarred me awake the next morning about 8 a.m. Unfortunately, I'd forgotten to put in my earplugs the night before. When I rolled over, I was surprised by the sight of Madeline sleeping topless on her bed. I wasn't used to women feeling so free about their bodies, but after the initial surprise, I thought, *Good for her for not giving a crap about what other people believe or think.*

I wasn't ready to get up yet and didn't think I could go back to sleep, so I found my headlamp, opened my latest book acquisition *Treasure Island,* and started reading. I had traded the disturbing *The Little Boy Under the Cupboard* for *Treasure Island* while in El Nido. I needed to read something that would take my mind off the awful things in that book.

After about an hour, two other dorm mates also woke up. We all introduced ourselves. Lila, from Spain was lovely with her olive skin and short curly brown hair. Margret, from England, had a peaches and cream British complexion and dark hair. It was her last day and she said her goal was to get some shopping done with Lila before leaving. We agreed to meet around 11 a.m. to catch a tricycle to Puka Beach.

After dressing, Madeline and I went to breakfast on White Beach and used our hostel discount to get a great deal. We ordered the breakfast special of a mimosa, fried eggs, bread, and fruit. We ate like champs for about $8 US, which is pricey for Southeast Asia. Boracay is super touristy, though, so I expected the inflated prices.

The sun shone bright and beautiful. I looked around and understood why it's called White Beach. The sand is stark white. Looking at all the people there, I imagined how beautiful it must have been before tourists discovered it—quiet, no resorts or large ships, pristine. But I pondered that even with all the crowds, the beach was still amazing. And it had perfect party potential. I looked forward to taking advantage of that by participating in multiple drinking shenanigans.

Still, I regretted that there was no chance for a quiet moment to listen to the water brush up against the shore. The sound was masked by the hustle and bustle of merchants hawking their wares or trying to attract customers to their restaurants.

At 11a.m., we met as planned, hired a tricycle, and headed to Puka Beach. I enjoyed our ride as we passed through local areas where the residents were going about their business and living their lives in spite of the circus of tourists that filtered in and out of their city. I saw merchants cleaning their shop windows, families having lunch, and a variety of day-to-day activities. I also noticed that most of the shops were closed because of the holiday.

After the driver dropped us off at the beach entrance, I saw that it was surrounded by vendors selling food and souvenirs. We browsed a few, but our main goal was to lay on the beach, swim, and relax.

The closer I came to the actual beach, the more I liked it better than White Beach. This place was quieter—no resorts and fewer tourists. As I looked around, I saw more locals than travelers. The golden sand was checkered with seashells and crabs.

I helped set up our "camp" at the edge of the palm tree forest then headed to the ocean, leaving Lila with first watch over our belongings. The glacier-blue water was a bit rough, but I didn't mind. It was refreshing and peaceful. I loved the crisp, cold sea splashing against my legs. *This* was paradise.

Madeline and I bobbed around in the water and talked about guys. I told her about Chad inviting me to Songkran in Thailand but wasn't sure if I should go.

She told me she'd been seeing someone while living in South America, but he turned out to be a complete asshole and, at the moment she was *so* over guys. She didn't elaborate so I figured she was either completely over it or the memory was too painful to discuss.

I decided to tell her a "guy" horror story from my home in the states. I thought it might make her feel more comfortable about sharing her South America woes. I told her about Don in San Diego and how I thought I'd found someone really great.

He'd moved there from Philadelphia a few months before I'd met him and he had what I like to call a 'partial package.' He had a good job, dressed well, had a nice car, played intermural sports, was social, and had his own place near the beach. Part of the attraction, I think, was that, in my experience, most of those qualities are hard to find in a man—especially in San Diego. I liked him, and he seemed to like me, but I later discovered that he had a wandering eye and Peter Pan syndrome: stuck in Neverland, can't commit, acts like a boy rather than a grown man.

Later, I realized that I liked the idea of him. I thought he had his life together because I had *my* life together. I thought we were a good match. It was painful to find out that he didn't care about me, but I am glad it didn't work out because now, looking back on it, I am right where I want to be.

Madeline seemed to relax and started to share more of her story when *BOOOOM*, without warning, a huge wave slammed into us. It shoved me underwater. I tumbled around, trying to swim to the surface.

When I finally came up, I saw my swim top wrapped around my neck and my *chi chis* exposed to the world! What could I do but laugh?

Madeline and I both giggled, fixed our suits then walked to our towels, chafing from the sand that had found its way into all the crevices in our bodies.

At the camp, Lila had music playing and had bought coconuts for us to drink. I cleaned up as much as I could then read my book a while before dozing off.

The rest of the day, we went in and out of the water, took several walks along the shore to admire the scenery, and enjoyed each other's company. I soaked it in and thought, *Such a great place.* I remembered how nervous and unsure of myself I'd been when I made the spur-of-the-moment decision to explore this paradise on earth.

It was late afternoon before we were ready to leave. Madeline suggested that we take our things to the hostel and go right back out to watch the sunset at White Beach—a spectacular sight.

I said I wouldn't miss it for the world, so we packed towels, sandals, clothes, books, and coconuts into our bags, and walked to the tricycle stand. I stopped and bought a fresh mango smoothie for the ride back to town. When we arrived, we cleaned up a bit, ditched the gear we didn't need, and ran back out again.

Crowds of people still blanketed White Beach—sitting on towels or chairs, in sailboats, and frolicking in the water. We managed to squeeze into a space with a full view of the sunset show. The sea had turned a deep-blue-and-purple mass, painted with the sun's orange-red fiery reflection. It looked like the sun would be engulfed into a liquid abyss.

I glanced around at the silhouettes of people sitting, laying, and standing in various postures as if they were posing for a photo. Everyone focused on this magnificent nightly event. As I turned my attention back to the water, sailboats—as if on cue for a perfect picture—slipped across the sun's painted pathway. It was breathtaking and mind-blowing.

I shot at least a hundred photos, but no camera could completely capture this beauty. After the lights faded, I took my time walking back to Frendz, trying to embed that spectacular sunset in my memory. There was something so soothing about what I had seen, I felt like I was walking on clouds.

Sun set, stars out, back to reality.

In the dorm, waiting my turn for the shower, I browsed the internet searching for where to eat for dinner and found a place that sounded interesting.

Shortly, we all headed out to find Crafty's, an Indian food restaurant off the main street. To get into the restaurant, we had to go into a grocery store and walk up four flights of stairs. Crafty's was on the rooftop of the store.

It had a nice view of the coast and a killer ocean breeze. All the furniture was made from beautiful dark wood. The bar had soft white lighting and the tables were spaced out enough for guests to have a little privacy.

The four of us sat at the center table. It was topped with three multicolored candles. I knew exactly what I wanted—tikka masala with chicken and cilantro garlic naan.

We were all so hungry, we split a veggie plate and dug in with little conversation. Dinner was excellent, and I left full and happy. Madeline finished my tikka leftovers. I've never met a girl who ate so much and stayed so slim. She finished her dinner and the rest of mine and was still hungry.

We gathered at our hostel bar to round up some friends for the night's shenanigans. Margret was stoked to go out since it was her last night on the island. She introduced me to Meril and Thomas, from England, who said they were on a long-term travel trip and just living their best lives. They invited me to go on a booze cruise with them. I accepted and signed up right then and there.

After filling up on cheap drinks at the hostel, thirty of us made the one-minute walk down the alley to White Beach. At least ten of our group had been in town for a week, so they knew exactly where to go. The first bar we stopped in was filled with so many fake trees and vines, it reminded me of a jungle. I ordered my go-to beer, San Miguel Pale Pilsen, and got to know my hostel mates a little better. A lot of them were going on the booze cruise, too. I was super excited to be joining them.

Out of the corner of my eye I saw a group of four children around ages 3 to 9, begging for money. One of the first things I'd read about Southeast Asia was to never give the children money. It was hard not to. They just stood there, dirty, sorrowful, and looking tired. So upsetting. But, if people wouldn't give them money, they wouldn't beg.

It's sad that kids in so many places are horribly exploited, but nothing is ever done about it. In other countries I'd visited before the Philippines, I'd been told that children were sometimes abducted from their villages by the local mafia to make money for their organization. The worst crime in my mind was that many of the little girls were sold into the sex trade. But since I couldn't fix the problem, I forced myself to put those dark thoughts aside and not contribute to it by giving them money. I hope that someday this abuse will be stopped.

☙☙☙

The next morning, Madeline and I got up early and walked along White Beach to The Sunny Side Café, a cute little breakfast spot. We had the beach to ourselves, probably because most of the shops weren't open yet. I'd assumed that was because a lot of people were still sleeping the night's festivities off.

The food was amazing, but most importantly, there was air conditioning. *Ahhhhh!* I ordered Eggs Benedict with a bacon/avocado smash. The portion sizes were huge, but since I was with Madeline, I knew my food wouldn't go to waste. Another guest opened the door to the café and let in a wave of thick, hot air from outside. I cringed at the thought of going back into it. The air seemed warmer and stickier than the day before and it was still early in the morning. I dreaded the scorcher that the afternoon would bring.

A few minutes after our last savory bites we paid, steeled ourselves to dive into the heat, then sprinted to the beach, ditched our outer clothes, and plunged into the water.

Escapade 48:
Booze Cruise Boracay

Everyone going on the sunset cruise gathered in the hostel bar. There were more people than I had originally expected. Meril and Thomas waved me over to chat. I spotted Emily and Thea across the bar and gave them a wave. I ask Meril where her next move was and somehow, we drifted into talking about the Thai Water Festival—the one Chad had been practically begging me to see. She insisted I shouldn't miss such an amazing event.

Something in me always knew I would be going, but for some reason I resisted. So, before I waffled again, I sent Chad a Wi-Fi message that I was in for the Songkran festival and interested in traveling to Nepal afterward.

I finished writing my message just in time for the cruise director to march in and herd us all through the crowd of White Beach vacationers to the tricycle stand. I hoped this would be better than my first booze cruise. After all, I wasn't the green newb I was before. I knew the ropes now. No time to reflect on that, though. The cruise director seemed all business. With little-disguised impatience, he stuffed us—three at a time—into the tiny vehicles. No problem for us. This was just a part of the fun.

Fifteen bumpy minutes later, we were at the boat dock. After everyone poured out of the tricycles, I had my first "huh?" moment. Surely the dilapidated boat I was staring at couldn't be the one that would ferry thirty—soon to be booze-sodden—party animals over deep water. It looked as if one little bump would sink it like a rock. I wasn't the only one with misgivings; others voiced their own WTF grumbles. I thought the boat must have been an old, yellow fishing vessel repurposed for tourists. It had an upper and a lower level, no windows, and a big open deck that I thought might have been used to bring a catch aboard. At least the seats, which looked hastily scattered on each level, had a life vest underneath each of them.

Should we turn back? Of course not. This was a party. We'd be fine. We shook off our concerns hoisted our bags and booze then splashed through shallow, rocky water to the slightly rickety, wooden ladder and climbed up. Most got off at the first deck. Some of us continued up a flight to the second level.

I took a look around. Although the boat was worn and shaky, the view was great. But, then, what view in this part of the world wasn't beautiful? It was all heavenly. My concerns fell away and I looked forward to a great experience.

After everyone was safely on board, the captain and his deck hands cranked up the music then got busy preparing the ship to head out.

The weather was perfect, with calm turquoise water and a bright, shining sun as we cruised to Puka Beach. When we came closer to it, I noticed that it looked even more beautiful from this vantage point, showing off its crystal-clear water that ebbed and flowed, depositing sparkling golden sand to hug the palm forest.

Someone announced that we would be anchored at Puka Beach for about an hour. Wonderful! Everyone vaulted off the top of the wheelhouse into the water. We were a little too far out to swim to the shore, but I didn't care. It was all so magical.

Hazard 49:

Conquer My Fears and Jump

After a while, when the boat hadn't fallen apart, I let my concerns go and focused on enjoying the trip. Our next stop was a snorkeling and cliff-jumping spot on Carabao Island. Everyone was excited about it. Everyone but me, that is. I'd had a traumatic experience with cliff jumping on my first trip to Thailand a few years before. It happened when a friend invited me to go cliff diving....

Sure, why not? I'd thought. *Adventure is my middle name.* The five of us talked about it but only Daisy and I went. The others decided on hiking instead.

We boarded the boat with four Irishmen who proudly brandished a handle of rum. They were in a sharing mood and greeted us with shots that we gladly accepted as we steamed out to the jumping grounds.

At the site, the guys boasted about other dives they'd taken. They convinced me that they were experts and that we were in safe hands as we climbed the slick, dark rocks to the first jump—about a 10-foot dive.

It looked easy. Only ten feet. Not like jumping off a skyscraper building. So I dove off the cliff and sliced perfectly into the water. What a rush. No backyard pool diving board could ever be this cool. *Piece-o-cake!* I felt confident enough to go a couple times more. The guys, of course, showed off and jumped in one after the other, striking poses and doing fancy moves in the air.

Daisy was a little braver than I was and climbed up to the next spot—a 20-foot dive. After she survived just fine, I was still hesitant. But, of course, the boys taunted me to "graduate" to the next level. "Come on Tam," they said, "you can do it, Daisy did. Do you want us to hold your hand?"

Well, I couldn't just stand there like a wimp, could I? So, I mustered up the courage to take the 20-foot plunge and nervously trekked to the next site where I paused and took in my surroundings. Still breathtakingly beautiful. The water was like a mirror reflecting a perfect blue sky. The neighboring islands were all topped with deep-green vegetation, covering the black volcanic rock.

I looked down at the five people shouting encouragement. I couldn't turn back now. *Go for it, Tam,* I thought. So, before I could come to my senses, I took a deep breath, pushed off with my left foot and dove toward the ocean. This was a much bigger rush than the "bunny" dive. *Whoo!*

When I hit the water all I could see were white bubbles. I swam up. No pain. That was a good thing. I was okay. As I surfaced and took my first breath and heard everyone cheering, I couldn't remember ever feeling so amazing.

The guys moved up to what looked like a 30-foot ledge. Without hesitation, they dove off one after the other, each releasing a loud yell as the adrenaline rushed through their bodies.

It was an amazing thing to see but there was no way I would dive from that monster height, so I was content to float and watch. Daisy jumped off the 20-foot edge a couple of times before climbing to the 30-footer. We all shouted our enthusiastic support as she dove. It seemed forever before she hit the water, and I mean HIT. She slammed into the ocean at a strange angle. I sucked in a gasp, hoping she was okay.

She wasn't.

When Daisy surfaced, all we could hear were her screams. We swam out as fast as we could. Nope. Not okay. I was really scared for her. She couldn't move. All of us teamed up to get her onto the boat to be rushed to the hospital. On the way, the guys gave her rum shots to numb the pain. I was so freaked out that I took a few shots as well and mentally urged the boat to go faster.

When we finally reached the shore of Phi Phi Island, I leapt off the boat and ran into the hospital for help. When I rattled off what had happened to the staff, a few men, acting as if this sort of thing was just routine and happened every day, grabbed a stretcher and hurried to the boat. They expertly scooped her up and headed back.

I quickly thanked my fellow divers for their help and followed the stretcher guys. I was sure Daisy was going to be paralyzed and probably gnawed off my fingernails while waiting to hear about her condition.

It seemed to take forever.

When a nurse, or doctor, or someone...I don't remember who, told me she was fine, and the injuries weren't serious, I nearly fainted with relief. They'd examined her and had given her pain killers. After a few minutes, she limped out and said she was all right but a little sore.

I was never so glad to see anyone in my life. What a tough cookie she was.

Even though Daisy hadn't been seriously injured, the whole episode was so traumatizing, I was sure I'd never go cliff-diving again.

Never say never.

Carabao Island, like nearly all the islands I'd been to, was beautiful. It seemed more like a spot for locals than tourists. I waded through the water with the others, clutching my gear as we trekked up the hillside to the official island entrance.

Ughh. Environmental fee scam again. This time I just paid the fee along with the other booze cruisers and continued on. Well, I sighed, grumbled under my breath, and rolled my eyes a bit, but I didn't make a scene. We walked through a tiny village and spotted a group of wild chicks following behind their mother hen. This made my face light up with happiness.

In my mind I had pictured a behemoth cliff with a rocky outcrop, but when we reached the jumping area I laughed. No majestic cliffs. Only wooden diving boards held up by worn logs that resembled stilts—like the ones that hold up houses near the coast. This was too funny. I had pictured a magical, remote jumping location. This odd set-up wasn't even close.

After the surprise at how different this was from what I'd expected, I realized that it had its own coolness. The top board seemed pretty high. Just because it was man-made didn't make it any less fun to dive from.

Most of our cruisers jumped off the first three levels with heights ranging from 10 to 20 feet. Walking out on the board, I pushed the Daisy incident behind me and vowed to just go for it. It felt like walking a pirate's plank, except no ship and no pirates. The first two levels were a breeze, but I was still nervous and asked one of my new-found friends to take a video. Before I could talk myself out of it, I jumped off. It was amazing. I made a big splash but was okay. Fear gone.

The next plank was around the 20-foot mark, so I was a little nervous, but I bravely climbed the ladder to the board and tiptoed towards the edge. Gripping the railing, I peered over to see how far the drop was.

I could feel everyone watching as I hesitated. Suddenly, they started cheering and urging me to jump. Thomas, called down from the highest plank that he would dive simultaneously with me. Well, now I *had* to jump or be humiliated and that just wouldn't do, so I pushed off the board, Daisy lingering in the back of my mind.

Splashhhhhhh! That one hurt but I was okay…except that I had lost my swimsuit top. I frantically searched high and low for my purple top with silver hearts. When I spotted it behind me and latched on, I discovered that my cheeky bottoms were down near my ankles. I quickly pulled them up and tugged on my top, glad that I wouldn't have to emerge wearing only my skin.

I finally decided diving was just too much fun to hold on to old trauma and headed for the highest platform. Besides, I rationalized, what happened to my friend in Thailand was a freak accident. I didn't want to look back on this and regret not taking the big thirty-foot plunge. At the plank I walked as fast as I could and didn't look down, pushing Daisy out of my mind. If I hesitated, or let myself think about her, I knew I'd chicken out.

At the edge, I crossed my arms over my chest, hands on shoulders, then took a big bounce off the board. As I fell my arms moved to my sides. This time, when I hit the water, I plunged down farther than on the previous plank. My bikini top was whooshed off again. At least this time it stayed around my neck and didn't float off into oblivion. When I surfaced, I repositioned my top and climbed the wooden ladder to the bench where I'd left my stuff and thought about the amazing thing I'd just done. *Good girl!*

Some of the group stayed to do more diving but I'd had enough. I hiked to the other side of the island to do some snorkeling. What a contrast to the adrenaline rush of diving. Here the peaceful waters were full of colorful fish displaying a rainbow of bright oranges, blues, and yellows.

I wasn't ready to stop when someone came out and told me it was time to board the boat and head out to the sunset viewing area. Okay, sunsets are a favorite of mine. I dried off, grabbed my bright green dry bag, boarded the boat, went to the second level and glanced up at the wheelhouse. No one was there yet, so I nabbed a chair, threw a few beers in my bag and climbed to the top. A short time later, some people joined me, so of course, we made it a party.

The sunset looked like a molten marble slowly sinking into a warm liquid that reflected its shining colors. Viewing the sun's disappearance from the water instead of the shore made it a million times better. I felt like a part of it—like I could slide down the horizon and follow it to the southern hemisphere. Wow!

Later, I met up with Madeline for dinner at the Smoke, a spot filled mainly with locals. We sat outside on the street and ordered Bulalo—beef stew with vegetables, rice bowls, and fresh mango shakes. The price, since this place catered mostly to locals was next to nothing. I'd passed this restaurant a few times before and notice that it always seemed to be packed, so I was sure the food would be good. I was right, it was delicious.

We took a long walk down the beach, soaking in the scenery, and exploring a new part of town. We found a karaoke bar filled with locals and went in. I love karaoke; so does Madeline. We signed up for all sorts of '80s and '90s pop. The locals sang to the saddest love songs I had ever heard—some deeply sorrowful American, but most were just depressing Filipino songs accompanied by equally sad music videos. In my mind, not a party.

When at least an hour and a half went by and none of our requested songs came on, we were borderline depressed and left. What a disappointment. I was really looking forward to a fun night. Now I felt like I was wearing a coat of sad.

As we headed to the louder, more popular side of town, we kept our eyes peeled for another karaoke spot. We found one but discovered that this one also played downer music, so we kept searching, eventually giving up and joining our hostel mates at some nearby regular bars.

👓 👓 👓

The next day, Madeline and I explored the island, sampling beaches. A couple of them were private, so no access, but we bravely crashed one private beach. It was large and clean, and we had it all to ourselves. None of them were disappointing. They all had powdery white sand and crystal-blue water.

We found a sushi restaurant and ordered whatever the chef wanted to make for us. I'm not sure what we ate, but whatever it was, it tasted like heaven. While we indulged in the chef's choice, I connected to the extremely slow Wi-Fi to devise a plan for exploring another region of the Philippines. I searched for plane tickets to Manila because I wanted to check out Taal Lake—the one I'd missed seeing weeks before. *Voila!* I found a ticket and booked it. It turned out Madeline was heading to Manila the same day as me. Super.

A while back, at Sheebang hostel, Mark had told me Pink Manila hostel was highly recommended, so I booked it and reserved a bed for Madeline as well.

Next, I checked my Facebook Messenger. It was filled with messages, one from Chad. He was happy I'd changed my mind and would set up our accommodations in Chang Mai. He also mentioned that he was down to travel to either Nepal or Burma afterwards.

I told Madeline I'd decided to go to Songkran after all and hoped that she could join the festivities. I had also received a message from Ally saying she was heading to Manila and that we should meet up and explore Northern Luzon together.

I wrote her back and said, "That sounds great. Meet me at Pink Manila hostel and we can figure out the details then."

Our last night in Boracay was fun but we didn't let it get too crazy because traveling hungover is the worst experience ever. Thea and Emily were heading to the airport at the same time as Madeline and me, so we shared a tricycle and a ferry to the mainland and vanned it to the Kalibo airport.

We presented our passports to the counter agent, who put us next to each other on the flight. I don't remember falling asleep but woke up when the wheels touched the ground for a rocky landing. I knew I was back in Luzon. The de-boarding process was full of the same chaos I'd experienced on all the planes in Asia, people jumping over seats, getting up during our taxi to the terminal gate, pushing past other passengers to try to get off the plane faster. It was nuts and super annoying, but thinking back on it, really comical.

When we arrived at baggage claim, nothing looked familiar, then I realized I was at a different airport than I'd been at before. I panicked a little, hoping it wasn't too far away. For some reason, it didn't dawn on me to look at the airport name when I bought my ticket. I just selected the cheapest flight to Manila. *Okay. Just take it one step at a time.*

We retrieved our packs from baggage claim and headed out to hail a taxi. It was way past sunset, so we hoped the hostel wasn't too far away. A white taxi pulled up and we gave him the address for Pink Manila. He turned on the meter before I had a chance to ask him to do so. That's when I knew the taxi was legitimate.

262

I'd learned that the white taxis were usually the reputable ones in Manila. The others often tamper with the meter or try to offer a flat rate and refuse to use them at all. I had been ripped off too many times before I learned to make sure cab drivers used their meters. If they refused, I just left and found a different ride.

Hazard 50:

Pink Manila Weird and
Lobster Liberation

On the way to Pink Manila hostel, I gazed out the cab's window. From what I could see in the dark, we were in a sketchy part of town. Soon, we stopped at a place that looked nothing like Mark's glowing review. I must have hesitated too long or had a quizzical look on my face because the driver pointed to the building and said, "Your hostel is in there."

I glanced at Madeline, who also looked doubtful. *Oh, well,* I thought, *nothing can be done about it tonight.* We retrieved our bags from the cab, paid the driver, and climbed five steps that led to an opening in a wired fence. This took us to what looked like the bottom level of a parking garage. Very weird.

Madeline spotted an elevator with a sign that read:

> Pink Manila hostel level 5.
> Use stairs. The elevator is broken.

Stairs!! Ughhh. "Okay," I said to Madeline, "stairs it is." We both shrugged and headed up. Normally, I wouldn't mind five flights of stairs, but it was late, and I was really tired.

Once there, I saw that the place wasn't as shoddy as first impressions had me thinking. Check-in was near the entrance and opposite a room with a billiard table and a huge library. The kitchen and bar area stood to the side. There was a comfortable-looking common room with lots of couches and chairs and an open deck with a pool. The walls were, of course, pink.

Our room was on the seventh floor, two flights up. As we started for the stairs, the owner warned us not to go to the other floors or the rooftop because a fire had broken out earlier in the week. *Fire? Not a good sign.* I was too tired to make new plans, so I pushed my concerns aside and started climbing. Madeline, who looked as tired as I was, shrugged in resignation.

On the seventh floor, I saw a mattress covering the accessway to the upper levels and scorch marks on the walls. I turned to Madeline. "It must have been a pretty bad fire but not bad enough to close the entire building."

Looking a bit worried, she stared at the soot-darkened walls and said, "Well, we can rethink this place tomorrow. Right now, I just want to settle in and relax."

Inside the dorm, we made our beds up with the clean sheets the hostel had provided. Mine were *Little Mermaid* sheets and pictured Ariel perched on a rock looking off into the distance. Cute. Madeline's had Smurfs. Not sure how she felt about that.

We freshened up and went downstairs to mingle with the other backpackers. I connected to the Wi-Fi and scrolled through my messages. There was one from Ally. She'd made it to Pink Manila but wasn't feeling well and would see me in the morning. Another message was from Natasha. She was heading to Manila, too. I hoped we could get together before I made the trek up north. Reading on, I burst out in a genuine belly-laugh when she wrote that she'd been arrested for freeing restaurant lobsters from their tank. I laughed so hard I cried. Natasha was passionate about the well-being of animals. She told me her get-out-of-jail fine was 20,000 pesos ($432 US). "Eek! They must really love their lobsters."

Next, I sent a message to my parents assuring them that I was alive and well in Manila and would be heading to northern Luzon to explore the 2,000-year-old rice terraces.

With business done, I set my mind on relaxing and meeting new people. It all turned out to be a fun evening after all. I didn't even think about the fire.

HAZARD 51:

SET A BUILDING ON FIRE

That night, in the hostel common area, Madeline and I met Jessica from New Zealand who said she knew how the fire started. As she told the story. It sounded like a movie plot…

"There was an American guy…

Just great, I thought. *Why did it have to be an American? We already have such a bad reputation. Ughhh....*

Jessica continued:

"…he was staying at the hostel—practically living here, and somehow, he got deep into drugs. The owner asked him to pay up because he hadn't paid her in a month. She told him he couldn't stay anymore unless he came up with some money.

The guy, who was clearly all drugged up, started yelling and acting crazy. He went to the library,

269

grabbed a bunch of books, took them to the roof, and set them on fire.

Well, as you can see, the fire got out of control and burned the top few floors. The fire department put it out, and the police came to take statements. They arrested the guy and left.

Everyone staying on those top floors had to evacuate and sleep in the common area. It was a crazy night. The guy must not have been charged with the crime, or was released, or something, because the next day he showed up at the hostel, acting all crazy and yelling at the staff. The police were called, and they took him away, again.

I guess his family had been looking for him for months, but because of his drug habit, he just seemed to vanish. I heard he's back in jail and might be deported."

Madeline and I sat there, stunned. It was more drama than I'd heard in all my travels so far. We stayed up for a while longer, getting to know some of the others, then headed up to bed.

In the morning I was up before Madeline and Ally. Not wanting to disturb them, I quietly dressed and left the dorm to check out the hostel-from-hell. It wasn't really bad but the vibe felt uncomfortable—crazy guy setting fire to the building, mattress blocking the stairway, scorch marks on the wall. I just didn't feel good about being there. So, one thing I knew for sure—I would find a way to get out of Manila as fast as possible. But where to go? While eating breakfast I thought it over and narrowed it down to two possibilities—Taal Lake or Batad. I was just finishing up my meal when Madeline came down and dropped into a chair at my table. She'd decided to go on a cycling tour of the Manila slums.

I shivered inside. Not my idea of a good time. I gave her a hug and said I might not be there when she returned but it was great to have met her. She didn't let on whether she was disappointed that I wouldn't be joining her on a slum-run or not and wished me well.

After she left, I read through my *Lonely Planet*, weighing options. When Jessica came down, she said she wanted to go somewhere North. The more we talked, the better that sounded and decided on Banaue, a city outside Batad.

A few minutes later Ally slumped down the stairs, looking like hell. I asked her if she wanted to stay here for a few more days or if she was up to catching the night bus with Jessica and me.

Sick or no, she said, "I want out of here. I'd *love* to go with you."

I knew how she felt about the bad vibes in the hostel and was glad she'd be coming with us.

Jessica booked three night-bus tickets to Banaue Ally decided to stay in and rest for the day.

To have fresh reading material for the bus ride, I scanned the hostel's book collection. My options were limited. It seemed that nut job used most of the books in the library to stoke the fire. Sighing, I swapped *Treasure Island* for *Something Blue*.

Madeline came in just as we were about to catch a cab to the station. It was good to see her before we left. I asked how she liked the slum tour. She was a bit noncommittal, so I let it go then said to look me up if she ever came to San Diego. She seemed a little sad that we were going so soon, but smiled, and carried Ally's bag down for her. The three of us squeezed into the taxi and waved to Madeline as we drove away.

I glanced around the small bus station waiting area and spotted the help desk behind a transparent window—outside the building. The station attendant behind the glass asked where we were going and checked our tickets. He kept them and handed us slips of paper to give the bus driver. So far, so good.

All set to go, we had an hour before the bus would depart so we scoped out some places to eat. Normally bus stations are filled with tons of vendors selling food and snacks, but not there. Ally sat down on a bench and volunteered to stay with the bags while Jessica and I headed across the street to a gas station, hoping they had food. They didn't. *Don't travelers eat in this part of the world?* We had to walk down the street about a mile before we found someone selling food. Very bizarre. Although there were no restaurants or food carts in sight, we spotted a tiny building with a woman standing behind a wood-framed, glassless window.

That seemed a bit odd and I thought she might be selling food. This was so surreal, it felt like a Fellini film. But, what the hell, we asked if she had food for sale.

She did—sort of. She showed us a puny selection of chips, popcorn, and Filipino candies. Okay. At this point, we couldn't be picky. I bought a couple bags of popcorn.

There *had* to be more. Someone else surely had food for sale. As we tramped a little further down the street, we hit the jackpot—a man with a cart, grilling sausages, peppers, and onions. It smelled *amazing*. We both bought some. I thought about getting a sausage for Ally but remembered that she wasn't feeling well and probably wouldn't eat it.

I was starving and hungrily bit into mine. It tasted a bit odd, not like pork and I wondered if it might be made from something I didn't *want* to know about. Then Jessica blurted, out, "This tastes good, but I'm not sure what kind of meat it is." I laughed and told her I was just thinking that and said, "You probably don't want to know."

Back at the bus station, we flopped down onto our seats next to Ally. I handed her the popcorn. She thanked us and dug in like she hadn't eaten in weeks. I hoped that meant she was feeling better.

When the bus finally arrived, we were all more than glad to be leaving Manila behind.

Escapade 52:
2,000-Year-Old Rice Terraces and Ex-Headhunters

We arrived in Banaue around 6 a.m. and transferred to a minibus to the town center. After a short ride, the bus dropped us off outside a hotel. The driver tried to get everyone to go inside. I guessed he got paid if tourists stayed there. Although I thought it a clever way to get business from exhausted travelers, we knew better and decided to look around for more affordable accommodations.

Although not always the best practice in other parts of the world, in Southeast Asia, being dropped off somewhere unfamiliar and not having room reservations was part of the adventure. I loved it. Jessica was a great travel buddy—always up for anything and well prepared. She found the Greenview Lodge—250P per person ($5 US). What a steal! It was half the price of the hotel the driver had wanted us to stay in.

Tired and sleep-deprived from the bumpy, noisy ride, we gladly checked in, found our room, and promptly took a nap.

A few hours later, we awoke refreshed and ready to explore. The tourist information center gave us maps and suggestions for what to do in town. I discovered that Banaue, in Northern Luzon, is nestled in the steep mountains of the Bontoc Province. It's a small town, with only one main street—the one we were standing on. People generally travel there to see the 2,000-year-old rice terraces and to experience the Ifugao people. This sounded interesting. The Ifugao were once fierce war-like headhunters but now spend their lives maintaining the terraced rice paddies that have been called the eighth wonder of the world. They are also sought out for their beautiful wood carvings and exquisite textiles. I was in heaven. This place was going to be awesome!

The weather in Banaue was green and lush, but oddly cold and a bit gloomy—so different from most of the rest of my travels in Southeast Asia.

Ready to explore, I gazed around at a lush hillside village, dotted with colorful houses of all shapes and sizes. I'd read that in the 16th century, the Spaniards invaded Southeast Asia, but when they tried to take over this area, they failed. Oddly, they were impressed enough with the houses built by the Ifugao to write about them. They were constructed without nails of any kind, and looked like an elevated pyramid, supported on four wooden posts but proved strong enough to withstand typhoons and earthquakes.

Their modern houses, though, are built using contemporary methods. And, like anywhere, some of the houses we saw looked dilapidated and some looked well kept. I especially liked the three, four, and five level buildings where each floor was painted a distinct color. These bright homes scattered across the land in picturesque clusters on green, dew-filled grass.

Pointed, tin-roofed buildings with uniform stripes of rust that made them look like circus tents lined the main street. Most of the buildings were covered in metal sheets giving the area an industrial zone feel. Although it wasn't especially attractive to look at, it was interesting. I enjoyed this unique place.

We traipsed about, exploring the mountain and trekking up the newly paved road to the rice terraces in the crisp, cool air. The terraces are stunningly beautiful, like emerald steps leading to a mountaintop. As I gazed in amazement, I thought *"I can't believe these rice terraces are two-thousand years old."*

The little village nestled within this maze of green was filled with wild chickens, pigs, and cattle roaming about. I loved being there to see and experience these people who, after thousands of years, still held onto their simple way of living.

After that awe-inspiring feast of beauty, we realized how hungry we were and went off to a village restaurant. Fortunately, the menus had pictures because they were not in a language we could read.

I pointed at what I wanted, hoping it was chicken adobo. As we waited for our food, I could have sworn I heard the cook strangle a chicken in the back of the restaurant. If that was correct, I had a very fresh lunch.

After our meal we headed down the mountain, gawking at the terraces as much as possible. I couldn't get enough of this place. Every scene was a masterpiece of jaw-dropping beauty and a surreal juxtaposition of ancient and modern life.

Hazard 53:

Zombie Teeth and

Emerald Beauty

For dinner, we found a nameless hole-in-the-wall eatery that offered a couple of great surprises. First, this tiny restaurant looked plain on the outside, but inside it was full of color from the vivid curtains that draped the walls to the bright tablecloths and bountiful fresh flowers.

Second, we discovered that, in addition to a regular menu, the owner's mother had made special food for a holiday and brought in the leftovers.

This would never be allowed in the US, but there, regulations are more relaxed—perhaps even non-existent in some places. I would guess the main food law for public safety in many parts of Southeast Asia is *caveat emptor*—buyer beware. So far, my friends and I had been lucky. Only a little food-born illness had plagued our travels. Remember tuna fish pizza?

This restaurant served beans, several types of stew, and bread. I don't remember the names of the dishes we ate, but it all tasted amazing. After dinner, we shopped and bought fresh pastries for our journey to Batad the next day.

After dinner, we walked around town. At first, it was just like many other small towns I'd visited, then I noticed red splotches along the road. A minute later, a man with what looked like clotted blood all over his teeth approached. I cringed and backed away. My expression must have looked like I'd just smelled a bad fart, but I had no idea what was going on. Red gunk coated and stained his teeth.

I walked away as fast as I could but saw more men with the same scary, red smiles. Had I stumbled onto the TV set of *The Walking Dead?* Was this an epidemic of some sort? Fortunately, it was nothing that dramatic. The red turned out to be a substance made from a betel nut, called *moma*. Moma is a stimulant like tobacco and thought to have some medicinal properties. Locals believe that chewing moma increases energy but also causes a mild, stimulating "high." I wasn't curious enough to try it for myself, though.

I wondered,*Does this also rot their teeth?* Looking around, I guessed it did. Many had teeth in bad condition or missing. I later learned that moma has cancer-causing properties like tobacco and the little health benefit it has doesn't outweigh the risks—or how ugly it makes your mouth look.

I imagined that arriving in Banaue at night could be freaky with its dilapidated buildings and abandoned-looking warehouses that screamed *The Hills Have Eyes.* Luckily, we were there during the day. It was all charming, so no frightening scenery (except for the red-gunk teeth), and everyone was friendly and greeted us as we passed.

We explored a little more then returned to the Greenview Lodge for the night. This place was one of the best. Built from rich-looking mahogany, it reminded me of an old boarding school, especially with its communal bathrooms and dorms that had two or three twin beds in each room. The most amusing part about this place, besides having to pay extra for hot water, was that the walls were not flush to the ceiling, so we could hear everything said or done on that floor—and did—including people having sex in the room across from us. We all giggled like schoolgirls before putting in earplugs so we could sleep.

After breakfast the next morning, we took a Jeepney to Batad but because of road construction, the driver dropped us off a couple of miles from the old trailhead to the village. Undaunted, we retrieved our bags, paid the driver, and began our hike through the meandering hills to the village.

The dirt road grew narrower as we walked along. We passed a few tourists but saw mostly locals. As the path meandered around the hill, the vegetation became thicker and more interesting with bright flowers and exotic insects dotting the landscape. It felt like being in a rainforest as we crossed over tiny wooden bridges without railings and passed by the village's fresh water supply.

The way grew steeper and we had to climb up the mountainside by holding on to branches and rocks for balance, trying not to look down. Then, after a short while of feeling like Sir Edmund Hilary scaling Mount Everest, the land suddenly flattened out.

We gazed at the distant, tiered pyramids of rice terraces carved out of the mountainside and draped in fairytale green. I'd thought the terraces we'd seen the previous day were awesome, but these massive, giant steps? Majestic. They took my breath away and gave me chills. I stood there, transfixed, in mouth-gaping awe.

Of course, just when I thought the day couldn't get any better, it did. At the entrance to the Batad rice terraces, my camping buds Alissa and Courtney from El Nido showed up. Surprise! We screamed with excitement, jumping, and hugging with abandon.

After paying the fee, we all continued our exploration together. Walking along the skinny ledges of the terraces, I remember thinking it was like balancing on the edge of a curvy, vertical sidewalk that thickened and narrowed depending on the shape and location. No terrace was exactly like another. Some were full of water and mud because the rice had been harvested, but most of these hand-carved rice beds were bright green, and in some areas of the rowed pyramids, water flowed down to the lower terraces like slow-moving mini waterfalls.

We traipsed around for hours admiring the beauty, climbing up and down steep green cliffs as we made our way around the mountain to the valley that held Batad village.

On the other side of the staggered plateaus, we found a dirt path that hugged the mountain and led to a heavily forested area, teeming with exotic plants, flowers, and insects.

After a while, the weather turned warm and we were soon covered in sweat, making us a tasty banquet for swarms of mosquitoes. Bloodsuckers or no, we continued up the steep, rocky trail to the top for the promised reward on the other side—a magnificent waterfall.

When the trail led downhill, I was glad to give my glutes some relief. I knew we were close to the falls when the smell of moisture grew stronger. Soon the land leveled to a smooth-rock covered ground. I nearly cried with happiness when we rounded a bend and saw the prize—an incredible waterfall that looked to be about a hundred feet high. The roaring sound of fresh water hitting the pond at the bottom was deeply soothing after the ordeal to get there.

I didn't have a swimsuit on, so I changed under my clothes because there were other tourists around. No problem, though. I had become highly skilled at changing in and out of clothing without exposing skin.

Ally waded into the water first. "Aaah!" she screamed. "It's ice cold!"

I cringed and thought about a strategy for the best way to enter the pool without getting thermal shock, or if I would go in at all. I looked around for a low spot where I could jump in but didn't see any. The shallow water's edge was covered in coarse pebbles that were unkind to my feet. They threw me off-balance and I stumbled in.

I had wanted to cool off, but not like that. The frigid water made me gasp. But I wasn't a wimp. I wouldn't run out screaming like a baby, so I bravely swam to the falls and stood underneath. Its heavy weight pounded my body, but in a good way. It felt therapeutic. The other girls joined me.

Later, Alissa asked a tourist to take a group picture of us in front of the falls. After we dried off and dressed, we hiked to Batad for lunch. At a small eatery with a dirt floor and wooden covering, we settled around a tiny table. There was no menu, but an adorable, petite woman made us a chicken dish with rice.

From there we had a full view of the terraces. This time, though, gazing up at them instead of down. They looked like an emerald colosseum.

After such a long day, we stayed in Batad for the night instead of making our way back to Banaue. The whole experience of the mountain and the village had been surreal. I wanted to know more about the people who lived there so I wandered off and explored. I loved observing the daily habits of the locals. Everything about their lives seems so simple. I wondered how the rice farming differed from the terraces I had worked on in Laos. At first, I was amazed when I learned these were carved using hand tools, but after considering their age, I realized that, of course, they used hand tools; there wasn't anything else back then. To me, that made the terraces seem more like a work of art than industry.

Most everything in the village was mired in tradition. The people still used the age-old methods of cooking, cleaning, and farming the rice. Fascinating. It felt like I'd been transported back in time.

We stayed in a traditional-style Ifugao hut—thatched roof, no windows, and wooden floors. Our host taught us some traditional ways of village life and told us the fascinating history of the once fierce Ifugao people and how their culture now revolves around rice. Harvest season is a big deal and social status is determined by how many rice granaries a family has, the number of water buffalo they own, and the value of their family heirlooms. Rice is the livelihood of Batad and of the Ifugao mountain people. Because it's sold mainly outside of that province, the village economy depends on it.

On our hike back to Banaue the next day, I noticed a man carving a piece of wood with a symbol that looked like a small horseshoe and asked him what it meant. He said it was an amulet and a sign of love and luck. I had seen this symbol in several Banaue shops and was glad to finally know its meaning. I bought the one the man had carved. He told me that amulet was especially powerful because the wood had a hint of red in it.

After a delicious lunch, we retrieved our belongings from the hostel and walked down the street to the Jeepney line-up area. I approached the first driver I saw and asked him which car was going to Sagada. He pointed at his own vehicle then hoisted our bags and tied them to the roof.

Jessica and Ally left to buy snacks for our journey. I waited at the Jeepney to make sure it didn't fill up and drive off with our things.

When the girls returned, the Jeepney was nearly full. We were in for a six-hour ride, so I wasn't happy that we had to sit in the back, crammed, shoulder to shoulder with more people and their stuff than the vehicle should have been carrying. One man had two 60-pound bags of rice with him. Someone else had an overly fragrant pig. At one point the Jeepney was so crammed, some passengers had to ride while standing on the back bumper and I counted at least six people sitting on the roof.

Since I had no choice in the matter, though, I decided that grumbling would only make me feel bad, so I chose to enjoy it (as much as possible). With that mental filter in place, I found it all fascinating. How many others from back home, I wondered, would ever have a chance to experience—up close and personal—a culture with such colorful, down-to-earth people?

I enjoyed watching them as they hopped on and off the Jeepney, listening to them chatter away with each other, or ride in silent resignation. Sometimes I made up little stories in my head about their lives. Was the pig a gift for someone? Would it soon be dinner? I loved catching a glimpse of the colorful shops and tiny villages we passed along the way. I was curious about the items the passengers brought on board. You won't find pigs, live chickens, and big bags of rice on any U.S. public transportation. Well, on hindsight, I think maybe that's a good thing.

As we ascended higher, my ears plugged but I barely noticed because the view, with its dense forest of trees was so spectacular. When I wasn't gawking at the scenery, I tried to read but the road became too curvy with seemingly endless switchbacks, so reading made my stomach lurch. I had to put the book down or puke all over the person in front of me.

I was relieved when we passed a WELCOME TO SAGADA sign near a school and church. The town center was much smaller than Banaue, but prettier. The buildings there were made of wood instead of large metal sheets. I already liked this place. It seemed like a peaceful little mountain town cut off from the rest of the world.

We stopped directly in front of the town hall, a small yellow, two-story building that included the post office, tourist information, bus station, and everything else the residents might think important.

Everyone got off the Jeepney and congregated outside in a ragged clump as the driver unloaded our bags and belongings onto the sidewalk. One of the first things I noticed was a sign that read

No Moma and thought, *Good. No red-stained teeth here.*

Ally wasn't feeling well, so Jessica and I left her to rest and watch the bags while we ventured out to find somewhere to stay.

We inspected two places that had been highly recommended in the *Lonely Planet* guide and decided to stay at the one closest to the town center then headed back to the Jeepney for Ally.

Once there, I had to hold back vomit. While we were gone, someone hacked a loogie on the ground and part of it ended up on *my* bag. I swallowed hard to keep from throwing up.

This reminded me of something similar that happened to my friend, Spence...

> Spence worked in a fish processing plant in Alaska and one day, as he headed down the stairs to the cafeteria, he placed his hand on the rail and heard a squish. When he looked down, he saw a big, green-yellow loogie oozing between his fingers and all over his wedding band.

Even now, thinking about it makes my stomach lurch. By comparison, I guess the situation with phlegm on my bag wasn't that bad.

I dug through my backpack and retrieved some bleach wipes. Cringing at the thought of some jerk's sticky, germy phlegm touching my stuff, I wiped off the goo. With my now sanitized bag in hand, I left the crisis behind and we headed to our new digs.

Inside, I scoped out my new "home." Not bad. Clean, and it seemed as good as, or better than, some I'd stayed in. The only glitch was that there were no three-bed rooms available, so Ally and I stayed in one room and Jessica had her own.

The family who owned the place lived downstairs, making this place feel more like a bed-and-breakfast than a hostel. The spacious common area's mahogany walls were pretty, but what excited me the most was their huge library. A veritable Garden of Eden for any avid reader.

After dropping our bags in the rooms, we walked to the tourist information center to discover what there was to do around Sagada. There were interesting possibilities, but it was late in the afternoon, so we decided not to venture out on any big excursion that day.

The town hall and our hostel sat on top of a hill. Restaurants, shops, and hotels sprinkled down the slope along the main street. We roamed around, walking in and out of shops and restaurants, pricing items, and searching out dinner options.

We ended up settling on a deli that served huge portions of yummy sandwiches and pastries. I ordered a chicken club with bacon and avocado.

On leaving the restaurant, we found that the sleepy town had come alive. People filled the streets. Children ran around; men and women gathered to socialize, eat, and laugh.

It was lively in a town-community way, but we soon discovered that Sagada isn't a party town. There wasn't much for us inveterate merry-making folk to do. So, after dinner and roaming around a bit, we went back to the hostel and made arrangements for the next day.

Escapade 54:

Caving but NOT on the Crawlie Route

The next day, we rose early, excited about exploring the caves at Sumaguing and Lumiang. After much discussion, we hired two guides. Ally and Jessica wanted to crawl through the small tunnels in the cave complex. That didn't appeal to me. In fact, the thought of doing that freaked me out. I decided to take the actual cave tour that started at the front entrance on the other side of the crawly opening.

The entrance was large and looked like most others I'd visited in Southeast Asia. Inside was also spacious, but as my guide led me deeper inside, the walls narrowed. I'd previously experienced that, so I wasn't concerned. As I looked around, I reveled in how amazing it was. One thing I love about cave exploring is that no two ever look exactly alike.

Since I had arrived early, my guide and I had the cave mostly to ourselves. It was so quiet we could hear the bats screeching, and water drops echoing as they hit the floor or splashed into water puddles. It was so eerie. The flickering lantern my guide carried, played tricks with the light and cast spooky shadows as we walked and moved about. Delightfully creepy. I remember thinking that this was much better than being assaulted by echoing clatter from a bunch of human voices.

The brown and cream walls with large, impressive formations nearly took my breath away. Somehow, they seemed even more amazing because the cavern was so devoid of others and their noise. Water-carved, tooth-like sculptures stood out impressively on the cave landscape, like giant dragon's teeth, and some of the walls and formations were artfully striped from water erosion. No human sculptor could have done better. We crossed through icy-cold puddles that glimmered in the lamplight. I only wish it had been possible to capture the magic of this place with my camera.

Occasionally, a mysterious movement, caught from the corner of my eye, startled me. But, when I looked at it directly, I had to laugh. It was always just another lantern shadow.

We stopped in an area that looked like a dead end at first, but the guide pointed out a rope dangling from the top.

I can't climb that. I have no upper body strength. "Well," I muttered while chuckling to myself, "This is going to be interesting." The guide didn't comment as he grasped the rope and scurried up like a ninja. That's when I noticed small notches on the wall to help with the climb.

I let out a breath and grabbed hold. Climbing was a workout. Not as hard as I'd thought but I was relieved to reach the top, which opened into a small chamber that shimmered like the walls had been painted with diamond dust.

We crossed over a deep pond by hopping along a line of rocks strategically placed to create a path to the other side then hiked the rolling formations to a larger chamber with a massive pool of water.

My guide asked if I wanted to swim. I declined at first, knowing how cold the water probably was. But after thinking for a minute and silently chastising myself for being a wimp, I jumped in. It was just as cold as I had anticipated but also refreshing and invigorating.

As I swam, I heard voices that seemed to be coming from inside the wall. It creeped me out and I scurried to the shore. Then someone called out, "Tam!" When the shouter came close enough to be in my light, I was glad to see that it was Ally and Jessica. They'd come through a tiny opening in the wall. This made me doubly glad I hadn't joined them for the crawly tour. They stopped only long enough to say "Hi" then continued through the cave by squeezing into another small crevice.

My guide said that it was time to go back, so I pulled on the hiking boots I'd taken off for the plunge, and followed him to the entrance, enjoying the cave even more on the way out.

The girls and I had prearranged to meet up at the little shop on the street. I arrived just after they did. We browsed the store and I bought my mom a bracelet that had her birthstone in it. A little tired, and with nothing else to do, we headed back to Sagada.

We weren't sure how to get to our lodging but weren't worried. This was a small place and getting hopelessly lost was unlikely. So, we enjoyed the scenery of huge trees and tiny cottages sprinkled around a majestic landscape with a view of spectacular rice terraces and colorful farmhouses clustered together in a vast valley of a green terraced garden. The thought struck me that the scene would make a great jigsaw puzzle.

A few hours later we reluctantly left the "Nat Geo" panorama behind and traipsed into town for some of their famous blueberry and lemon pie before heading to the hostel. It was delicious.

Escapade 55:

Drift Off Under the Milky Way

At the hostel, we cleaned up and relaxed for a bit. I settled into our small room that reminded me of a college dorm minus the bunk beds then opened the book I had taken from the Pink Manila library, *Something Blue*. Shortly into it, I remembered that I'd seen the film based on the book.

When it was time for dinner, we chose a place just for its Wi-Fi. Luckily, the food was good too. After eating, we left the restaurant and discovered that like the night before, the street bustled with activity from locals and tourists enjoying the cool evening. Some people Jessica knew surprised her on our walk. After a minute or so of OMGs and chit chat about "what'r the odds," she decided to go with them to the local rock bar.

Ally and I kept exploring the area. We passed the town hall and headed towards the school. I crinkled my nose at how many vendors along the road were selling balut—a partially developed duck embryo, boiled in the shell. I remembered my travel friend, May from Canada, had tried to get me to taste it while we were in Cebu. *Yuck*, gag! As before, I politely declined.

We ended up on the basketball court, a perfect spot to gaze at stars on such a crystal-clear night. I spread my jacket on the court and laid down to look at the stars. Ally did the same. Multiple shooting stars sliced through the sky. This was the brightest and clearest view of the Milky Way I'd ever seen—no light pollution or loud noises from a big city. I was mesmerized by outer space until a loud, raucous *Vroommmm* from a passing car jerked me out of my near hypnotic trance. A bit dazed at first, I sat up and realized Ally and I had both been asleep. We must have been more exhausted from our cave adventure than I'd realized.

I let Ally sleep a little longer while I resumed my sky watch. She woke up looking just as confused as I was when the car noise had jolted me awake. We laughed about it and decided to head back.

Arriving at the hostel, we realized that our nap under the stars had lasted at least two hours. When we passed Jessica's door, her light was off, so we slipped her a note that we were okay and would see her in the morning.

Escapade 56:

Hanging Coffins

The next day, we went to the laundry, so Ally could drop off her things for washing then headed for the Yoghurt House—delicious yogurt but pricey.

Our plan for the day was to see the hanging coffins, take a ride to the Red Mountains, then hike to the waterfall. We stopped at the hostel for our day packs and water before trekking to the school with the basketball court where Ally and I had fallen asleep the night before.

We weren't sure where the hanging coffins were, other than on a cliff somewhere in the area, so when we saw a church that had a cemetery, we guessed it was near there.

Hanging coffins are from a pre-Spaniard-invasion burial practice that comes from a tradition of burying the dead in coffins attached to the side of a cliff face. This protected them from headhunters who would steal heads and take them home as trophies. Also, people were afraid that animals would eat bodies buried in the ground. They also wanted to be interred closer to "heaven" and their ancestral spirits. I found it all so fascinating.

We spotted a path behind the church that led to a normal cemetery but couldn't take it because a man blocked our way demanding a fee to tour it. This screamed scam, so we decided to find a different way in.

We set off toward the school at the base of a small hill and soon found others there with the same idea. Joining forces, we climbed the hill to a fairly level, grassy area then followed a small trail into an area dense with trees. The flat ground abruptly gave way to a steep, uphill trail.

Since we were all wearing flip flop sandals, the thick leaf-litter on the ground made our going difficult. Determined, though, we kept going. Onward and upward we went, carefully scaling the cliffside, holding on to rocks, tree branches, shrubs, and sometimes sitting down and scooting our butts along the ground.

At the top we examined the damage, relieved we'd made it with only minor scrapes and bruises. I felt like celebrating our amazing feat and thought about the episode of *The Fresh Prince of Bel Air*:

> Will, after returning home to Philadelphia, tries to prove to his old friends, especially the bully, Omar that he's not chicken because he ran off to California. He trains like Rocky Balboa—falling and getting up again several times.
>
> He finally feels ready and runs through town to the many flights of "Rocky" steps that lead to the Philadelphia Museum of Art. The Rocky theme plays throughout. At the top, he does a victory dance. He was a survivor.

Gazing around, we discovered that we were at the back end of the graveyard the scammer had so dearly guarded. It overlooked a great valley and a beautiful forest on the far side of the mountain.

This wasn't a hanging coffin graveyard but fascinating in its own right. As I explored, I thought about how interesting old graves are. I love the history and craftsmanship. I think people used to take more pride in their work. I'm guessing it wasn't just a job to them. It was a way of life, a part of themselves that showed through their work. I was glad that so much of the past was still around for me to see.

After viewing the graves, we asked some other tourists there if they knew how to get to the hanging coffins. They said to follow the trail down and we'd find our way to it.

So, down we went. We passed a few rock climbers and asked if we were on the right track. They said we were. After about twenty minutes we finally found the cliff coffins. I was surprised to see the coffins actually attached to the side of the cliff.

I counted eighteen. It looked odd to see chairs mounted on the cliff next to the coffins. Later I found out that these are "death chairs." During a ceremony celebrating the person's life, their body is placed in one of the chairs so loved ones can pay their respects. After the vigil, the body is removed from the chair and placed in the coffin. What an amazing tradition—so macabre and beautiful at the same time.

.

Hazard 57:

Lost in a Dark Cave and Jessica Goes Missing

After viewing the hanging coffins, we continued down the moist dirt path in our unstable flip flops. The terrain gradually turned more rugged and vegetation began to overtake the trail. I thought that most people probably hiked down to the coffins then headed back up the way they came. Not us. We were intrepid explorers, so we trudged on, undaunted by the gradually disappearing path.

About an hour later, we came to a fast-running stream. As we continued, the trail and stream crisscrossed several times, making us have to tiptoe across the wobbly rocks to avoid getting our sandals wet. In some places, fallen logs made natural bridges over the rapid water but most often we had to hop across on rounded stones. I tried to keep my leather sandals dry, but a lot of the rocks were covered with slippery algae, so sliding into the water was a regular occurrence.

I'd fallen so many times that my sodden flip flops squeaked with every step I took. I had to laugh about it even though I suspected that, after a few minutes of hearing my feet go *squeak, squeak, squeak,* everyone else found it annoying.

To their credit, they didn't gripe but laughed about it with me. Where the rocky ground gave way to mud, I took my sandals off so the squish/squeak wouldn't drive us all nuts.

After what seemed like hours of hiking, the trail ended at a pile of large boulders. Looking around them, we spotted a shallow cave to our right. After peeking inside, we saw it was just a large hole and resigned ourselves to climbing up and over the big rocks. The other side looked much like what we'd just passed through except for the much-welcomed sight of a tour guide giving his group a talk about the area.

With no idea where we were or how to get back, we followed behind the tour group trying to be as inconspicuous as possible. The guide, however, noticed us freeloaders and seemed a bit annoyed but said nothing.

We followed behind them at a distance safe enough not to invite a confrontation with the guide. When they entered a cave, though, and went into a side chamber, we lost their light-trail. We had lights, but only a couple.

Continuing without guidance from someone who knew the cave was a bad idea, so we turned around and exited to see if there was another way. There wasn't. Resigned to navigating the cave by ourselves, with dim light, we sucked up our fears and doubts and headed back in.

Jessica and I led the way because we had the lights. There were pools to cross, so we splish-splashed and slipped on the wet rocks as we crossed. Alone, I might have been terrified but being with the group helped. We all found humor in our predicament. Laughing and joking about it kept the fear away.

The cave was beautiful, but we were more interested in finding our way out, especially since daylight was fading and trekking through strange wilderness in pitch dark with our feeble lights would be near impossible.

As we wandered around, hoping to see a glimmer of daylight indicating an exit, Ally and I took advantage of the time to talk about her escapades in El Nino after I'd left. She told me that Tuni had taken her to some interesting spots on the island she'd not seen before. He even mentioned that she could work at his new restaurant in Melbourne, Australia in the fall to earn travel money. I think she had a crush on him but didn't say anything.

For much of the journey we walked in silence, listening to moisture trickle down from the cave ceiling and hit the standing water. It sounded like slow, heavy rain.

Intermingled with the water drops were bat screeches, the snapping sound of flip flops, and footfalls on uneven ground. It all created a surreal symphony.

At one point, Ally noticed that Jessica was missing. She'd been right in front of us. Where did she go? We knew she wasn't behind, so we assumed she had gone ahead. Hoping that was the case, we picked up our pace. Finally, we literally saw the light at the end of the tunnel.

Exiting the cave, we thought for sure Jessica would be waiting for us. But there was no sign of her. We called out then went back in to look around and shout her name. No Jessica. It was as if she had simply vanished.

None of us wanted to go back into the cave again. Night was falling and without the light beacon at the exit, we could get hopelessly lost inside. Our only choice was to keep going along the path, hoping that we'd somehow find her and come across a road so we could get help in case she was injured—or worse. If we never found her, we could send a search party back to the cave for a rescue. After a while, we came upon a small waterfall and stopped to wash our feet and rest. I wondered if Jessica had passed this way.

There was some discussion about which way to go. But without any information, and in a strange land, we had no other options but to follow our intuition, so we chose a direction that felt right and started walking.

Just beyond the waterfall we saw people walking through distant rice terraces. We trailed after them and called out, asking if they'd seen Jessica, but they were too far away to hear.

Clueless, we were traveling through who knows where to who knows where, our friend was missing, and the sun was close to setting. If we didn't find a road soon, we would be in pitch dark. Scary, but I couldn't deny that the land was beyond beautiful with its ancient tropical green terraces and small pools along the way that were filled with frolicking frogs and tadpoles, indifferent to our plight.

Even though I loved the peace and quiet of the area, a million questions raced through my mind. *Would the locals take us in if we needed to spend the night there? Where was Jessica? Was she safe? Was she also lost?* I experienced a roller coaster of emotions but deep down, something told me everything would end well.

As we made our way to the top of the green gardens, we finally spotted a road. I was beyond relieved! Now, however, we needed to choose which way to go—left or right. We agreed on right because, well, it just felt "right!"

Our hunch was correct. The first sign of civilization we found was a museum of weaving. Since Sagada is well known for its fabric weaving, a museum of this sort wasn't much of a surprise, but certainly wonderful to find. It meant we were no longer lost and wouldn't have to beg a local family to take us in for the night.

Inside, we browsed the wonderful but overpriced items and asked the woman who worked there how to get to town. She told us to continue along the road. Relieved we were on the "right" track home, we still worried about Jessica.

Finally arriving at the hostel around mid-evening, we decided to clean up then regroup with our new friends for dinner at a place we'd heard was good—The Log Cabin. Perfect choice, considering it was the only place open that late.

When we went to our rooms, I nearly jumped for joy. There was Jessica. It turned out that she *had* gone ahead, somehow found the tour group, or maybe a different group, and followed them to another road. At first, she thought we were close behind, but when she looked and didn't see us, she felt it was best for her to just stick with the guide and his group. She was sorry she'd caused us so much worry. I was so glad she was okay and that we didn't have to form a search and rescue party for her.

We all ate dinner together at The Log Cabin then went to a rock bar for a beer. I was so exhausted, though, I didn't stay long. In retrospect, I mused that getting lost wasn't so bad. We'd scaled a cliffside, snuck into a graveyard, found the hanging coffins, trekked through a jungle, slipped in a creek, navigated through a dark cave, found a waterfall, traipsed through rice terraces, and misplaced our friend, all while wearing flip flops. What a great day!

The next morning, I felt it was time to make my way down south. I asked the girls if they were interested in coming with me or if they were staying north for a while. Lucky for me, they wanted to come along, so we decided to visit the 100 Islands (Alaminos), making a quick stop to visit San Fernando on the way.

We split up and ran errands for our journey. I stopped in several stores searching for deodorant and soap but failed because everything had whitening agents in them. Not what I wanted. I wasn't out of those items yet but getting close. I just hoped my supply would hold out until I got to Chiang Mai.

The next day we were on a four-hour bus ride to Baguios—the major city in Northern Luzon. Quite a culture shock after so long in small towns and open country. Baguios was bustling with locals. It didn't seem like many tourists passed through there. I thought it might be great to check the place out on a future adventure. From the main bus station, we walked to another and waited in line two hours for our bus to Alaminos.

Jessica stood in line while Ally and I found a restroom. Of course, it cost to get in. Squatting over a floor toilet never got boring but paying for it did. Business done, we found a couple carts selling food, so I bought popcorn and a fried bread thing.

Seeing how short everyone in this area was made me feel like a giant. I wondered if Jessica, who is a few inches taller than my five-foot, seven inches, experienced the same. Heading back to the line so Jessica could use the hole in the ground, a lot of eyes stared at me—but there were also a lot of smiles.

The bus was a local, meaning it wasn't like a standard coach. The seats were benches set up like mini church pews. The spaces between the pews were so narrow that us Amazonians had to sit at an angle because our legs were too long to fit.

I was a bit bummed to be leaving Northern Luzon. It is immersed in such beautiful culture, and much of it is cut off from the rest of the world, giving it a timeless feel. But I appreciated the crisp cool mountain air after having spent so much time on beaches.

The bus ride was so uncomfortable it bordered on painful, so when we pulled into Alaminos after a ride lasting more than three hours, I felt like celebrating.

We hired a tricycle from the bus station to take us to the street where all the accommodation places were. With no reservations nor a specific hostel in mind, we just showed up—true backpacker move. Although I made reservations for many of the places I'd stayed on my extended journey, showing up in a new town or village and not knowing where I would be staying was more fun.

I think there's a part of me that has always been spontaneous and ready for anything. Even though traveling this way—unplanned and in the moment—can sometimes be stressful, especially the time I showed up only to find out that the hostel was completely booked, it always worked out fine in the end.

Escapade 58:

The 100 Island National Park

We soon discovered that accommodations in Alaminos were few and far between, perhaps because this wasn't a wildly popular tourist destination. But, us hopefuls found a tricycle driver who knew two places he said we might like. The one we chose was owned by a lovely, elderly woman, who rented an upstairs room in her huge two-story house.

We entered a side door through a patio enclosed in mosquito-netting. Right away, I noticed a piano next to the stairs. The walls were covered in striped pink and cream wallpaper. Artificial-flower bouquets covered most flat surfaces. A large wooden table stood in front of a massive window next to the front door. The bathroom where we were supposed to shower was opposite the entrance. All in all, a comfortable, attractive place. After the "tour," the owner left to prepare dinner.

Ally and I wanted to explore the town, so we hired a tricycle to take us to the main street. The driver said he would wait for us while we explored in case we wanted a ride back to the hostel.

As we walked around, I noticed that most of the people out and about were locals. Not too far up the street, we found a karaoke bar. The place was awesome! I loved that we got to see a full-on show when a crew of regulars stumbled in and jammed on the mic. They turned out to be really good and tried to get us on stage with them. But Ally and I gave each other the look of terror. Too shy, I guess, or not drunk enough. Anyway, we said no but told them how much we liked their performance.

★★★

The next morning, we enthusiastically ate breakfast at the large table by the front door while the woman's son, "the dentist," kept us entertained with conversation. We told him we were headed to the 100 Islands. He gave us directions to the ferry dock that was only about a five-minute walk from the house. *Good. No long drive in a Jeepney, at least.* No reason to delay, we left our backpacks there and headed out.

At the dock, we compared boat prices and searched out people who might be looking to split the cost with us. Jessica found a group of campers and asked if we could share their boat. They agreed. Camping sounded like fun, but we didn't have any gear with us. The guides for the group said no problem and they kindly gathered tents and food for us then said the boat would be ready to leave in an hour or two.

We decided to use that time exploring and discovered a large market next to the ferry dock, so, of course, we shopped. Ally found some restaurants that had fresh-caught seafood. Who could resist? We chose one and ordered crab, mussels, fish, and naturally, it all came with rice. *Yum.* I especially loved the unusual seasoning they used.

After we'd filled up on food, it was time to set sail. We paid our share of the fare money and hopped on board.

I've always found that the people I meet on my travels are largely what make my trips truly wonderful. This was no exception. Our boat buds this time were French and traveling during their summer break from school. Good people and so much fun. I feel lucky to have met them.

The 100 Islands were small, but beautiful. I had never seen such tiny islands. Some of them looked more like big rocks. There are 124 islands during low tide and 123 islands during high tide. Each one has a name, but the main attractions are Bat, Turtle, Scout, and Governor Islands. They are mushroom shaped with green vegetation on top and a grayish green limestone at the base. The sea turtles swimming about were a highlight for me.

After sailing around for a while, our captain took us to a cave-jumping area—basically a big hole in the ground with a pool of water at the bottom—about 12-20 feet down. Pretty cool, but I'd done *real* cliff diving, so I wasn't all that thrilled.

Next, we rode around Bat Island, called that because it is thick with bats. So thick they have the rocky, gray land mainly to themselves and hang, like ripe fruit from the mostly bare, tree branches. It was neat, but I wondered—if we had passed at night, would we see glowing eyes all over the place?

I thought the 100 Islands was beautiful, but after the stunning landscape of El Nido, this seemed mediocre in comparison.

Next, we beach-hopped to several of the miniature islands. On the "largest," we followed a trail that led to the highest point where there was an expansive view of the green-covered mounds protruding from the bright blue ocean.

Just before sunset, we docked at Scout Island and set up camp. Our guides made a fire. We drank whiskey, played cards, listened to music, and got to know one another.

After a while, I felt like taking a swim, so I changed into my suit and headed for the water. It was wonderful, a few degrees warmer than the air and I could see the bioluminescent plankton. I went back and told Jessica and Ally they *had* to experience this. Jessica tried to get the others to join us, but they seemed uninterested. She grumbled about their attitude, but Ally and I

307

laughed and said it was their loss and we shouldn't let them spoil our fun. She calmed down and enjoyed our "secret" swim in the glowing water.

After everyone went to bed I sat on the beach, listened to the ebb and flow of the sea and gazed at the silhouette of the neighboring islands against the moonlit sky.

One of my first thoughts the next morning was that later, I would be catching a night bus back to Manila for my flight to Chiang Mai. But I soon pushed that thought into the back of my mind as we sailed around and explored more islands.

At the end of the tour, the boat dropped us off at the dock a lot later than I'd anticipated. I needed to hurry or miss my bus. I ran back to the house, changed clothes, paid the owner, grabbed my backpack, and rushed out, hoping to hail a tricycle.

I felt awful, running off without saying goodbye to Jessica and Ally, but I had a plane to catch and the last bus to Manila was due to leave in thirty-five minutes. Luckily, just as I was about to climb into the tricycle, the girls showed up. I gave them big hugs and told them how happy I was to be able to say goodbye. We all vowed to keep in touch, and I rode off on the tricycle toward the bus station.

Escapade 59:

Unexpected Delay

At the bus station, the tricycle driver must have seen that I was close to frazzle point and went with me to the counter to make sure I bought the correct ticket and boarded the right bus. It's a good thing he did because we were at the wrong station. *Eeekk!* We got back on the tricycle and rushed to the other station.

I thought for sure I was going to miss my flight because of this delay. When we arrived, the driver, again, went with me to the ticket counter then to the bus and loaded my bag underneath. As I boarded, he wished me luck and scooted away, probably to the next clueless traveler. I was grateful for his help and mused that along with the scammers and hucksters in this part of the world, I'd met a lot of genuinely decent people.

Almost as soon as I found a seat, the driver started the engine and we left the station. Really glad the racing was over, I settled in for a three and a half hour journey to Manila. It wasn't quite dark yet, so I gazed out the window at little houses nestled among tropical plants and trees lining the coast. This was nice.

So many other shores in the tourist-clogged areas were lined with crazy, big resorts, standing like modern-day Easter Island giants, looking out to sea. This, I thought, was a true paradise—quiet and mostly untouched by tourism. I hoped the next time I came for a visit it would still be the same.

I set my alarm for three hours then rested my head on the seatback and went to sleep. When I woke, it was almost like I'd landed on a different planet, one full of city lights and urban noise. *Goodbye quiet, peaceful countryside. Hello, city.* I glanced at the time and breathed a sigh of relief. I could make it to my flight.

I asked the driver how far to the airport. He said about forty-five minutes. What? My heart sank to my knees. I had thought I'd been dropped off at the *main* bus station. *It's always something.* I quickly hailed a taxi, telling him to get me to the airport as fast as possible. Luckily, traffic wasn't too bad, but my heart pounded the whole trip.

When we pulled up at the airport, I paid the driver then shot out of the taxi, grabbed my bag and sprinted to the check-in counter. When I gave the gate agent my passport, I nearly screamed when she told me I was at the *wrong* terminal. The other one was fifteen minutes away. *Ughhhhh! How is this happening today?*

At this point, there was slim-to-no-chance I would make my flight, but I didn't give up. I caught a taxi to the other terminal. When I got to the door the security guard asked for my passport and flight information. He looked at his monitor and said that I could not enter the airport unless my flight was departing within three hours. What? I *was* there within three hours. My flight, in fact, was about to leave. Could this man not tell time! Was I in some weird existential loop?

I reminded myself to calm down and think then dashed to a monitor and checked my flight. By some miracle, it had been delayed by more than three hours. "YES!!!" That's why he wouldn't let me in. I think that's the first and, perhaps, the only time I was glad my flight was delayed.

After retrieving my passport from the guard, I sat in the outside waiting area and took a nap. When my alarm buzzed, I headed to security. This time there was no problem. He smiled and let me in. I calmly headed toward the check-in counter for my boarding pass. All was right with the world again.

It seemed my stretch on the obstacle course had ended. I breezed through customs, boarded the plane, and dozed off. When I woke up, it was morning and the plane had just touched down in Chiang Mai.

"Okay!" I affirmed. "On to the next adventure. Everything will go smoothly now."

Escapade 60:
Baggage Woes and
a Lost Tuk Tuk Driver

Still in my seat, I watched this episode of the "chaos show" as everyone shoved, pushed, and scrambled to get off the plane as fast as they could, which, of course, meant using the slowest way possible to accomplish what they wanted.

When the circus calmed down, I casually exited without having to fight my way through. Inside the terminal I breezed through immigration then headed to baggage claim and waited. About fifteen minutes later, I noticed that everyone else had retrieved their luggage and left. *Okay. Stuff happens. It will be fine.* At the help desk, I filed a claim and left the address and phone number of my hostel.

I ran a gamut of emotions about this. First, I felt relief that I hadn't arrived without planning ahead. I'd heard horror stories of luggage taking days to be found.

Sitting in the airport until my bag was returned conjured up a picture I didn't want to see. Next, after I'd done all I could, annoyance took over. *I cannot BELIEVE they lost my bag. Ughhh!!* After huffing over this a moment, I pulled myself together and went into planning mode. Finding the ATM, I withdrew some Thai baht to pay for the hostel then walked outside to find transportation.

I approached a tuk tuk driver, showed him the address of the Living Space 2. He said he knew exactly where it was and could take me there. An hour later, though, he was still driving around looking for it. My temper was quickly simmering toward a boil. *What a waste of time!*

Finally, after the driver had asked the fifth person where the hostel was, he found it. Then, he had the audacity to ask for 900 bhat—because it took a long time to find!

Well, I wasn't some newb. I'd learned how to deal with situations like that. I laughed and gave him 100 baht like we'd originally agreed then strode, head held high, into the hostel.

Later, when I calmed down, I remembered that those drivers make very little money and they wouldn't want to miss a fare just because they didn't know the location of a place. I felt a little bad about how I'd reacted, but only a little.

Escapade 61:
Surprise!

I gave the hostel manager of Living Place 2 my passport and reservation information. She welcomed me with a warm smile and expressed understanding and sympathy when I told her the airport had lost my bag and would deliver it as soon as they found it.

On the way up to my room I heard "Tam?" When I turned to see who it was, I screamed with joy. "Russel!" My friend from Warung CoCo stood there with a wide grin. I gave him a great big hug. It had been months since we'd seen each other. *What're the odds,* I thought, *after all this time that we'd be staying at the same hostel in a totally different country?* At that moment, I didn't care, though. This was awesome!

He told me he was on his way to the hospital to get a second round of rabies shots because a dog bit him while he was in Pi the day before.

"Wow. Dog bite. Bummer," I said, but he didn't look worried about it, so I let it go. After a short catch-up chat, we agreed to meet later for food and fun. Walking on cloud nine and thinking that even though this trip started out troublesome, it was going to be one of the best yet.

My room on the 3rd floor was nearly full. I spotted Chad napping on a top bunk and headed for the only empty bed left. Claiming it with my carry-on bag and the statue I'd bought for my dad, I heard a sort of snort/cough. It was Chad, pretending to be annoyed. "Thanks for waking me up," he grunted. But he couldn't really pull it off and his bright smile broke through.

I laughed then told him the story of my lost baggage and lost tuk tuk driver adventure.

He climbed down from his top bunk. "I'm sooo hungry."

"That makes two of us," I said.

"What are we waiting for?" He grinned and signaled another roommate. "Hey, we're going to find food and buy water guns for the festival. You in?"

The guy hopped off his bed, quickly introduced himself as Jack, from Seattle, then without another word, the three of us were on our way.

On the road, a couple of people squirted us with their water guns. Even though the festivities wouldn't officially start until the next day, some celebrators didn't want to wait.

Our hostel wasn't the only one on the dead-end street that connected to the main thoroughfare where the festival would take place, so dousing was inevitable.

On our way back, we made a run for it, but several people chased us with buckets of water and super soakers. It felt like a water-zombie apocalypse. Nowhere outside was safe.

Drenched, we finally made it back to the hostel. Inside, another great surprise! My roomie from Boracay, Madeline, stood chatting with some friends, super soaker in hand.

I was beside myself with excitement.

Seeing me, she screamed; I screamed; she screamed; we both screamed together.

This might have gone on longer, but the manager came in and invited us all to a big BBQ she was having. I told Madeline my baggage and tuk tuk story and gestured to the wet clothes I was wearing. "This is all I have so I hope they find my bag soon."

She told me that she'd arrived in Chiang Mai a few days before I did, had gone ziplining, and volunteered at the elephant sanctuary. She remembered me telling her where I was going and where I'd be staying and, on a whim, she decided to show up and surprise me.

I was surprised—in the best way possible.

At the BBQ, we pigged out on steak, chicken, salad, beans, veggies, bread, and booze. There, I met Jeremy from Maryland, and Blair and Sue, from New York. Jeremy, around 6-feet tall, had deep-green eyes and sandy brown hair.

Jeremy played a really impressive guitar. Blair and Sue were being their fun selves, telling jokes and in general, putting out a good vibe.

I mused that a lot of experiences are shaped by who we're with, and that the energy of the people staying at this hostel was amazing. Everyone was fun and full of the spirit of adventure. It felt like we'd all known each other forever.

Chad had invited some friends, including Gloria, a woman he'd met while partying in Ko Pha-ngan and Koh Toa. After the BBQ, we all went to the night market. I remembered when Casey, Valerie, and I were there in January. We had a fabulous time. It hadn't changed—jam-packed with large tables full of hand-carved trinkets, magnets, scarves, lamps, jewelry, and just about everything else. The streets were lined shoulder-to-shoulder with vendors selling paintings, drawings, clothes, and food. This all made bartering so much fun.

Street-eats are my favorite, so even though I was stuffed from the BBQ, I couldn't resist. The food section was amazing—skewers, fried insects, fruit, smoothies, fried rice, noodles, curry, morning glory, things I had no name for and, of course, beer.

I downed a kiwi strawberry smoothie, a few skewers, curry, and an unknown dish that turned out to be Thai spicy. It just about killed me. We ate with Madeline, Gloria, Steven, and Kyle, from Ireland. Steven and Kyle were staying at the Living Place 2 as well. After an hour or two of fun, we went back to the hostel to round up the rest of the group for some pub crawling.

We all packed into a couple of big tuk tuks and jostled over the road to the main strip, which was full of bars and clubs, all sidled up next to each other. It made it a large outdoor party. When Chad's wingmen arrived, he was stoked and beyond ready to go hit on the girls. He'd been talking about it all day like a kid waiting to go to Disneyland. So adorable. Well, I knew I wouldn't be seeing much of him that evening and joined some of the others for drinks and dancing.

When I heard a familiar tune playing in the distance, I went to check it out. Sure enough, it was a band performing '80s pop music. YES!!! I was ecstatic and thought others in the group would be, too. But no. Only Damian from Ireland was as excited as I was. So, naturally, he was my partner-in-crime that evening.

We headed to the bar with the great music and had a blast, even getting on stage and dancing with the band, occasionally checking in with our group at the bar next door. But the '80s were calling us, so we kept going back to that. When the band left, we decided to join a group at the reggae bar. But when we walked in, we only saw Chad and his posse picking up girls. None of the others in our group were still there, so Damian and I checked out some other bars with live music and enjoyed the cool evening.

When we arrived back at the hostel, I went to my dorm and discovered that Damian and I had been the last ones standing. All the beds were filled with passed-out people.

Awesome night!

Escapade 62:

Songkran (Thai Water Festival)

Today was the day! Songkran! Stoked, I headed down to breakfast with my buds, Chad, Jeremy, Gloria, Steven, and Kyle. Chad's friends, Blair and Sue rounded out our group of carousers.

Water guns loaded with H2O, we were ready to rumble at the water festival after we ate. But as poet Robert Burns said, "Best laid plans of mice and men often go awry," things did not go as expected.

We left the hostel with full confidence of having a great day. The festival was due to start soon and already we heard a DJ somewhere in the distance blasting music in full swing, bumping jams.

Right away, we found ourselves having to run a gauntlet of water squirts. The streets were filled with people having a blast. We joined in the fun and came through with no serious casualties as we dashed toward the DJ, where a full-on dance party was happening.

Even being doused with buckets of water hurled at us from passing cars didn't put a dent in our good time. Some of the water was ice cold and some warm and brown from the river that ran alongside the major street. It didn't matter. We just squealed, laughed, and kept on having fun along with everyone else.

We danced a while then moved on, fully intending to find a restaurant for breakfast. Hah! Heading down the street was like a war zone, full of ice-cold water bombs and people fighting squirt-to-squirt skirmishes. It wasn't long before we were soaked through and through. I loved it—except for the torture of icy water.

I'd been drenched since I'd set foot outside the hostel but didn't care. Songkran was exhilarating. Think about it. A huge, water fight celebrated by a whole country. A week when everyone gets to be a kid, what could be better than that? Next to nothing, in my mind.

I imagined how the little kids felt on this day. They love water and love playing. Squirting grown-ups and not getting in trouble for it must have been magical for them.

It was a good thing that there were a lot of refueling stations around because we reached one just as I ran out of water. I soon found out, though, that stopping to fill my squirt gun made me an easy target. I was a victim without ammo— and fair game. As I stood filling my giant-size yellow and navy-blue super soaker, someone dumped a bucket of ice-cold water over my head. I gasped and screamed but laughed when I saw that the others in our group had also been hit.

Armed again, we headed out. On our way, we passed multiple DJ booths, dance floors, and fill-up stations. We stopped at most of the dances, joining in for a bit before moving on.

Hours later, breakfast had been totally forgotten. So, when hunger threatened to zap our energy, we took a break from the fun and ate. We found a food place and grabbed something quick. As soon as our stomachs were filled, it was back to the action.

We weaved in and out of cars and tried—unsuccessfully—to dodge water attacks. I didn't mind, though. The water war was the most fun I'd had since...ever! All around me people were laughing. I was surrounded by the sound of happiness and never would have imagined having so much fun without alcohol. Wow! Songkran was beyond awesome! I just wish everyone could experience the water festival at least once.

Fun or no, after a while, I finally wore out and headed back to the hostel for a nap. At the door, I was relieved to see my lost bag. "Yes!" Before going in, I peeled off my wet outer clothes, left them there, then hurried—backpack in hand—to the dorm to drop it off, then dashed back down to wring out my drenched clothing. That's when I ran into Madeline. She'd showed up with her hostel mates and a super soaker.

At that point, a nap was not in my immediate future, so I forgot about sleep and focused on play. I put my wet clothes back on, refueled my squirt gun, and filled a bucket with water balloons. I was ready to hit the streets again. This time, with Madeline and her dreaded super soaker.

We targeted mostly those who didn't look wet enough and people who doused—or attempted to douse—us. No one was safe. We squirted passing cars, people on bicycles, little kids, and oldsters. We were equal-opportunity dousers. We refueled from filling stations with ice-cold water. Seeing the look on someone's face when they felt the freeze was priceless.

Sometimes it got a little more personal. Jeremy and I had our own war going. Every time we got within shooting range of each other we'd empty our guns in a one-on-one fight. It was all beyond the most fun I'd ever had, especially when we found a foam party. It had to be the biggest one I'd ever seen. Booming music and showers of froth slowly drifting down on a sea of people—astounding! We danced until we'd had enough then moved on from foamy fun to rejoin the watery war zone on the streets.

At one point, I turned around to ask Madeline something and discovered she was nowhere to be found. I headed back to the foam party to see if she was there but didn't find her, so I backtracked a few blocks. No Madeline. I was a bit concerned but remembered that she was a big girl and could take care of herself. I shrugged and carried on with my battle plan to squirt EVERYONE!

Well into the night, we withdrew for dinner at a tiny street-food place. The vendor station looked well-worn and rundown, but I remembered that sometimes the worse it looks, the better it tastes. Sure enough, it was some of the best Thai food yet—and for next to nothing.

We all squeezed into the tiny tables and chairs on the sidewalk. It was hilarious seeing Chad's 6-foot 4-inch body stuffed in a chair that even some American children would have to squeeze into.

As I dug into the food, flavors exploded in my mouth. The combination of noodles, sprouts, peanuts, spices, and veggies in the pad thai was unbelievable. I knew there was fish sauce in it because of the cooking class I'd taken but was glad I couldn't smell it. That stuff is strong enough to clear a room.

After dinner we headed back toward our hostel to chill for a while. On the way, we grabbed some drinks at the corner market. At the hostel, we listened to music, relaxed for a while, and swapped war stories.

When we were ready to head out again, Jeremy and I wanted to go to a karaoke bar, so we looked up one that seemed perfect. Chad was feeling sick, so he stayed at the hostel. Madeline, who had mysteriously shown up again while we were still in the fray, had something else to do and agreed to meet us there.

Our first disappointment of the night came when we arrived at the karaoke bar. It was closed. Bummed, we walked down the street to a place blaring 90s pop music from a live band. Jeremy and I looked at each other with wide-eyed excitement when they played *Teenage Dirt Bag*. We sang all the words—as if we were on stage. Steven, Kyle, Jeremy, and I did a lot of singing and dancing at that bar.

The one thing that put a chink in it being a perfect place, though, was that the beers there cost four times what they did at a bar across the street. In truth, the beer wasn't that expensive by American standards. I was on a backpacking budget but liked to party hard, and I did so as cheaply as possible. Fortunately, there were no strict laws about alcohol there, so I did a beer run.

Back at the bar, with cheap beers safely secured, I connected to Wi-Fi and let Madeline know the karaoke bar was closed and that she could meet us now at the '90s place down the street or later, at the reggae bar. She joined us for some '90s.

After the band left, so did we. On our way to the reggae place, I mused on how nice it was to be able to leave the bar with my beer and not worry about having to down it before moving on to the next destination.

Hazard 63:
Perfect Last Day and a Slap on the Face

Our last full day at the water festival was so perfect it felt almost surreal—like a scene from a movie. We were all throwing water at each other and everyone else within firing range. It was great, except for when I accidentally swallowed a mouthful of water someone had thrown at me from a bucket. I had a fleeting, *I'm-going-to-be-sick-later* thought.

Overall, I was having the best time of my life. One unforgettable moment stands out from that day. Chad and I had the deliciously evil idea to hop onto the bed of a slow-moving truck and squirt people from there. We got away with it, too, until the owners discovered their uninvited hitchhikers and kicked us off.

Undaunted, we found another truck. This one already had people in back who welcomed us aboard. We especially took pleasure in squirting our hostel mates on the sidewalk—naturally we used the ice-cold water for this.

All the bright, beautiful colors made the day even better. It was like a kaleidoscope had burst over the city and everyone was happy.

I loved that our group hung together—Russel, Kyle, Steven, Jeremy, Chad, Gloria, Blair, Sue, Chad's friends (the bro's), and Madeline. There was a lot of laughter that day. It was one of the most memorable events of all my travels.

That night, people went really crazy! Our troupe grabbed food and headed out to the street for a final hurrah. I stayed with the group because I knew it was probably the last time we would all be together. We danced, drank, talked, and laughed in the overcrowded street.

Madeline hadn't come out with us, but I was sure she'd join us later. When she didn't show, I wondered what happened. Shortly after that, a friend of hers approached and said Madeline was looking for me but didn't know where she was at that moment. I searched for her but the crowds in the street were huge. No sign of her anywhere. I decided to continue celebrating and keep an eye out for her at the same time, thinking that Madeline had a talent for disappearing.

Dale, one of Chad's friends, offered me a beer. I gladly accepted. We were talking about the book *Game of Thrones* and how we were waiting for Martin to finish the next book when *whackkkk!* A girl came up and slapped Dale in the face. Unfortunately, her aim was off and she slapped me too. I'm not sure she even knew because she just turned and stomped away. "What was that?" I shouted while rubbing my face in disbelief.

I looked at Chad. His mouth gaped open as if he was about to inhale an entire sausage. I turned to Dale. "Do you know that girl?"

He got a funny, embarrassed look, tinged with a hint of defiance and said, "I wasn't very nice to her earlier and it appears she's pretty upset about it."

I was not happy about getting hit in the face and walked over to her. "Do you realize you hit me, too?"

I calmed down a bit when I saw her shocked look. She apologized and explained that she'd just snapped because of the degrading things Dale had said to her.

I don't know what he'd said—I didn't want to, but I gave her some sage advice. "Don't let people make you react in a way that could get you into trouble." *Hell,* I thought, *he probably deserved it. The way some guys talk about women is pretty vulgar.*

After the drama was well behind us, I put it out of my mind and danced and partied like the slap never happened. Nothing was going to get in the way of me enjoying my last night in Chiang Mai with friends.

Chad woke me up from a deep sleep by yelling "Taaaam wake up!!! We have to go to the airport."

Foggy brained, I stumbled out of bed, packed my bag, and dropped it off downstairs, then returned to the dorm to say bye to Jeremy, Russel, and Gloria. A little more awake by then, I joined Chad in the lobby.

Giving the manager a huge hug, I let her know I appreciated how sweet and helpful she'd been. Then Chad and I walked to the corner store, picked up some toiletries, and hailed a tuk tuk to take us to the airport. Still swimming in my fuzzy brain, I looked over at Chad who seemed a bit green around the gills and decided that we were either still drunk or hungover. It was hard to tell.

At the airport, we checked in and went through customs then waited at our departure gate. I must have dozed off because something jolted me awake. Looking around, I saw that all the chairs around us were empty. The PA system announced a final announcement to board and called out our names. I nudged Chad a few times. He didn't budge, so I hurried over to the counter and told the attendant we were there and ready to board.

Dashing back to Chad, I lifted his head off the seat, ready to slap him when his bleary eyes creaked open. When I told him we were about to miss our flight to Burma/Myanmar, he said a few choice words and leapt out of his seat. We grabbed our things and rushed to the plane.

Escapade 64:

Become a Celebrity in a Steam Bath City

On our flight to Burma/Myanmar, Chad and I sat next to each other. I was both excited about our trip and hungover. The flight was almost empty, so, since we had plenty of room to spread out, I took a nap, waking up when the flight attendant offered water and snacks.

Someone, talking behind me, sounded like he was from the western United States. Without looking back, I asked, "Are you from the West Coast?"

He was silent a moment then answered in a friendly tone, "No. I'm from Toronto, Canada. The name's Collin." I turned around to see him—tall and thin and with a runner's body. He reminded me of actor Omar Epps in the movie *Love and Basketball.*

After landing and working our way through customs, Chad and I asked Collin if he wanted to share a cab with us. He said yes. Since Mandalay was about an hour away, we were glad to split the fare three ways. Collin seemed like a nice guy and it looked like we had a potential new travel friend.

After withdrawing money from an ATM, the three of us were off to Mandalay. Outside the airport, the unbearable heat hit me like a sledgehammer. After the relatively cool, dry temperature in Chiang Mai, this was a scalding steam bath.

Collin hadn't booked accommodations, so he came with us to Fortune Hotel. Chad and I shared a two-bed room and Collin booked his own. After our trip in the soul-sucking heat, we all needed a power nap before heading out to find food. I was asleep almost as soon as my head hit the pillow.

We woke up rested and refreshed—as much as we could be in the heat—then fetched Collin and headed into the city to find a place to eat. On the streets, people stared at us like we were celebrities—surprised and curious. I figured it was because we looked so different from them. They would point and stare at us then laugh and wave. A lot of people took our pictures or wanted pictures with us. I guess the selfie is a world phenomenon. I loved that these people *liked* us because we were different from them.

We stopped for food at a spot a few blocks from the hotel. I ordered pork with rice that turned out to be just fried pieces of pork with unseasoned white rice. Disappointing, but I ate it because I was really hungry. After having such wonderful, flavor-complex food everywhere else, this was a let-down.

Lunch over, we braved the sweltering heat again to explore the sleepy city. I noticed that nearly everyone wore classical Burmese clothing. I'd never been to any other large city where so many people were in traditional dress.

The men wore a masculine *longyi* (pants-like garment), tied in a side knot to keep it in place, a collarless shirt, and sometimes a head wrap. The women wore blouses that covered their shoulders and most of their arms and a feminine *longyi* (more like an ankle-length skirt). The clothes were made from thick, colorful material with elaborate designs, embroidered with gold and silver thread.

I loved it. One of my favorite things is to be immersed in a traditional culture.

Escapade 65:

Visit the World's Largest Book

We decided it would be cool to see the world's largest book but didn't know where to find it. We asked local people where it was, but since so few locals spoke English, this was a challenge. And there was no sign that read THE WORLD'S LARGEST BOOK. Burma isn't set up for a lot of tourism, so finding the attractions can be a challenge. Frustrating at times but their lack of rampant catering to tourists is one of the reasons I like Burma so much. It's more real.

We walked through the little markets searching for the Book. No luck, so we continued on to the Royal Palace, brick-red and yellow with pointed-cornered roofs and well-manicured lawns that had turned brown in the heat. Still no luck finding the Book, so we gave up.

The next attraction on our "to see" list was the nearby Kuthodaw pagoda. After asking a few people where it was, one person finally directed us to a group of pointy structures—well maintained and painted gold. What a surprise. This housed the world's largest book. There's a good reason we couldn't find it. This book is not bound paper. It is 730 stone slabs (each five feet tall, a half foot wide, and five inches thick) inscribed on both sides with the text of the Theravada Buddhism canon—*Tipitaka*, which means "three baskets," referring to the baskets that held the original Buddhist teachings.

The three of us took plenty of pictures of ourselves with the "book" to capture its size. It was incredible.

After leaving the pagoda, we met brother and sister, Tomen and Cara from Denmark. Both of them are typically Danish with lovely blond hair. We asked if they knew where the hiking trail was that led to the top of Mandalay Hill. Cara checked her map and found it, so all five of us hiked to the top and watched the sunset. This 734-foot hill has been a major Burmese Buddhist pilgrimage site for about two hundred years. In fact, the city of Mandalay got its name from that hill.

When the sunset had faded into night, we hiked back down and asked Cara and Tomen to join us for the evening. They had other plans but agreed to meet us in the morning to tour Mandalay and its neighboring villages.

With all that exploring, we'd worked up an appetite— especially Collin and Chad. They were "brothers from another mother" for sure. Sometimes they would completely nerd out on computer tech-talk or international politics. It seemed like they'd known each other for years. I would just look at them and laugh, happy to not participate in those conversations.

Scouring the town for a dinner place, we spotted a restaurant full of people and decided to check it out. Inside, it looked good and smelled like great food. Collin headed to the buffet to pick out some items then took them to the cook to be barbequed. He brought back a huge plate for us all to share. We also ordered other dishes. The menu was in Burmese, so we pointed at the pictures to tell the server what we wanted.

When our food came, Chad and I busted out in laughter

because we had both ordered the exact same thing we'd had at lunch. That disappointing pork and rice dish was again, staring me in the face. Collin chimed in with, "That's why you never order the same dish." Smug.

Mid-dinner, two guys came up to our table. One of them wore traditional Burmese clothing. His face had thick make-up and vibrant eyelashes. The other guy was dressed in jeans and a t-shirt. Odd but fascinating. They both spoke English and struck up a conversation with us, but it was clear that they really wanted to talk to Chad and Collin. They seemed smitten with them. I felt invisible. Fascinated, I just sat back and watched.

They offered to take us on a tour of the city and gave us tips on things to do. We said something noncommittal. They handed Chad an email and phone number and said he hoped we'd keep in touch. After they left, I just stared at him with a huge grin on my face. He smiled and rolled his eyes.

Anxious for the next bit of fun, I mentioned that I'd read about the Moustache Brothers and their must-see show in *Lonely Planet*. Chad said he'd read an article about the show and suggested we go.

Back at the hotel, the front desk filled us in with more details. The Moustachze Brothers, actual brothers Par Par Lay and Lu Maw, and their cousin, Lu Zaw, spent nearly seven years in prison for criticizing the Burmese totalitarian military regime.

After their release, they were put on house arrest and were only allowed to perform their show for tourists from their home's garage in Mandalay.

The performance was great. It included jokes and criticism about the Burmese government and traditional dances, songs, and stories performed by family members. How could we resist?

I met Lu Maw after the show. He asked where I was from. When I told him I was from the United States, he seemed really excited and told me he was a big fan of President Obama then bragged that he and Obama looked very much alike. *Not so much,*

I thought. Other than dark skin, I didn't see the resemblance. Lu Maw said he wanted to give the First Lady, Michelle a kiss on the cheek because POTUS gave *his* wife a kiss on the cheek during a visit to Burma. Not sure if he was serious or not, I stifled a laugh.

Lu Maw scanned Chad from head to toe and back again, commented on his towering height, and asked him where he was from. He said he liked Chad's Australian accent then told him to take care of me. Traditional values, I guess.

He asked Collin where he was from and when he said Canada, Lu Maw commented that Canadians were nice and that it was a beautiful country.

I'm glad that I was able to experience that performance and meet the family. Sadly, Par Par Lay died in 2013 from kidney disease, probably from the lead paint on the walls of a water tank he drank from during his arrest. The others continue to perform.

I have collected foreign currency since my first international trip and wanted to add some currency from a country that had been isolated until 2011. I bought a few 1950s and 1960s Burmese bills from Lu Maw. They had, "from the Bank of Burma" printed on them. Burma became Myanmar in 1989 making the Burma money collectible.

After the show, we headed into town on our way to the hotel. The Burmese had been celebrating a water festival just like in Thailand, so there were still a few squirters around and we were easy targets. I didn't mind at all. Even though it was well into the night, the air was still hot, and a cool-to-cold dousing felt really good.

At the hotel, we tried to buy water, but our money denominations were too large for them to give us change, so we started a tab.

We climbed the mahogany steps to our room then gathered to plan our trip for the next day. It turned out that the cheapest way to explore Mandalay was to hire a driver.

Plans set, Chad and I watched a few episodes of the *Chappelle Show* and died laughing then decided it was time to turn in for the night. I read some of the book I'd picked up in Sagada. It was about alleged UFOs and government cover ups in the 1940s and '50s that led to the unexplained disappearance of a lot of people. I wish I could remember the name of the book because it was so interesting, I had a hard time putting it down.

For breakfast the next day, I met Collin on the rooftop. Chad wanted to sleep a little longer so he didn't join us. I ordered fried eggs, toast, fruit, and coffee. The view from the roof was wonderful and we soaked in the sight of the landscape. Collin thought it was awesome and took as many pictures as he could.

After eating, we went down to fetch Chad but before we got there Cara and Tomen joined us and we gathered forces to wake him up. We shook him and called his name. Finally, he groaned and snorted, "Wha?"

I said, "If you're going to join us today, get up and meet us in the lobby."

Bleary-eyed, he moaned and mumbled something like, "Okay. See you in a few minutes."

Escapade 66:

Hustling, Fake Monk and Lost in a Banana Farm

Driver-guide hired, our first stop in Mandalay was Sagaing, the home of Sagaing Hill, one of the most important in the world for Buddhism. The devout swarm there for religious and meditation retreats. This place has around six hundred monasteries and convents, over six thousand monks and nuns, and is home to numerous pagodas. Its most famous one, Soon u Ponya Shin Paya, was built in 1312 and sits on top of the mountain.

Our guide dropped us off at the base of Sagaing Hill and said he would be back to pick us up later.

Step after step we climbed in sweltering heat, stopping at various pagodas to admire them and take an occasional rest. As we continued upward, sweat dripped down my back.

We passed several monks making their way down after having gone to the top to pray or give alms, but there was one odd monk I'll never forget. He wore the standard brown robe and like all monks, his head was shaved. He approached us on the steps and asked us for a donation. He then took out a pack of cigarettes and lit one up. We told him we didn't have any kyat (pronounced *chaught*). This didn't seem to bother him and he continued down the steps asking others for money.

This annoyed me at a deep level. Monks—real ones—don't ask for money. Most travel books warn about fake monks. I guess these charlatans count on gullible tourists who haven't read those warnings.

I didn't want this incident to spoil my day, so I just shrugged, glad no one in our little group gave him anything.

My favorite pagoda was U Min Thonze, situated in a crescent-shaped cave-like structure. It is famous for its gallery of forty-five gilded Buddhas lining a crescent corridor.

The higher we climbed the better the view. I'm always excited when I reach the top of a mountain—it means my strenuous hike is over and I can relax and enjoy an amazing view just waiting to take my breath away.

When we reached the top of Sagaing Hill, I wasn't disappointed. A spectacular view opened up for us of the Irrawaddy River and the Yadanadon and Inwa bridges that lay across it. In the distance, opposite the river, I gaped in awe and admiration at the lush green vegetation dotted with stupas and monasteries. I especially remember the Soon u Ponya Shin Pagoda with its giant Gautama Buddha. It sits on a frog-shaped hill, which is how it got its name. It also solved the mystery of the frog-shaped donation box. Best of all, though, it's covered in glass tiles that sparkle in the sunlight.

When done exploring, we stopped at a little restaurant on the hill to rest and have something to drink then headed down the steps. It took about thirty minutes to reach the bottom.

I was glad to see our driver waiting to take us to the next destination. He drove us to a restaurant just outside the river-crossing to Inwa village. The food was excellent. I ordered dried chili pork. It wasn't actually dry but a sauce covered the pork dish. The menu was in English, so I knew it was a place that catered mostly to tourists. I had a suspicion that our taxi driver got some kind of commission for bringing us there. But the food was good, and not too overpriced, so I didn't mind.

After lunch we hiked down the riverbank to a small ferry and boarded for a two-minute journey across the river to Inwa. This place was definitely set up for tourists. Horse carriages filled the streets and we were inundated with offers to take us anywhere we wanted to go. But we all agreed that we'd prefer to walk and explore. One carriage though didn't want to take no for an answer and followed us for about twenty minutes, probably hoping we'd get tired and ask him for a ride. I admired his tenacity, but it wasn't going to work on us. Eventually, he gave up.

This was a beautiful place and bigger than I'd thought it would be. When a sudden rainstorm hit, we were lucky to be near the lovely and well-maintained Me Nu Ok Kyaung Pagoda. It was the perfect shelter from the storm. We all watched the hard rain beat down on the stone from the open-air windows. It was bewitching. The downpour lasted for about thirty minutes then the sun came out and the clouds disappeared.

We decided to walk along a muddy, puddle-filled dirt road to see where it would take us. Such intrepid explorers, Indiana Jones had nothing on us. Green bushes and plants grew along the roadsides and chickens, cows, and pigs freely roamed around. I liked this place.

After a while, we came on a sign that read WATCH TOWER and continued, curious about what that meant. It turned out to be a massive tower standing in a copse of small trees.

Very cool.

We wanted to climb the crumbling stairs to the top, but it was closed—probably because the staircase was falling apart and held up by a wooden post that looked like a light breeze would blow it over, collapsing the whole staircase, and maybe the tower with it. After considering the danger versus the adventure factor, we decided not to risk it.

The Royal Palace was nearby but sadly, in ruins. Still, it was interesting to see what was left of it. The most striking thing was the massive royal swimming pool that had been used by the Princess. I imagined it full of water on a warm summer day and thought it would have been a beautiful place to relax and cool off.

Wandering around, we stopped to see the deep, burgundy-red, brick Yadana Hsimi Pagodas. They are surrounded with a brick wall and enclosed by palm trees and a variety of tropical plants. Built in the early 1400s, they were damaged by an earthquake in 1485 but rebuilt. In 2012 they were left to decay into ruins.

We dinked around there for a bit then continued along the road and into the unknown, which led us to a farm in the middle of nowhere. Tall banana trees grew everywhere and I felt like I was on a remote island, untouched by the rest of the world. As we walked along, the "forest" grew thicker. By the time we thought about turning around to go back, we were lost. There were only three hours before the last ferry of the day would leave the island and we needed to be on it. How? We didn't know which way to go, let alone how far it was to the horse-and-carriage filled town we started out in.

The thick and humid air was a haven for swarms of flying bugs trying to feast on our sweat and blood every chance they got. We almost collapsed in relief when we finally found what looked like a well-traveled and maintained trail. Following it through a field dotted with grazing cows, it took us to an area with a few small local shops. No time to stop, though. Still lost, we kept on, hoping to find a clue that would tell us where we were.

After about an hour, we came upon a weathered building in the middle of a paddy field, surrounded by banana trees and bright-green tropical plants. This was the Bagaya Monastery.

Built in the 1500s, it had been seriously damaged in an 1821 fire. Most of the building had been restored but it still felt ancient with its elaborate Burmese carvings, artwork, large teakwood pillars, and the gold-trimmed décor that lined the pointed rooftop along with statues of the Buddha.

As I walked around Bagaya, the wood creaked under my feet reminding me of its age. It gave me goose bumps. We didn't stay long to gawk. It was important to keep moving but none of us knew where we were in relation to the shore, so how long it would take us was impossible to gauge. At that point we had less than forty-five minutes before the last ferry would shove off.

We finally managed to reach a familiar area that looked like the touristy spot where we'd refused the carriage ride but we couldn't be sure.

Now, though, there was no horse and carriage in sight, so we dashed down the road. I spotted a carriage and we tried to get the driver's attention. He moved past us as if we were invisible and I thought maybe it was the driver we'd ignored earlier and he was snubbing us. We followed it, hoping it would lead us in the right direction, but eventually it disappeared into the distance.

Still not ready to give up, we continued on the muddy road through rice paddies and farms with cows, chickens, and smoke coming out of chimneys. I liked that it was quiet and peaceful but wondered if we would have to swim across the river to get back to our taxi.

We came upon a small, well-kept cluster of tourist shops and found a parked horse and carriage. We asked him for a ride to the water's edge.

I sat up front with the driver. The others rode in back. Putting my concern about missing the ferry aside, I enjoyed the fifteen-minute ride to the riverbank.

Arriving just in time to see the ferry pulling away, we yelled and waved our hands to get the captain's attention, but it kept going. We glanced at each other in disbelief, but Chad hadn't given up. He kept yelling, waving, and jumping in the air. His only reward was a comical pratfall in the mud. I laughed so hard my sides hurt—until he pulled me down with him. We all started laughing and it turned into a fun, all-out, take-no-prisoners mud fight.

All was not lost, though, another ferry showed up. We marched our mud-caked bodies aboard, relieved to be on our way back across the river.

The day's adventure behind us, we cleaned up at the hotel then went out for dinner where we bid Tomen and Cara farewell. Chad promised them we would meet up for their birthday shenanigans in Yangon in a few weeks.

We ventured out for a little night-exploring but there wasn't much to do, so we stargazed. Mandalay is a quiet, dark place at night. There aren't many streetlights, the shops and restaurants close early and no one else was outside at that hour. I don't know if it is always that way, though. It could have been because it was a holiday week.

Back at the hotel, I called home for the first time in a long time. My dad answered. I was glad to hear his voice and he sounded happy to hear mine. I told him about my time in Thailand at Songkran and about all my new friends. I talked about my travel friends, Chad and Collin, and that we were in Burma and planning to take a night train to Bagan to visit the pagodas.

Chad, who was sitting close to me, grabbed the phone and said hello and something else I'm sure he thought clever and charming, but Chad has a thick Australian accent, so the message was probably not understood. I told Dad to send Mom my love and that I would call as soon as I had Wi-Fi again. I packed my bag. Chad and I watched some YouTube videos then went to sleep anticipating a good trip to Bagan.

Escapade 67:

Worst Train Ride of My Life

The next day, we weren't in a hurry and lost track of time until it was almost too late to catch our train. Grabbing our things, we sprinted to the station then tried to figure out where the train to Bagan would depart and where the ticket counter was. Asking around, we were directed—twice—to the wrong ticket counters. The third time, luckily, was the right one. The low ticket price was a pleasant surprise and I forgot about how difficult it'd been to find the right place. The fare was equivalent to about $1.30 US for a twelve-hour train ride.

While we waited to board, we met Maggie from France, Amelia from Spain, and Bridget from Scotland—I loved her dark straight hair, golden brown eyes, and thick Scottish accent. They were also heading to Bagan, so when the train arrived, we all sat together.

Looking around at the odd seating, I understood why tickets were inexpensive. The tan seats stood straight up like church pews and were evenly spaced between the windows. Chad and

Collin sat opposite me and faced forward—the direction we traveled. There was no air conditioning, so it was stifling hot and our car was starting to smell. I put my feet up on the window ledge to feel the cool air on my legs, but cautious Chad insisted I take them down for safety reasons.

As I tried to settle in, I reflected that it was going to be a long, uncomfortable ride. Our seats, obviously made for smaller people, didn't recline, the lights wouldn't go off, and the air was hot and sticky. Grumble, grumble. It was almost comical, though, to see Chad and Collin scrunching their long legs up against the seats in front of them. Collin turned on his iPad and focused on watching some *Game of Thrones* episodes. With nothing else to entertain us, we huddled up to watch with him.

The most annoying things about that ride were that the horn blasted every fifteen seconds or so, making it impossible to get any sleep, and at crossings, the guards had to lift the safety gates manually. Thinking back on it now, it seems more funny than annoying.

As I was mentally grousing, Chad asked me something. When I turned to answer, an untrimmed tree branch from outside the open window smacked him dead in the face! I'm ashamed to say that even though I was concerned, I found it comical. I laughed then caught myself and changed to concern. He looked a bit dazed but said he was okay. I was glad of that and grateful he'd made me take my feet off the window ledge.

Together we pulled down the shade to prevent that from happening again. Unfortunately doing that made it even hotter in the car. Chad and Collin eventually stretched out on the floor and I laid along the benches. I put in earplugs and slipped on an eye mask to try to get some sleep. Real sleep never came but I drifted in and out of consciousness enough to get some rest. One of the worst train rides of my life and I thought, *You most certainly get what you pay for.*

Hazard 68:

Ambushed at a Hidden Check Point

When a train conductor came up to us and spouted something in Burmese, we thought he might be telling us we'd arrived at our stop. Without being completely sure, we got off along with some of the other passengers.

Outside, I had a moment of panic when I glanced at my watch and saw that it was 3 a.m.—four hours earlier than it should be for our destination. I suddenly realized that we might not be in Bagan after all. The only thing to do was to find the town and get more information.

A man approached in a van and offered to give us a ride to Bagan. *Good,* I thought, *we are in the right place.* Transportation schedules in this part of the world are often more a suggestion than a fact.

We negotiated a fair price for all of us—Collin, Chad, Amelia, Maggie, Bridget, and me. After about ten minutes of driving down the road in inky darkness, he stopped and the van was immediately surrounded by a group of men. I bit my lip and thought, *This can't be good.*

One of the men opened the door and counted the people inside. I felt tension creep up my spine. He demanded that each of us pay the kyat equivalent to $20 US. We had no idea why he was asking for it, so we refused. The driver sounded panicked and annoyed as he insisted we pay up. In an over-the-top drama-voice, he said it was required by the government as an entrance fee into Bagan and insisted that the money was to help preserve the temples.

I wasn't completely convinced but recognized that we really had no other option. Grudgingly, I pulled out the fee and thought, *Why didn't they say that first? I wouldn't have been so scared, thinking it might be my last day on earth.*

After we all paid, they handed us tickets that were good for four days. I wondered, sarcastically, what would happen after that. Would they sacrifice us on the altar of some ancient temple for being freeloaders? More likely, they would boot us out of town, or worse, throw us in jail to rot or be held for ransom.

Escapade 69:

A Pagoda to Myself and
Lost on a Bike

Before our van arrived in town, Amelia suggested we have the driver take us to two of the most famous pagodas in the area. We all thought this a great idea, since it was the middle of the night and we'd have them all to ourselves.

The driver might have thought we were looney to want to visit pagodas at that time, but he didn't say so and off we went.

Manned only with headlamps, we stepped into the first temple. The cool, quiet, stillness of the old, red-brick place seemed to echo its centuries of existence. The musty air smelled faintly of incense. That, coupled with the quiet, made for an awesome, eerie atmosphere. It was a completely different experience from trekking through during the heat of the day with crowds of noisy tourists. I loved it. We explored hallways, openings, floors, crevices, tunnels, and stairways—just about anywhere open to the public. I regret not taking pictures, though. They would have been incredible!

After poking into every nook and cranny we could, we headed back to the van for the trip to the second pagoda to explore and watch the sunrise from its rooftop.

After removing our shoes (only bare feet allowed in temples), we wandered around, oohing and gawking. The staggering immensity of this place gave me a sense of its power and age. I vividly remember the feel of cool brick under my feet. Since so little in Burma is cold, this felt *really* good.

In the dark, lit by our headlamps, the shadows on the stairs, the large entryways, and the elaborate Burmese art seemed to come alive.

When we discovered corridors that led to several ascending staircases, we each climbed a separate one. They all led to the roof but came out at different spots.

It was still pitch dark, so after carefully exploring the "top of the world," we gathered together, faced east, and waited for the sunrise. I stretched out on my back to watch the stars fade out of view and disappear into the dawn as it slowly crept over the sky.

In the grey twilight before sunrise, I sat up and gazed at the landscape below. Silhouettes of what seemed to be hundreds of pagodas sprinkled across a desert dotted with trees.

When the sun first peeked its fiery orange head above the salmon-colored clay earth, I sat mesmerized and dazzled by the breathtaking sight of Bagan bathed in a golden glow and suddenly knew why people from all over the world traveled there. How many others over the centuries, I wondered, had come to this rooftop at dawn and marveled at the same beauty filling my senses in that moment?

We took at least a thousand photos. Sadly, no photo can completely capture the extraordinary landscape like seeing it in person and having the place all to ourselves.

Our trance-bubble burst when a busload of tourists pulled up in front. Show over, we realized how hungry and tired we were. Pushing to our feet we reluctantly descended a staircase and left our fairy castle behind.

Just outside the entrance, the tourists heading toward us stared at our motley crew with curiosity. It didn't matter, we all felt content and a little smug at having had an incredible, private time with such magnificence.

After the driver dropped us off in town, we scouted for a breakfast spot and found one right away. I ordered my customary fried eggs, coffee, fruit, and toast. As usual, I cut out the egg yolks and put them on Collin and Chad's plate. In Laos, I tried telling a server that I only wanted egg whites, but he either didn't understand, or thought the request so insane he didn't believe me. I stopped asking for it after that.

Stomachs full, it was time to turn our attention toward finding somewhere to stay for the week. We headed for a place that Bridget suggested. It turned out to be perfect for us—and affordable, so we checked in. Once settled, we all napped until about mid-day, visions of Bagan at sunrise dancing in our heads.

Waking up rested and ready to explore the town, one of us had the brilliant idea to rent bicycles. We all agreed and marched to the rental place to pick out our wheels.

It was so much fun. The six of us peddled around the area, visiting every temple we saw, took pictures, raced to the nearest pagoda, sang Disney songs, and enjoyed each other's company. Whenever the intense heat got to us, we stopped for water and a moment to cool off before heading out to the next site.

The bricks outside the pagodas' entrances were scorching hot, so after taking off our shoes, we would run like firewalkers, rushing to get inside before blistering our feet.

All the pagodas in Bagan are red brick. Even though they're hundreds of years old, they are well preserved. I noticed that some of the walls even showed parts of the original painted murals. I thought maybe the entrance fee really did go to maintain the temples.

Each pagoda is unique, and they range in size from massive, with several entrances, windows, corridors, passageways, and levels, to tiny, with a single entrance and shared exit.

After having traveled for hours to complete our first loop around the temples, it was time for dinner. We headed into town to return the bikes and find somewhere to eat.

The place we chose offered a dish I'd never had—tea leaf salad. It's made with dried green tea leaves, fresh vegetables, peanuts, and an amazing dressing. It was delicious. We also ordered nearly everything else on the menu and shared. After that meal, Burmese food topped the list of my favorite cuisine.

Next, we walked to a local bar, ordered 30-cent beers, and played cards—Irish Snap and Rummy. Chad and I combined our personal game-rules to create a super, new game. It was fantastic! We kept a running tally of our scores. Chad was in the lead and he proudly let everyone know it.

When it was time to head back to the hotel, we talked about what a great day and a fun night it had been. Inside, we went straight to our rooms for a good night's sleep.

🍽️ 🍽️ 🍽️

The next morning, Bridget and I got up before the boys. We decided not to wake them and had breakfast together in the hotel restaurant, which offered mouthwatering choices—several kinds of omelets, fried eggs, pancakes, French toast, yogurt, cereal, oatmeal, bacon, sausage, fruit, bread, and coffee, juice, or tea.

While munching down on the wonderful food, Bridget and I talked about travel plans and how great the pagodas were. I could see she had something else on her mind, though, and after a moment of hesitation, she asked me how I could stand to be around Chad. She thought he was vulgar, disrespectful, and the most womanizing guy she'd ever met.

I mulled that over a moment then shared with her that I saw those behaviors in him, too, but realized he acted that way, sometimes, to get a reaction. For whatever reason, he liked to do that. So, when he sensed her discomfort at his bad-boy behavior, he revved it up to get a stronger reaction. Twisted? Maybe. With me, though, Chad dropped all that and acted like a grown-up, well maybe a semi-grown up, but none of the vulgar rudeness came through. He was friendly and funny, and we had actual conversations. I'm not sure why he was so odd around others. Not my job to judge, I guess.

I wasn't sure if my explanation helped Bridget or not. She didn't say. I did hope she understood that his behavior wasn't a personal attack on her. Now, I wonder what would have happened if she'd turned the tables and volleyed back. Maybe, he was just looking for a worthy opponent. Or not.

The boys finally rolled out of bed and joined us for breakfast on the covered patio. As soon as they sat down the skies opened up, dumped buckets of rain, and blasted thunder that shook the building. I accused them of causing it. Yeah, Thor and Zeus at their best.

I loved the smell of the rain as it pelted the concrete and filled my senses with earthy, wet aromas. Then just as I was really getting into the whole Zen of the experience, the power blinked out. So much for exploring town that morning, but all agreed that we weren't going to let it spoil our good time and decided to play cards until the storm let up.

I hurried back to the room for my playing cards. First, though, I headed into the bathroom in our dorm and was slammed with a sight I can only describe as—UGH!!—a dysfunctional toilet. Chad had been the last one down, so I had a few unpleasant thoughts about him. *How did he break the toilet? Danggg.... Chad??? And why didn't he call housekeeping to have it fixed?* But there was no use just standing there and griping. I called the front desk and asked for it to be repaired or give us a new one. They said they'd take care of it.

Still annoyed, I used the bathroom in Bridget and Collin's room then, cards in hand, headed back to the group.

Putting my disgruntled fuming behind me, I sat down to enjoy myself. We played rummy for a few hours and Chad was in the lead. But after a while his crown as lead-gamer toppled when two others scored more total points. Chad didn't like to lose. I looked at him, wondering if he was going to make a scene. Fortunately, although he didn't like not being top dog, he wasn't too much of a dick about it.

When the rain finally let up, we decided to rent electric bikes this time and ride around the big loop to see the other temples in Bagan. Amelia and Maggie didn't join us because they'd planned something else to do first.

This loop was long but our powered bicycles made the ride a lot easier. We explored all day, popping in and out of temples and burning the bottoms of our feet on the scalding bricks. Close to the halfway point we came to a massive pagoda or temple— several levels high and with multiple passageways, staircases, windows, and corridors.

Climbing to the topmost level to get a daylight glimpse of old Bagan from up high, we were rewarded with a spectacular view. But what made me smile the most was when Chad befriended some children. He let them climb all over him like he was a human jungle gym. It was so cute. In that moment, my mind flashed on what Bridget had said about him being a boorish knuckle-dragger and wondered at the two extreme sides of his personality.

We took the stairs back to the ground floor and were ready to leave when a kid approached and asked if we had foreign bills or coins to add to his collection. I gave him a US quarter. Chad handed him some Aussie currency. Collin gave the boy a Canadian dollar and Bridget contributed a 1-pound coin.

The boy grinned from ear to ear and proudly showed us his collection, pointing out the foreign currency still missing. He had a long way to go. We expressed how impressed we were and gave him encouragement to continue searching. He was a cool kid.

Leaving the pagoda, we continued along the loop and ran into Amelia and Maggie who joined us for the rest of our ride. First, though, we stopped at a vendor just outside the temple and refreshed with some fruit juice. It was the best lemonade I'd ever had.

On the way back to the hotel I somehow found myself alone—separated from the group and lost. Taking a breath, I thought, *Okay. Don't worry. Keep going and you'll eventually find the others.* Feeling more centered and confident—sort of—I pushed off and continued on the path. Sure enough, I eventually spotted Amelia and Maggie ahead of me and followed them as they rode back into town. On the way, my bike broke down. I was some distance behind the others and the wind was blowing too hard for them to hear me when I called out.

I reminded myself that there was no reason to worry. I could handle this. I left the bike on the side of the road and walked to a nearby hotel to ask them to call the bike agency and request a new one for me. That done, I headed back to my no-go bike. I must live under a lucky star. Less than five minutes later, Chad and Collin showed up. Chad stayed with me while I waited for the new bike to arrive. When it did, I told him to go on and that I'd follow in just a minute.

Of course, after he was out of sight, I discovered that the *new* bike wouldn't start. *Sheesh!* What the hell was going on? Fortunately, the bike's owner was still there. He fiddled around for a few minutes with what I thought was false confidence but somehow, he got it to start. Good. I was off and on my way back to town.

At the hotel, I turned in the bike, cleaned up a bit, then joined my friends for dinner. Bridget and Amelia had discovered an amazing restaurant that served authentic Burmese food. More importantly, though, it offered tea leaf salad.

While we waited at our table for service, Bridget and I walked to the bus station to get tickets to Inle Lake for a few days later. From the start, the agency owner tried to cheat us, but I wasn't having it. I was tired of being ripped off and told him so. He loudly protested his innocence. I raised my voice to match his and finally put my foot down and told him, "You either want our business or not. If you do, give us a fair price." After a few feeble attempts to defend his "honesty," he finally recognized he'd met his match and sold us four reasonably priced tickets.

When we arrived back at the restaurant, I was still a bit annoyed and told the rest of the group what had happened. They understood my frustration and shared their own stories about being cheated. That unpleasantness behind us, we all cheered to friendship and long travels as we sipped our drinks. We ordered dried chili pork, cucumber salad, tea leaf salad, curry, and an assortment of other delicious food.

The restaurant was upscale. Our table looked like a movie set with its beautifully colored cloth and mats embroidered with intricate patterns. The red, blue, yellow, and purple plates and bowls had intricate designs in white. Shiny, exotic lamps covered the ceiling, and the walls were draped with rugs similar to those in India. The ambience, as well as the charming little town, made the evening perfect.

Escapade 70:

An Aussie's First Squirrel And Strange Canoes

For a few more days we biked around Bagan, popping in and out of temples and museums, eating at a new restaurant every night, and playing our own version of Rummy.

At the Bagan Archaeological Museum, Collin, Bridget, Chad, and I were the tourist attraction. Groups of locals came up wanting to take our pictures and say hello. I felt a little like a rare and exotic exhibit. It was fun.

What wasn't so fun was Chad and Collin nearly boring me to death with nonstop talk about world politics. I know global events are important, but there's a time and place for a political bitch-fest and I felt that a museum was definitely *not* one of them.

I was taught that museums are quiet places to enjoy the exhibits and learn, but apparently not everyone had that same upbringing. Bridget went her own way straight from the start. I thought she might have been feeling the same way I did about talking politics in a museum. I tried to go off on my own, but it turned out to be a futile attempt. Chad and Collin were like magnets seeking metal. They found me no matter how far away I ventured. It was more than annoying. I swear they could talk for hours without coming up for air.

Eventually I managed to escape them. Off I went without a CNN debate shadowing me and found Bridget in the Buddha room—my favorite part of the museum—filled with hundreds of Buddha statues, some dating back to ancient times. They displayed a variety of Buddha's postures and poses. The one I noticed most was the Earth pose. The Buddha sits, legs crossed right over left with the bottom of his right foot facing the sky, his right hand touching the ground, and his left hand resting palm up on his right leg.

My favorite posture is the one where Buddha is cutting off his ponytail. He holds his long, dark hair in his left hand while chopping it off with a sword in his right hand. There are many Buddha postures and mudras (Buddha's hand positions), including the Teaching Buddha, Meditating Buddha, Turning the Wheel of Dharma, and more.

Bridget and I enjoyed learning and practicing the postures and mudras. We were there for at least an hour before Chad and Collin showed up, chattering on about who knows what. I silently chastised myself for staying so long in the Buddha room that the boys found us. When they got close enough to hear, I whispered, "Quiet in the museum."

They just smiled, a bit indulgently, and kept talking, so I shrugged and decided to let it go. They were clueless.

Bridget and I, followed by the chatter-monkeys, left Buddha behind and walked to a spacious room in the back corner of the building that had a huge window nearly spanning the entire wall. From there we were treated to a spectacular view that included beautiful trees and an abandoned structure of some kind.

Out of nowhere Chad shouted, "A squirrel!" His outburst was so loud, it almost gave the three of us a heart attack. He turned around, wide-eyed and grinning like he'd just seen a UFO offering candy. "It's a squirrel—guys, check it out!"

Chad had never seen a squirrel before. They're so common in most parts of the world, I'd never even considered that a grown man might never have seen one, and thought, *Don't they have squirrels where he comes from?* I later learned that squirrels are not native to Australia and were introduced to the western part of the country in the 19th century. They are considered environmentally dangerous intruders. *Huh?* Watching Chad eagerly watch the creature's every move was hilarious. I even captured a few pics for him, glad I was around to witness Chad's first furry rodent.

As it turned out, there were a lot of squirrels in the area and we spotted them all day. Chad couldn't have been happier.

It's the little things that make life worthwhile.

When it was time for us to leave beautiful Bagan behind, we checked out of the hotel and enjoyed a delicious breakfast while waiting for our bus to Inle Lake, excited about the trip. I was especially looking forward to swimming in beautiful freshwater and breathing crisp mountain air. Inle Lake would be 20 degrees cooler than in Bagan and I pictured it as clean and majestic, nestled between huge mountains with towering pine trees littering the area—similar to Lake Arrowhead in California. I was so looking forward to getting out of the stifling heat.

When our bus arrived, there were just enough seats left for the four of us, Collin and Bridget sat together, and Chad and I sat in the two seats in front of them. The trip was about 187 miles which should have taken three hours. Of course, it took longer because the bus made several stops along the way.

On the ride, I read, took a nap, woke up and read some more, then napped again, waking up just in time to witness the girl in front of me vomit into a bag. *Not Awesome,* I thought as I plugged my nose and turned up the volume on my headphones, hoping she would feel better soon.

The show really started, though, when the driver slammed on the brakes and a sleeping man catapulted out of his seat and smacked straight into Chad.

No one was hurt, and I howled with laughter along with many of the other passengers.

Thanks to that incident, I met Emily, from England, and Nigel, from Northern Ireland. When we arrived at Inle Lake, they joined our group of intrepid explorers. Our new friends had already booked accommodation but went with us as we shopped around to find the perfect spot.

Inle Lake is a quaint, small place. Some of the roads are paved but not maintained very well. The people appeared to live simple lives—very different from Mandalay.

After choosing a place to stay, we checked in, dropped our packs, and went out to discover the town. One of the first interesting things I saw was children playing soccer in an open field. We stopped and watched for a while then continued on.

A short time later, we turned our attention to food. Discovering a tiny restaurant filled with locals, we agreed it looked good and smelled like heaven.

I ordered chicken, pork, and seafood kabobs as my main meal and as a group we decided to share dried chicken chili, tea leaf salad, mango salad, cucumber salad, tomato salad, rice, and an assortment of other delicious, colorful food.

When we'd finished our feast, we strolled around town admiring the dark, clear sky, filled with illuminating balls of gas. When the others turned in for the night, I was still full of energy, so I went in search of the actual lake but it proved too elusive.

I settled for a small pond we'd passed earlier. The pond reflected the sky like a mirror. It was incredible. I stood transfixed in the silence and the eerie, yet perfect darkness.

The next day, I got up excited to finally see the actual Inle Lake. Waiting was torture. I could already feel the cool water on my skin.

After breakfast, Collin, Chad, Bridget, and I hired a boat to tour the lake and the neighboring villages. Our boat turned out to be a canoe with a motor. The lake was bigger than I'd expected, and completely different from what I'd imagined. No pine forest like at Lake Arrowhead, but amazing scenery of floating gardens, wooden structures, and homes on rickety stilts to keep them above the water.

Fishermen in canoe-like boats propelled across the lake by wrapping a leg around a tall oar, resembling a flamingo perched on one leg. It looked difficult and I thought it must take a lot of strength and discipline. Some of the boats carried produce, others had fish, and some covered their cargo in large gray tarps. On land, weather-worn, spikey stupas dotted the hills.

Inle Lake is extremely shallow in places and occasionally the propellers of passing motorized boats kicked up a lot of mud. The engine in ours looked like it belonged on a lawn mower. A long, metal rod connected it to the propeller. People in that part of the world are certainly creative engineers.

To my disappointment, the lake was too shallow, muddy, and heavily trafficked for swimming. As our canoe-like boat cruised to a monastery, I let go of wanting to swim and decided to just enjoy the rest of the tour.

The Nga Phe Kyaung monastery was built in the 1850s and is completely made of wood. It rests on stilts to keep it just out of the water's reach. It has beautiful, gold statues and, most impressively, a 200-year-old Buddha. This monastery was originally known for having jumping cats. The monks trained the cats to jump through hoops. Even though the tradition had stopped years before, plenty of cats still live there. The old wooden structure was fascinating. We dinked around for a while enjoying the sculptures and artwork. Bridget spread a blanket on the floor, and we all sat down and ordered tea.

During our tea party some of the cats came by for a visit. They surrounded us. Bridget looked like she was in heaven but the boys were indifferent. I was delighted but a bit concerned about getting cat hair in my drink.

After tea we headed back for our "cruise" to the next destination. Getting in and out of the small boat was risky. At one point I worried it would capsize. That didn't happen, so I guess the Buddha must have been looking out for us.

Escapade 71:

Floating Village Garden and Farm

After the monastery, our next stop at Inle Lake was Ywama village where all the houses are on stilts and everything is made from bamboo and tree branches. Each house looked incredibly old but still standing strong and the people still live in them. They are all one-level but of varying lengths. Most have large, covered porches or decks. Each has a set of stairs underneath that lead to a small boat dock.

A boat is a necessity there. It's the only way to get around since the waterway serves as a brown, liquid road with all the homes lining each side of it. Fascinating—sort of an Asian Venice.

Children waved from some of the houses and we waved back. We also saw a lot of dogs on the decks. I was curious about how the animals got around or if they just stayed at the houses all day. I noticed wooden walkways on some of the homes leading to other parts of the floating village and thought that could be how the dogs got around, but from what I saw, most of the people who live on Inle Lake travel solely by canoe.

When our water-world tour was finished, we walked around the village and checked out a few of the shops. The lake was calm, and the village, hushed and quiet. After a while, our guide took us to his village, which was similar to Ywama. We met his mother, who gave us delicious, homemade treats. I loved seeing the inside of a traditional Burmese home. I'm always so curious about how people of a different culture live.

After lunch we went to, in my opinion, the best spot on the lake—the floating garden—incredible. Hundreds of long rows of vegetation look like they grow right out of the water. And, in a way, they do. The food grows out of large dirt mounds surrounded by water. The rows of growing fruits and vegetables sport bright green tops that look like they erupted out of a muddy, water-volcano.

We wove up and down the rows admiring their structure and beauty. Occasionally, fish would pop out of the lake, do a flip, and dive back in.

This place is incredible. Farmers travel by boat all day, every day, tending their crops. It seemed, to me, like such a simple and happy life.

Escapade 72:

Bicycle Race and
a Mystery Monastery

I opened my eyes the next morning—as I did nearly every day on this leg of my journey—with Chad shaking my shoulder and reminding me that he was my personal alarm and wondering how I had survived without him.

I could have told him to stop and just set an alarm like I did before we'd met, but I liked having him wake me—much nicer than being jolted awake by loud digital noise. I think he liked being my "personal awakener." Once, when he groused about it, I told him he could stop, and I'd start setting my alarm, but he ignored me and kept on shaking my shoulder each morning. Chad is a nice guy but, for some mysterious reason, he didn't want others to know it. I felt good that he let me in on his secret, true self.

We met Bridget and Collin downstairs for breakfast, and everyone did their usual morning Facebook browsing, emailing our family and friends, or writing postcards. After that, Emily and Nigel met us outside the hotel. They had their bicycles and were ready to go. I love cycling. It's one of my favorite activities and, in "real" life, I don't do it enough. My bicycle had a bell and a basket, so I loaded up my bag and water. Chad's bike didn't have a basket, so I volunteered to carry his things, too.

After meandering through the town, we found a road that led into the unknown—often my favorite kind. It was paved at first but gradually degraded into a narrow, dirt track. It led us through bright-green pastures, trees, and quaint little houses. I felt amazingly free. This area was so untouched by modern life that I imagined few had ever traveled it. We passed tiny, mud-brick homes with grass roofs scattered among banana forests and shrubs. It almost looked like a National Geographic film.

As we biked along, we took turns being the leader and would occasionally stop to check out an interesting bug or tree, or just to take a moment to soak up the magnificent scenery.

At some point, though, our journey turned into a race and my competitive nature kicked in. Chad, who had fallen behind because he'd stopped to tie his shoe, caught up with me and tapped my shoulder as he gleefully passed by. Well, *that* would *not* do. I kicked my legs into turbo gear and took off after him like Batwoman. I whizzed around him, then did a full-on sprint for a few minutes.

Wind and bugs flew in my face. It was exhilarating. Okay, just the wind. Not the bugs. For that short time, I felt like I was in another dimension, traveling through a green tunnel of fresh air. My heart pumped and my skin glistened with sweat. As I slowed down and came out of my competitive trance, the outside world became real again and I heard the whine of wildly spinning tires on the uneven pavement behind me getting closer by the second.

I knew Chad was near. He couldn't let *me* win. When he came up next to me, a challenging look on his face, I didn't have the energy to pull ahead. I needed a little more time to recover from my supersonic sprint and he knew it. He just smiled in his sardonic, "gotcha" way, dashed ahead, circled back, made another loop behind, then came up beside me again. He absolutely *had* to show that *he* was the winner and that I had no chance of defeating him. Adorable. I just laughed, and we continued on in friendly silence.

Chad and I were way ahead of the others and stopped at the base of a hill to wait for them. The hill had a track that led up to a monastery. I took a few sips of water and poured some over my head for a brief respite from the muggy weather. When everyone else arrived, they took a breather as well before tackling what promised to be a strenuous ride up steep terrain.

Biking the rough and difficult path was a struggle, but well worth it for the gorgeous scenery. One thing I vividly remember about that ride was that the fresh morning smell filled me with delight. As I continued up the rocky, pitted, rutted, and curvy road, I kept glancing behind to catch the beautiful view of a tiny town below.

The road cut through the dense, brilliant-green forest like a knife with a jagged edge. Eroding boulders poked through the squatty shrubs as if trying to inch their way closer to sea level. Oddly, we didn't encounter any animals. I was hoping to see a squirrel again so Chad could freak out and get all excited, but nothing, not even a bird. Odd.

Finally, we reached the base of the monastery and parked our bikes at the plant-covered stone wall then inched around it to find the entrance but found nothing. There seemed to be no way in. Finally, we decided to split up and search for clues, openings, trails, or anything that would lead us into this mysterious place.

After searching by myself a while, I realized I'd not heard a peep from any of the others for some time. I stopped and glanced around. The wall was no longer visible and I was surrounded by trees. Where was I? Nothing looked familiar. I searched around, trying to figure out where I was and how to get back to the wall, telling myself not to panic. *If I don't turn up, the others will look for me. After all, how far away from the wall could I be in such a short time?*

I was about to call out when I heard rustling in the bushes. Thinking it was a small animal, I felt sorry that no one else was with me to see it. The rustle stopped and I studied the ground, expecting to see a snake or a squirrel, but nothing showed. Then I looked up and shrieked. Collin had silently appeared out of nowhere and now stood right in front of me. *How did I not see or hear him coming?* I calmed down, glad he found me.

He said he'd discovered the entrance so, taking a deep breath and feeling a tad foolish for shrieking, I followed him. We called out to the others and they quickly appeared. Collin told them he'd found the way in. Yess!

Collin led us up a faint path of crumbled and weathered stone steps that gradually became more defined as we climbed. After a brief trek, we approached the entrance. I thought we must have found a secret place because most of the monasteries I'd been to had proudly displayed very visible and grand entrances. Why was this one so elusive? Secret society? Cloistered or renegade monks? Renegade Buddhists? There's an interesting concept.

Inside, we passed through an atrium into the main square. There wasn't another soul in the place, and it was eerily quiet. The gloomy clouds overhead made it even more eerie. The words *dark and stormy night,* echoed somewhere in the back of my mind. Asian *Rocky Horror Picture Show,* anyone? It was both creepy and magnificent. This stony fortress on top of a mountain in the middle of a thick forest was truly magical.

We walked through the unique, secret monastery, gawking at its beauty and soaking in the wonderful silence. After climbing stairs to the top, the reward for our persistence was a spectacular view of the lowlands. Vast expanses of green below us flowed to the water's edge. The lake reflected abundant, white clouds making the scene look like it was a sea of low fog. It felt like I had stepped through a portal into a fairytale. But peering down, we could vaguely make out the meandering dirt road we'd struggled to cycle up. So, not transported to Neverland, after all.

I thought it strange, though, that all the time we were in that monastery, we didn't encounter a monk, apprentice, or another living soul. I don't even remember seeing evidence of anyone living there. Abandoned? But why? What story did this place have to tell?

When it was time to leave the magical monastery, I said a silent thank you and farewell. We retraced our steps to the waiting bicycles and made our way down the mountain. Just as we were on our way, the sun split through the cloud cover, creating beautiful, luminous rays. *Maybe,* I mused, *the monastery was magical after all, and this was its way of saying thanks for the visit.*

In town, we enjoyed lunch at a local spot, beside a tiny walkway, and surrounded by banana trees. The menu was in Burmese, so we just pointed at the pictures and hoped for the best. Chad and I giggled after we ordered, remembering when we'd accidently ordered the same "unfavorite" dish and Collin had freaked out saying, "Hah! That's why you never order the same thing."

Hazard 73:

Fall off My Bicycle and Wake up in a Panic

After lunch we rode our lethargic butts to the Red Mountain Vineyard that was, of course, at the top of another steep hill. Bridget and Collin would be heading out of town that day, so the vineyard was a bit of a going-away celebration.

Up the gravel road we peddled to the guard shack then onward to the top of the hill. Parking our bikes at a structure that looked like a bus stop, we crossed the road to the wide, terraced stairway leading up to the winery. Each "terrace" was about four paces deep, making it an easy climb, and I loved the multicolored roses and poppies lining the way.

The stairs ended at a large patio area. I scanned around and saw that all the tables were filled with people enjoying their wine and the panoramic view of the valley below. With no tables available, we went inside and found one with a window view. There were six of us, so we ordered three bottles of wine.

The wine prices started at roughly 4000 Burmese Kyat ($3 US) per bottle. Talk about a steal, it felt like we were drinking for free. I pulled out my cards and we played Rummy—the "Chad and Tam version." This was the last time we would all be together, so we wanted to get a final score down—for the record. Of course, Chad won the first hand and became super arrogant. I won the next two, so he sulked and said he didn't feel like playing anymore.

Collin suggested the game Drunk Driver, sometimes called Asshole. A few rows of cards are dealt on the table. Each row is assigned a drink number, 1, 2, 3, and so on. The remainder of the cards are dealt to the players. When the dealer flips over a card, whoever has the corresponding number gets to assign any amount of drinks to their choice of players.

So, when the dealer flipped over a 2 of diamonds, Collin had a 2 and assigned Bridget a drink. But Bridget also had a 2 card and reversed the drinks back to him, so he had to drink even more. At this point we ordered another three bottles and were on the road to happy town.

It's curious how games so often end up turning into a boys-against-girls contest. I wonder if it's how our brains are wired or if it's a way of flirting. That's what happened to our game at the winery. I received the worst of it, or as some would say, the best of it.

After a few rounds Collin and Bridget needed to leave so they could catch their bus to Yangon. We hugged and wished them safe travels. That just left Chad, Nigel, Emily, and me.

Emily and Nigel stepped outside to smoke while Chad and I talked about places to check out next on our crazy adventure through Burma. I wanted to hike from Inle Lake to Kalaw. Chad immediately said, "Sure. I'm in!" He sounded a bit too enthusiastic. I could tell he really didn't want to do the hike, but I was glad he was willing to go with me anyway. I realized then that we had a special connection.

With me, Chad was a great guy, but with others, he often turned into a different person. I witnessed this when a group of five girls came in. Chad's whole demeanor switched. He was like a cat ready to pounce on its prey. I didn't mind and even found it amusing to watch his Jekyll and Hyde transformation.

Emily and Nigel were still outside, so with no wingman available, the role fell to me. I put on my "wing woman" face and asked the tall, dark-haired girl if she and her friends would like to join us for a round of cards.

They accepted. My job was done. The ball was now in Chad's court. He put on his most charming smile and explained *our* Rummy rules then dealt the cards.

We played a few rounds, but I wasn't having much fun without Collin, Bridget, Nigel, and Emily. With them it was more like we were a little family. These girls were nice, but they lacked "spark" and didn't seem all that interested in us getting to know each other.

Bored, I excused myself and headed to the bathroom. While there, I decided not to return to Chad and the girls. I figured he would rather pursue his prey without me hanging around, so I went outside to find Emily and Nigel. They'd made some new friends and invited me to join their table. Yesss! This felt much better. I don't remember much of what we talked about, but I do remember feeling content and happy. We sat there long after the winery closed, drinking, talking, and enjoying ourselves.

Finally, Chad joined us. He was not in the best mood and gave me an earful about leaving him at the table with *those* girls. I don't remember his exact words or my response. I probably laughed and told him I was bored but hoped he'd had a good time.

The last memory I have of that night was sitting at the table, staring off into the spectacular sunset.

The next thing I remember is waking up in bed at the hotel. I didn't have a clue how I got there or what happened after the sunset. Puzzled, I lay still. The room was quiet and dark with only a faint light filtering in. Asking myself what happened, I tried to fill in the missing time. Nothing. It was all a blank.

Without warning, a rush of pain gripped me. *Huh!* I sat up. Scattered ruby-red spots stained my white sheets.

I'm usually calm in a crisis, but this pushed me too close to scared. I took some deep breaths and told myself to calm down and figure this out. Something big happened to me and I needed to remember what.

Looking around, I saw Chad, sound asleep across the room. That somehow felt reassuring.

Trying to take a closer look at my body and the sheets, I realized it was too dark to see clearly. Since the light switch was on the wall above Chad's bed, I'd have to go over there and turn it on or wait until morning.

Ignoring my pain, I swung my legs over the bed, and stood up. Reeling a little, I realized I was still drunk and carefully made my way across the room.

Standing next to his bed, I took a moment to think about how to actually reach the switch. Gently waking him, explaining, and asking for more light didn't occur to my besotted brain. Only one way came to mind so, I went for it and climbed over him to turn on the lights.

The room lit up with blinding brightness.

Chad gulped in a surprised breath and stared at me with wide-open eyes. He whisper-shouted, "What *are* you doing?"

"Just trying to figure out what happened to me. I don't remember anything." I glanced toward my bed and realized that the ruby spots were blood—my blood. I had deep cuts all over my feet, legs, and arms. If I hadn't still had so much alcohol coursing through my veins, this might have really scared me, but since I was *not* sober, my reaction was confusion and mild concern.

Chad groaned. "Go back to sleep. I'll explain in the morning." He flipped out the light and turned over.

There would be no further talk that night, so I stumbled back across the room, climbed into bed and collapsed into a deep sleep.

When I woke up again to bright daylight, and Chad perched on my bed, I asked, "How long have you been sitting there?"

"A while, I've been waiting for you to open your eyes."

Sitting up felt like a truck had plowed into me. "Aagh! What the...?" I grimaced and glanced at the dried blood on the sheets.

"You're a mess," he said in a quiet voice, then, like a caring nurse, inspected my wounds and cleaned them out with an antiseptic he'd picked up that morning from the corner store. What a sweetheart he could be.

I had deep gashes all over my feet. The worst one was right over my ankle bone. It pained me just to look at it. I had smaller cuts on my arms and legs, and a huge abrasion on my side. The worst part, though, was that sitting really hurt my butt.

After Chad fixed me up, he grinned and insisted I call him "Doctor Daddy."

There's no way I would ever do that, so I just smirked, and calmly asked, "What happened?"

He explained that as we were leaving the vineyard, someone decided it was a good idea to race down the steep gravel road. "You turned on your headlamp, took off before me, then bolted down the hill. I got a late start because I ran back to the table to grab the wine."

I didn't remember any of that, but it sounded like something I would do.

He continued the story:

"When I reached the guard shack all I saw was your bike. My heart sank. I knew something was wrong. I found you in the guard shack and all banged up. You were in really bad shape and couldn't ride, so we ditched the bikes and started walking back to town. It was pitch black. We found our way by moonlight. You couldn't walk on your own, so I had to hold you up the whole time."

I took a deep breath. This was almost too painful to hear. But there was more.

"We tried hitchhiking, but the car that stopped tried to charge us. You weren't happy about that and loudly told them to get lost. We continued down the street on foot. At one point you were crying but had no tears, so I just held you until you stopped. You kept asking if I picked up your headlamp and RayBans. I lied and said yes."

I felt terrible and grateful at the same time and realized that Chad really was a good friend. What I couldn't figure out, though, was how I could have blanked all that out? I'd never been *that* drunk...or had I? I thought of college, and realized the answer was yes. This was a relapse. Were there other times in my life I have no memory of? Absolutely. But this wasn't the time to ruminate on them.

Chad interrupted my musings with the rest of the story.

"Eventually another car came along and gave us a free ride to the hotel. I tried to take you to Amelia, the veterinarian, so she could fix you up, but you adamantly refused, pronouncing that blood coagulates and you were fine. So, I knew there was no arguing about it. I checked to make sure you didn't have head injuries then put you to bed. I told the hotel where we left the bicycles and I think they sent someone out to retrieve them."

I was stunned. It hit me that if everything he said was true, I was lucky to be alive and not seriously injured. This was not one of my proudest moments. To this day I find it hard to believe I didn't hit my head or scratch up my face when I fell. My guardian angel was vigilant that night.

After thanking him and apologizing for being such a dope, I painfully dressed. It was too late for the hotel to serve breakfast, so we went out to find food.

Since Chad had confessed to lying about retrieving my Ray Bans and headlamp, I wanted to see if they were in the bushes somewhere. After breakfast, we started back toward the winery. About fifteen minutes into our walk, the heavens opened and dumped buckets on the small town. We dashed into a tiny bus stop structure and huddled inside, watching the streets fill with water.

We must have looked comical, squished under the tiny shelter in our shorts and tank tops. When a car drove by and sprayed street-water about ten feet into the air, I cringed at the thought of that disgusting bacteria cesspool touching the open wounds on my foot and hid behind Chad to shield myself.

We were stuck there for what seemed like hours. I wasn't willing to walk through the rain and aggravate my cuts, so we played thumb war and listened to music on Chad's iPad. I was impressed by his playlist, but even more impressed by his knowledge of the artists. I thought, *He's like a walking music encyclopedia.*

When the rain finally let up, we continued on to the vineyard. The flooded street looked like a chocolate river flowing in slow motion, so we tiptoed through, hopping to the high spots and trying to avoid huge puddles. The farther we walked out of town the drier the ground became. At the guard shack near the bottom of the hill, it looked as if it hadn't rained at all.

After asking if anyone had found RayBan sunglasses or a headlamp, the guards, who didn't speak much English, pointed to the vineyard. We thanked them and headed up the path. Inside, we asked around. I let out a great sigh of relief when they said someone had turned in my RayBans.

Outside, I searched the bushes near the crash site but never found the lost headlamp, so we gave up and made our way back to town where Chad and I booked the trek to Kalaw. We were happy that it included a guide and accommodations in an old monastery. The travel agent told us that people usually trekked *from* Kalaw *to* Inle Lake because it's an easy hike. Apparently, the way *we* were heading would be difficult and all uphill.

We were glad there were a few days before the guide would meet us. That gave us extra time to explore more of the beautiful mountain town.

Later that night we met Emily, Nigel, and Amelia for dinner, where we each ordered a bunch of food and ate it family style. Burmese food is extremely good.

After dinner we headed to a rooftop bar. On the way, we ran into the group of girls from the Red Mountain Vineyard and invited them to meet us there. Chad seemed giddy as a schoolgirl. His odds of hooking up was good since there were five of them and one of him.

The girls showed up at the rooftop bar and we all listened to music and drank while looking up at the stars. The girls were friendlier this time around and we joked and laughed, enjoying each other's company. When the bar closed, they invited us back to their hotel to continue the party on the patio area. We gladly accepted. Chad made a quick detour to *our* hotel to get the wine he'd bought the night before.

Their patio was on the second level and overlooked the street. The balcony wasn't large but was spacious enough for the ten of us. We played cards, danced, chatted, and enjoyed the view.

After a while, some of us faded and wandered off to bed. That left only five who were still up and lively, me included. But when Emily and Nigel announced they were heading back, I decided it was time for me to exit and let Chad and his "chosen" girl have some alone time. Unexpectedly, though, when I asked him for our key, he insisted on walking me home. Emily and Nigel volunteered to do that, so he could stay, but he insisted on doing it himself. When he stood and told the girl goodbye, she looked surprised but gave him her contact info.

On the way to the hotel, I asked him what was wrong. He said nothing was wrong. Well, I wasn't going to let it go at that and said, "You complain everyday about how you want to hook up with chicks. And now that you had the opportunity to do so, you wuss out. What gives?" I was pretty annoyed.

He just laughed and said, "Don't be mad at Doctor Daddy."

I smirked and rolled my eyes.

He let it go.

Back in our room, he poured antiseptic on my gashes, which stung so bad it just about killed me, but it was such a caring thing for him to do, I didn't challenge "Doctor Daddy's" kindness and concern. I thanked him then laid down and drifted off to sleep.

Escapade 74:

60-Kilometer Trek to Kalaw

The travel agency agreed to hold anything we didn't want to carry on our hike and dropped us off at the trailhead with our guide, Agung. He wore traditional Burmese clothing and had extremely curly eyelashes.

Chad insisted on bringing his backpack, so we loaded nonessentials into my bag to leave behind. I stuffed whatever I needed inside his.

At the trailhead, the village houses were made from bamboo shoots and banana leaves. They had bamboo-fenced gardens to keep out the critters and, of course, the ever-present free-roaming chickens. The beautiful red soil looked fertile—but I'm no agricultural expert. To top off this *National Geographic* photo op, big, leafy trees filled with chirping birds surrounded the tiny hamlet at the base of a gigantic mountain.

A deep layer of slippery leaves blanketed the trail and hid hazards like rocks and roots, so we had to travel carefully. The temperature rose fast and soon droplets of sweat flowed down my back.

We stopped by a massive bamboo wall for a water break and to cool off. I offered to carry Chad's backpack, but he said he was okay, so we continued up the hill following the not-so-clear path to Kalaw. We crossed through tiny villages with acres of farmland beautiful enough to be an inspiration for a painting. So many colors blended together with the mountains, and the layered, bent, and folded earth that had developed over millions of years looked like the bands in a vinyl record.

The trail was so enchanting and quiet, no one said a word for what seemed like an hour. I was enjoying the fresh air and the quiet of the countryside broken only by an occasional chirping bird. *Finally*, I thought, *a break from loud city sounds*. It was such a welcome respite from the incessant honking, and the hustle and bustle of locals trying to sell their souvenirs. But most of all, I was glad to be away from the god-awful street smells— the stench of rotting animal flesh piled up near drains, puddles of liquid that looked like old chicken broth and smelled of swamp. This hike gave my senses a much-needed rest. The fragrance of farmland was deeply quiet and soothing.

Beautiful or not, as the temperature quickly ramped up, we were drenched in sweat, Chad and Agung had gone ahead when I stopped to take some pictures of a small garden that appeared to be growing potatoes, carrots, and some kind of cabbage. As I stood there, I heard someone in the near-distance singing but couldn't see who. Then, when I started on the path again and caught up with the others, I discovered the singer was Agung, belting out a native Burmese song. I joined in as if I knew the words. This made Agung giggle and he asked if I'd ever heard the song before.

I said, "No, but I like your voice." This seemed to please him and he continued singing. When he finished, he asked if I knew any songs.

I love to sing, so without hesitation, I belted out:

Down by the bay,
Where the watermelons grow,
Back to my home,
I dare not go,
For if I do,
My mother would sayyyyyy...
Have you ever seen a bear...
combing its hair down by the bay?
Down by the bay,
Where the watermelons grow,
Back to my home,
I dare not go,
For if I do,
My mother would sayyyyyyy...
Have you ever seen a goat...
wearing a coat down by the bay?
Down by the bay,
Where the watermelons grow....

I was surprised at how at ease I was singing in front of him and Chad. I'm as tone-deaf as they come but, I love to sing. The only time I'm uninhibited enough to do so in front of others is at drunken karaoke or to a loud band or album playing. But being there with Chad and our friendly guide in the beautiful, quiet, and peaceful countryside made me feel comfortable belting out my tune.

When I was singing, Chad just looked at me, shook his head, and smiled.

I remembered Bridget, a while back, asking how I could stand being around him and that she thought he was a rude beast. Why, I wondered, couldn't he be the same great guy that I know when he's around others?

383

Hazard 75:

Chased by Angry Water Buffalo

Still trekking through astoundingly beautiful country, we carefully stepped along the edges of dried rice terraces. Trying hard to keep our balance on the uneven ground, it must have looked like we thought there was danger of falling into a boiling pool of lava or unforgiving quicksand.

We made it through without mishap but were stopped in our tracks by a group of not-so-friendly water buffalo grazing in the middle of the trail. Obviously unhappy to have their lunch interrupted, one of them gave us a steely glare and menacingly stomped its hoof to say, "Get out of here or we'll charge your puny human asses."

Agung sucked in a breath. He was scared. I looked at Chad and could tell that he was seconds away from ditching the heavy backpack and making a run for it.

Bad idea.

We slowly and carefully backed away through the terraces. The giant beasts weren't impressed. They kept creeping closer to us. I wondered if there was a mother and baby in the herd they were protecting. That would explain their uncharacteristic aggression.

I didn't get a chance to ponder that further when they suddenly decided we hadn't heeded their warning and charged us. It was like being in an old Western film with the cattle stampeding, kicking up clouds of dust and trampling anything in their way. We ran for our lives. Before we became a permanent part of the earth, we made a sharp turn and took a detour away from the trail to escape the angry buffalo.

When it was safe to stop and catch our breath, I was surprised to see that Chad still carried our backpack. Panting, he stripped it off and dropped to the ground. Agung and I sat with him. I was shaking from the adrenaline.

I broke out in uncontrollable laughter thinking about what just happened. "Did we really just get chased by a herd of buffalo? No one will ever believe that."

After a few minutes, we had recovered enough to get back on track. No buffalo stalked us as we continued on the trail.

Around mid-day, we stopped at a small village for lunch. Agung cooked up a local vegetable soup and a chicken and potato dish that I very much enjoyed. I took off my shoes and socks to let my feet breathe. Chad had a nap on the bench we were sitting on.

We'd been hiking for at least six hours but still had at least five miles to go until we reached the monastery where we'd be staying the night. After lunch I offered again to carry the backpack, but Chad said he was fine with it, so I let it go.

We finally reached our destination around 5pm. I looked at the so-called monastery and thought, *No way.* There might have been one near there, but this? This just looked like some guy's house in the middle of nowhere.

Inside, we saw a large man hobble into the room with the help of a cane. He could barely walk because one of his legs was massively swollen and he had to walk on his ankle bone. It all looked excruciatingly painful.

Without complaint, though, he led us to a one-room cabin. I was dismayed, but too tired to protest as I looked around the room and saw a table with a bench on each side, two twin beds in each corner and glassless cut-outs in the wall instead of windows.

The man offered us beer and bottled water then abruptly left, wishing us a good night.

Agung didn't show whether he was surprised at our accommodations or not. He just told us to relax then prepared dinner.

Chad flopped his tall body down on a bed built for a much shorter person. It was one of the funniest scenes I'd ever witnessed. His legs hung almost completely off the bed, nearly touching the floor.

I noticed that there were no mosquito nets and with the open "windows," we would most certainly be eaten alive in our sleep. While Agung was busy making dinner, I searched around the property for a shower or something that resembled one but had no luck. I asked Agung where I could rinse the dirt and sweat off. He led me to a large, round tank and said, "There's the water," as he handed me a bucket.

Okay…. I guess this is going to be more of an adventure than I thought. I smiled and thanked him.

After he left, I gathered my things and started to undress when I realized I wasn't alone. I heard strange noises and someone shouting. Turning around, I saw Chad sitting on a bench, hollering at a game he was playing on his iPad. *Jeezzus!* Glad I hadn't completely stripped, I asked my dear pal to go inside the cabin while I washed up.

I hung my beach towel on a tree branch for a bit of privacy. With my swimsuit still on, I dipped the bucket into the tank full of ice-cold rainwater and flinched as I poured it over my hot, sweaty body. After the initial shock, though, I found it invigorating. I dried off and dressed then immediately sprayed mosquito repellent all over me.

When I returned to the cabin, Chad had a funny grin on his face that said he'd snuck a peek at me while I bathed. I just rolled my eyes. He put on some tunes and we played cards until dinner was ready.

Escapade 76:

Sleep in a Real Monastery

Agung announced that dinner was ready. We initially thought that we would be eating in the room with the small beds, but he led us up a staircase to what resembled a living room with bamboo mats covering the entire area. A low table, set with bowls of rice, stood in a corner. Chad and I sat cross-legged on the floor facing each other.

I glanced around at family photos on the wall. Agung poured us tea and brought out the food. He'd made soup, curry, salad, and an assortment of other dishes. It was a welcome feast. For dessert he insisted we try some Mandalay rum, which was really rice wine, and poured us each a shot.

In the relaxed atmosphere fueled by good food and rice-wine rum, Agung gushed out a story about how his girlfriend had left him. We were appropriately sympathetic, but after one shot, Chad and I were ready for bed. We tried to exit graciously, but he kept filling our glasses and pouring out his heartbreak.

I'm not a fan of rice wine but we couldn't just leave him there, alone in his misery, so we kept drinking. When the bottle was finally empty, I thought for sure we would die tomorrow on the trek.

Instead of going back to the room to sleep, Agung motioned for us to get our things ready to leave. Chad retrieved our belongings and we stumbled out of the house and into the near darkness. I was pleasantly surprised to find out that the cabin was not the monastery after all. I was so happy we wouldn't be sleeping there.

At the real monastery, Agung took us into a large room, so dark we had to use our headlamps to maneuver. The room had bamboo walls and flooring. I checked all the corners for spiders and creepy crawlies. On the floor, there were two sleeping mats next to each other with real pillows and a mound of blankets. The night was already cold, so I was glad to see the covers.

We thanked Agung for a wonderful evening and got ready for bed. I left to use the toilet, which was outside in a tiny shed that didn't have a light. When I opened the door, my headlamp shined on a spider hanging down from the frame. I really didn't want to go in, but it felt wrong to pee outside, so I brushed the spider and its web out of the way and hoped nothing else was in there. I washed my hands with the rainwater, brushed my teeth, and went back to the sleeping chamber.

Chad and I giggled about the day. He made fun of my singing and I laughed about him being more scared than I was during the water buffalo encounter. We both felt bad for Agung and his girl situation.

After a while, we were ready to turn in for the night but before we did, Chad carefully patched up all my cuts and bruises, both from the drunken bicycle incident and the buffalo run. He was so different from how I'd seen him with others. It made me feel really cared about. Then, when we finally laid down and snuggled under our respective blankets, I dove into sleep.

In the middle of the night, I woke up to see Chad slapping his face and arms as if a bug had landed on him. "What's wrong?" I whispered. When he didn't answer, I realized he was dreaming so I burrowed back down into the blankets.

As soon as I relaxed, my skin itched and tingled as if bugs were crawling all over *me*. Too tired to get up, put on my headlamp, and check, I convinced myself it was all my imagination. That did the trick and I drifted back into a sound sleep.

☾✷ ☾✷ ☾✷

In the morning, we gathered our things while waiting for Agung to fetch us for breakfast. I thought for sure I'd be hungover, but surprisingly, Chad and I both felt fine. I told him how much I appreciated him doing the trek with me and carrying the bag. He sloughed it off but I'm sure he felt good about what I said.

Agung finally made an appearance but didn't look so hot— too much rum for him. We had fruit, eggs, coffee, and tea then headed back to the trail.

Around midday, we came to a small restaurant on a side road and had noodle soup as we rested our weary legs.

After lunch, we headed back to the trail. This time, it took us into a forest of tall, encompassing trees. It was so quiet we could hear animals moving about in the distance. Shortly we came to a large tree that had fallen over and blocked our way. It was so big, it must have been at least 150 years old. With no way around that seemed safe, we climbed over it. As we did, I noticed several marks on the trunk that looked like lightning scars and saw where new growth had sprouted up from the scorches.

The thick canopy provided shade but also masked the sky and cast a dark gloominess all around. I was reminded of fairy tales where the hero ventures into a magical forest full of danger.

My musings were interrupted by a thud and the sound of leaves scattering behind me. When I turned, Chad had taken a face-dive to the ground after tripping on something. As funny

391

as this looked, I remembered that he'd been carrying a heavy backpack and could be hurt, so I ran over to check on him. Before I could say anything, he shot to his feet and dusted himself off, swearing he was okay.

As we continued onward, I noticed that he walked with a slight limp and I offered to carry the bag, but he still refused. Looking around, I found a thick branch just the right size for a walking stick to help take the weight off his injured leg. He accepted it without complaint.

When we arrived in town, it was time to part ways with the broken-hearted, and all-around good cook, Agung. We thanked him and gave him a generous tip. He smiled and said something about enjoying our company then handed us over to our driver.

At the hotel, our belongings were waiting for us as promised. This time, the room price was low enough for me to get my own—6,700 kyat ($5 US). I showered then napped until dinner.

After Chad and I ate, we caught a night bus for Naypidaw, the new capital of Myanmar that had been built in secret. The air-conditioned bus with comfortable seats was a nice surprise. I had been expecting something similar to our Mandalay to Bagan train ride from hell, so this was a relief.

I stowed my pack in the storage compartment and hopped on the bus. It was dark so I turned on my headlamp and read. About fifteen minutes into the ride the girl behind me started vomiting into a bag. *Ughhhh.* I felt sympathy for her, but also annoyed as I gagged at the smell. When others started getting sick, too, I put on headphones, turned up the volume to drown out the noise, and breathed through my mouth.

Chad didn't seem fazed at all from the noise or smell and I secretly envied him. But maybe he was just putting on a macho façade.

Escapade 77:

Secret Capital

What's with buses in Asia? The schedule says a destination arrival is one thing, but they end up arriving hours earlier. I can't count how many times that happened to me. This trip was no exception. We were due in Naypyidaw at 8 a.m. but arrived at 5 a.m. So, since Chad and I didn't have accommodations reserved and it was the wee hours of the morning, we hired a cab to take us to *any* hotel. The one the driver chose was, of course, expensive. We were too tired to care, though, and shelled out the equivalent of $20 per night for the room.

On the way there, I noticed that the town seemed deserted. *But,* I thought, *it's early in the morning. Maybe it will liven up later.*

We hit the beds and slept until a phone woke us up. I grumpily answered. It was the driver who'd dropped us off earlier. He offered to take us around the city. Nice offer, but I wasn't ready and said we'd call him later. Afterward, I thought it was odd that the hotel gave him our room number, then I went back to sleep.

Around mid-day we rolled out of bed, showered, dressed, and had the front desk call the taxi driver so we could tour the city. While we waited, I touched up my nail polish and since Chad was glued to some game on his iPad, I decided to paint his toes a nice shade of pink. He was too engrossed in his game to notice what I was doing.

When the taxi arrived, we slipped on our flip flops and headed out the door. Chad saw his pink toenails and tried to rub it off.

I laughed until I nearly cried.

Chad just resigned himself to it and I thought, *What a trooper— or maybe he's planning revenge.*

The driver glanced at Chad's feet and immediately looked away. I feigned innocence. Our first stop was the water-fountain garden where the driver raved about how spectacular it was, "Like the fountains in Las Vegas," he proudly exclaimed.

The garden sounded amazing and I was excited to see it, but it turned out to be not-so-fabulous. Half of the fountains didn't work and those that did were less than spectacular. I remember thinking that the Bellagio Casino in Las Vegas has way better fountains. I glanced at him and thought, he had to be joking, but by the expression on his face, he was serious. Clearly, he had never been to Vegas.

The grass was well kept, though, and we went on a charming ride that took us through a large-scale map of Myanmar. There was a pool, and some swimmers but it wasn't exceptional—kind of ordinary. Again, I didn't understand how this driver could favorably compare the fountains to Las Vegas. He was clearly delusional, or hoping we'd never been to "Glitter Gulch," and wouldn't know the difference.

As we drove to the next attraction, I noticed that the city was still nearly empty. The roads were broad and had as many lanes as the Katy Freeway (Interstate 10) in Texas. Well, not that many exactly, but there were a lot. It was almost comical to see roads that wide with only a few cars on them.

Chad read up on Naypyidaw and discovered that the only embassy to move there had been Bangladesh. In general, the people refused to accept the "new" capital and remained loyal to the old, "unofficial" capital of Yangon. One of the rumors that had been floating around was that the government created those large flat and straight-as-an-airport runway roads as an escape route. If this was true, the roads could serve as a runway for planes to take off if the government was ever overthrown.

This place is strange but has a few spectacular sites. First, we visited the beautiful Thatta Thattaha Maha Bawdi Pagoda. It is painted gold and looks like a pyramid with a huge base and a skinny top. It's covered in designs that resemble hieroglyphs but are stories from Buddhist literature.

Next, we toured the Uppatassanti Pagoda. It's shaped like a huge, golden chocolate drop. The outside ground was still hot enough to flash-bake a pizza, so Chad and I would dash from shady spot to shady spot toward the entrance to prevent the bottoms of our feet from blistering. Inside, gratefully, the floor was cooler.

After touring the "chocolate drop" pagoda, we ran out of steam. Exhausted, we asked the driver to take us back to the hotel. He was huffy about it and gruffly told us that the tour wasn't done yet.

We insisted anyway. At the hotel he tried to bleed us dry. Chad said with a raised voice. "I am tired of being a walking wallet. Now give us a fair price or you will get nothing." The guy grudgingly cut his price in half and went on his way.

Dinner was the strangest situation ever. Since this so-called capital was like a ghost town and Chad and I were the only guests in the hotel, the servers waited on us hand and foot—as if we were royalty. It was so bizarre. Chad said the waiter practically held his beer to his mouth for him to drink it. Every time I got up a waiter would come over to pull out my chair. When I sat down a waiter would rush to help push in the chair and place my napkin on my lap.

During dinner, I received a Skype phone call from one of my besties from home—Casey—and headed into the lobby to chat with her for a bit. I filled her in on my whereabouts. She gushed about her latest crush (and now, husband) and asked about mine. I had no comment.

When I turned back toward the dining room, a server sprinted across the floor, practically breaking his neck to open the door for me.

Although it was nice to be treated like a rock star, it also made me feel uncomfortable. Well, we would be on our way to Bago the next day. I looked forward to leaving this eerie place behind. It seemed like a city that had been built for two million people who never moved in.

Our night bus to Bago was horrific and I didn't get a wink of sleep. When we finally pulled into the city, I was relieved to see that it was a bustling hub to just about anywhere anyone would want to go. We decided to stop for a few days and see the famous golden Buddha.

We had no hotel reservations but looked up some prospects via Wi-Fi. Our toothless tuk tuk driver, however, had his own ideas about where we should stay, and we had to haggle to get him to take us to our choice—the San Francisco. That sort of thing was commonplace with drivers and guides, though, and we stood our ground.

He eventually gave in and took us to the San Francisco and asked if we wanted a tour around Bago to visit the Pagodas. Chad and I were both keen and told him we would contact him later.

After settling in, we grabbed a bite at the restaurant next

door. I ordered dry chicken chili. It was amazing. It was obvious that few tourists came to that part of the city, so we were getting authentic food.

After eating, we went to our room and napped. When we woke up, we contacted the driver and asked his price and where he planned to take us. Satisfied, we hired him.

He took us all over Bago, mostly to the temples we wanted to see. I was really enjoying myself—until the guy asked us for an extra $10 US to enter the archeological sites. Chad and I called him out on it and let him know that we knew what he was up to.

He then laughed and apologized. After that we all got along fine and the rest of the day was great.

Escapade 78:
Bago Bus to Buddha Breaks Down

The next day we decided to see the reclining, golden Buddha. My first clue that this was going to be an unusual day was the weird bus station—I can't even describe it. Maybe it was a converted fruit market or an old shop of some kind. After waiting a short while, a "vintage" 1950s bus arrived.

We were assured this heap would take us somewhere close to the famous Buddha, so we boarded. Inside, the heat was nearly intolerable, and if I hadn't been already used to the smell of passengers packed in like Vienna sausages in a can with no air conditioning, I might have puked or passed out. But I was now a veteran traveler in these parts and my tolerance for hot, stinky situations was pretty high.

A lot of buses there are not built for tall tourists and the seats on this one were so close together, we could barely fit our legs in the space between us and the next row. Even though the windows were down, it was so hot outside it didn't make much difference.

The bus was filled but continued to pick up passengers along the way. To accommodate them, the driver placed tiny stools in the aisle. We were dangerously jammed in like pickles in a jar. I remember thinking that if a fire started or we were in an accident, it could be death to us all.

After about an hour, the bus pulled over. I'd hoped it was for *some* people to get off, but when *everyone* headed for the exit, we realized there was a problem.

No one in this backwater part of the world spoke English, so we hadn't the slightest idea where we were or what was happening.

As we waited, a couple of buses went by without stopping. The whole scene was both funny and strange.

At one point, I stopped a cab and told him we wanted to see the golden Buddha. He just looked at me, with a puzzled expression. Not only did no one speak English, I was wondering if they'd ever *heard* English.

There was nothing more to do but hang around, hoping another bus would come along and stop for passengers. After about an hour, one did. Enormously relieved, we boarded and continued our journey, hoping it would take us to the reclining Buddha.

When the bus pulled into a small town and stopped, the driver pointed to us and, with intonation and gestures, let us know that this was where we should get off.

Initially grateful to be done with that horrid experience, I quickly realized that we were *not* at our final destination. *Groan!* There was nothing we could do but hope another bus would soon come along. In the meantime, we were hungry and went to a little eatery on the side of the road.

Squeezing into the mini-chairs that faced the street, we scanned the menus. They were in Burmese but thankfully there were pictures, so we pointed at something that looked familiar and hoped for the best.

My choice ended up being an excellent pork curry but a little too spicy for such a hot day. I ordered an extra bottle of water to wash it down and to rehydrate myself after sweating like a squeezed sponge on that stifling ride earlier.

After eating, we waited for yet another, probably hot and uncomfortable bus. When one finally arrived, we hopped on, again, hoping it would take us to the Buddha. This bus was newer than the first but just as packed, so Chad and I had to sit on the tiny aisle seats. This was especially not fun for Chad. These seats were meant for much shorter people, and he looked like a giant perched on a toadstool.

I was amazed that, as crowded as we were, the driver kept picking up more people and they all seemed to take it in stride. This packing-in-of-passengers would never be allowed in the U.S.

I steeled myself and hoped the trip would be short. It was hot, crowded, and I was disgusted at the passengers who casually threw their trash and garbage out the bus window. I kept thinking that the reclining Buddha had *better* be the most spectacular thing I'd ever seen to be worth *this* horrible experience.

After a while, I had a strange feeling that we needed to get off the bus as soon as possible. I told Chad and we agreed to leave at the next town. I'm not sure if he believed in my hunches or he was just happy to have an excuse to get off the nightmare bus.

When we pulled into some hole-in-the-wall village, we fought our way to the exit. As we started to step off, a passenger called out, "Be *very* careful!" That sent a chill up my spine. I guess I'd seen too many horror films. Freaked out or not we were getting off.

As we watched the bus ramble away down the road, we looked around. I was a little dismayed. The town looked like no tourists *ever* visited. And we soon discovered that no one spoke English. Normally I wouldn't mind but the last bus to Bago was at 5 p.m. so there wasn't much time to see the Buddha and catch the last ride home.

We walked around, trying to use sign language to describe the Buddha but no one knew what we were saying or talking about. For what seemed like ages, we tried to find a map, a bus stop, a train—anything that could help us get to the Buddha. We looked for places with Wi-Fi, but no one knew what that was. A hostel or hotel would have tourist information but we didn't see any.

Were we in a time warp? I didn't see one cell phone, and everyone was dressed in traditional clothing. *Yep.* I thought, *Definitely been transported into the past.* Was our last bus a DeLorean with a "flux capacitor" in disguise? I wished there had been more time to experience the town. On the other hand, I was still pretty freaked out that the man on the bus had warned us to be *very* careful.

We finally gave up on trying to see the Buddha and just focused on finding our way back. Eventually another bus arrived. We just said the word "Bago" and a local man pointed to where we needed to go. It was all so frustrating. We'd gone through a lot to NOT see the Buddha.

Arriving in Bago about five hours later, we disembarked and found that the only transportation running that late at night were motor-bike taxis. It was either that or walk to our hotel, so we rode, three-deep on a motorbike. I made Chad straddle the driver and I sat behind. Chad wasn't happy about it, especially since people laughed at us and took pictures. I wish I had one of those photos now. It would definitely bring a smile to my face.

We were such a heavy load, the driver had to make a stop and put air in the bike's tire. Passersby gave us strange looks, laughed, or smiled and waved "hello."

When we finally arrived at our hotel, we decided to catch a mid-day bus the next day to Yangon or the coast. It was late and we were tired, so we left the final decision for the next morning.

The trip to Yangon was easy and without mishap—thank goodness. This was a genuine city with real-world people. Some wore Western clothes and others native—all roaming the streets together. Tourists to them, were just another common, everyday sight.

I was ready for a bustling city. It was busy and loud, making street-crossing a hazardous chore, but my time in Vietnam had prepared me well. I was a champ at dodging traffic.

Chad and I made new friends at our hostel and decided to split up for the day.

A fellow Californian and I went to a nice hotel with a pool and swam and drank. Chad went to watch the Mani Paquio/Floyd Mayweather fight. It was a great day.

Later that night we met up for dinner and made friends with Toke, an older Aussie gentleman. We decided to go exploring with him the next day. So far, Yangon promised to be a great time.

We were in the hottest part of the year, so I was super happy that our hostel had air-conditioning. We visited the famous Shwedagon Pagoda that has a 99-meter high, gold-plated stupa. We also discovered what our Buddha day of the week was. This was determined by our birthdate.

The pagoda was packed with people, so no roaming around with the whole place to ourselves like some we'd explored. A nice surprise was when we ran into our Danish friends Tomen and Cara and decided to have a bite to eat together. We ended up at a wonderful restaurant that had live music and ordered everything family style so we could all share. Burmese food is a hidden gem and I wish there were more restaurants that served it where I live in the United States.

Later that evening we went to a couple of bars and had a few drinks then planned to meet with the Danes for their birthday shenanigans the next day. It was so cool that they were five years apart but shared the same birth date. It was Tomen's 21st birthday so we wanted to make it really special. After breakfast, Chad, Toke, and I went to find a cake and birthday card for them. Although we tried our best, we couldn't find a cake.

Tomen wanted to eat at an ice cream shop he saw online, so that was our first stop. The best part was that they gave a birthday boy or girl free ice cream. The workers in the shop sang to Tomen and Cara then we gave them their card.

We were all hungry and decided to go to a speakeasy that we had to find by following inconspicuous paw prints around town. It was marvelous and we ordered fancy drinks and yummy burgers. To top it all off, Steven and Kyle from Songkran were in town and joined us.

This was the beginning of a crazy day. We spent hours in the speakeasy playing games and having laughs. After a while, we decided to move the party to 19th Street where there were bunches of bars. We secured a big table and ordered several rounds of beer.

This street was a lot tamer than Koh San Road in Bangkok. I think Burma is more conservative than Thailand. Steven and Kyle mentioned a reggae place they thought we should go to, so we headed there. Chad wasn't feeling well and went back to the hostel while the rest of us continued the party. The reggae bar played all types of music, and I danced the night away.

Hazard 79:

David Hasselhoff Dining Performance and Chad Turns Bad

While I was taking a breather from "dancing the night away," a guy from Arizona that Cara and I had met earlier bought us a round of Patron Tequila shots. A few minutes later he got us another round and I decided I needed to dance those off.

Later the subject of food came up and I realized, in my inebriated state that I was really hungry. Bravely, I took it upon myself to go out and find some food. Considering how much I'd had to drink, Kyle thought wandering the town by myself was a bad idea and tried to talk me out of it.

No use, though, when I drink, I think I'm Superwoman. I assured him that I would be *just fine*. Arizona said he was hungry, too and would come with me because he knew a perfect fish and chips spot. Okay. I flagged a cab and off we went.

If I hadn't been so drunk, I would have seen it coming. The "perfect" fish and chips spot turned out to be at his hotel. And it just "happened" to be closed. Right! How convenient. I wasn't *that* drunk. I glared at him in a way that said I knew what his game was.

Caught off guard he fumbled and mumbled, finally choking out the words, "Room service is 24-hours." If I hadn't been so angry, I would have laughed. Maybe this move had worked in the past and he didn't expect resistance.

I thought, *What kind of a numbskull does he think I am? He's trying to pull a fast one on me. I'll fix this guy.* I dropped the scowl and decided to pretend to play along for a bit. We went up to his room. He ordered food like he said he would and we watched *Survivor* on TV while we waited.

When the meal finally came, I was relieved. I had formulated a plan to get my dinner and put Arizona off his game at the same time. I grabbed the food with my hands and stuffed it in my mouth like a drunk David Hasselhoff eating a hamburger *(see YouTube.com)*. I could hardly keep from laughing when I saw the look of disgust on Arizona's face. My plan was working. Then I upped the game and talked to him with my mouth full. Chunks of food fell to the floor and all over my shirt. At that point, I think it was all he could do not to run out of the room screaming. I howled with laughter—on the inside.

Glancing at my watch, I was surprised to see it was past 2 a.m. *Damn,* I thought. *I missed my hostel curfew and would be locked out.* Just getting another room in the hotel didn't occur to me and, in my mind, I only had two choices—either sleep there or on the street. So, I brazenly curled up on one of the beds, wrapped myself in a sheet burrito—just in case this dude got any ideas—then went to sleep.

When I opened my eyes in the morning, I didn't remember where I was. I saw a piece of modern art on the wall. *Nice frame, ugly painting.* I figured out that I was in an upscale hotel but had no memory of how I got there, of Arizona, or my performance the night before. I *did* notice that the bed was amazingly comfortable.

As I turned my head, I saw a large TV tuned to a local channel but with the volume on mute. Then, I rolled over and saw Arizona on the other bed, typing on his laptop while sitting cross-legged with his back resting on the headboard. Memory flooded back. Groaning inside, my only thoughts were of escape.

When he saw I was awake he simply said good morning and offered to order breakfast from room service. I'm sure he was hoping I would decline. I did, then glanced at the dinner cart from last night and chuckled to myself. My plate looked like a four-year-old had mashed all her food together and then spread it around the dish and all over the floor around the cart. Ironically, there was an unopened bottle of wine.

Arizona acted as if I hadn't been a lunatic the night before and with a calm, friendly voice said he was finishing a work report and that I could sleep for as long as I needed to.

What an amazing guy. I'd expected him to be mad or at least annoyed about the night before. I thought maybe he'd figured out my game of gross-out and knew I wasn't always like an off-the-diet Richard Simmons. On the other hand, I remembered a time when I woke up with a half-eaten burrito lying next to my face. So maybe that behavior wasn't totally out of character.

I decided to take him up on the offer to sleep in. After so many stiff dorm mattresses and sharing my quarters with lots of people, the quiet room and soft bed were heaven.

After I woke up again, Arizona and I had a nice talk. He told me he worked in Yangon and was living in an apartment with roommates. They were evicted because of some shady business one of the roommates was into, so he decided to stay in a hotel until he found a new place to live.

He showed me a swollen foot from when a car ran over it while he was crossing the street a few days before. It was better, but still swollen. He was leaving Yangon for a few days to go to a hospital in Bangkok and get his foot checked out.

How did I not notice that the night before? Oh, yes. I was blind drunk and pissed. Crossing the street in Southeast Asia is always a dangerous business. In most of the places I'd visited, it was like playing Russian roulette—just a matter of time before my number came up and I would have a really bad encounter with a car. So far, my luck had held.

For the rest of the morning, we talked, watched Australian YouTube videos, shared stories of places we'd visited, and the people and cultures that we'd interacted with. He turned out to be pretty cool and even paid for the cab back to my hotel.

When it was time to leave, Arizona walked out with me. In the elevator I noticed that we were on the 12th floor. I had no memory of that and thought, *Wow. I must have been in an altered mind-space.* On the ground floor, we went outside, and I saw the name of the hotel—Shangri La. Very nice! I smiled, thanked him, and climbed into the cab.

Chad was asleep when I arrived around 3 p.m. I showered and changed clothes. When I came back into the room, he was awake and looked a bit worried, or annoyed (I couldn't tell which). He asked where I'd been. Before I could say anything, though, our friend, Beverly came in. I told them the story of my performance to teach the guy that "I wasn't that kind of girl," and how I'd missed hostel curfew and crashed at the Shangri La.

Bev thought my story was hilarious, but Chad looked dark and broody. Maybe his stomach was still upset. I offered to get him an antacid, but he said he'd prefer to just rest.

He had asked me if I wanted to explore Vietnam with him, so I spent some time researching things to do there. After I had agreed to go with him, he booked the plane tickets to Hanoi with a layover night in Bangkok.

Our last few days in Yangon were low-key. I thought Chad's moodiness was because he still wasn't feeling well. We decided to take a cooking class, which turned out to be a private session because no one else showed up. In his mood, I thought that was a good thing. We learned how to make our favorite dish, tea leaf salad, which turned out to be way easier than I'd imagined. All the ingredients are prepackaged. Our instructor said that it's hard to learn how to prepare tea leaf salad because the ingredients are secret, so everyone just buys the prepacked items and mixes them together. We made an array of other dishes, filled our stomachs, then headed home.

Chad was silent the whole way back, and for a second, I wondered if I'd done something wrong but couldn't think of anything that would have upset him so much. I brushed it off and just went with what he told me, which was that he wasn't feeling well.

The next day we met up with Kyle and Steven for lunch and ran into the girls from the Inle Lake Vineyard, I was happy to see them because I knew this would cheer up Chad! We all went out for drinks that night. Chad and I gave them tips on what to do around Yangon. Cara and Tomen met up with us as well and I filled them in on my shenanigans the night before at the Shangri La.

Cara said she got locked out of her hostel as well and had to stay with Kyle and Steven. It was such a fun night! Beverly joined us and it turned out to be a last hurrah for us all.

The next day, at the airport, Chad said some guy was staring at me and pointed to someone over my shoulder. I just brushed it off thinking he was imagining things but looked anyway. It was Arizona. I smiled and waved but he just glared at me. I thought it might be because he was upset about me sitting with someone else but dismissed that idea, thinking, *Maybe he didn't recognize*

me. I called out in a room-appropriate voice "Hey Arizona." He looked even more upset and said, "That's not my name."

Oops. After I sat down and pulled my foot out of my mouth, I glared at Chad, who found this all too funny. I thought he was laughing a bit much for what just happened and wondered what was really going on in his mind. Did the two of them cook this scene up to get back at me for my performance in Arizona's room? I decided to put it out of my mind.

The plane ride was, gratefully, uneventful, except for being delayed. We landed in Bangkok late, and headed for our hotel, looking forward to getting massages and sleeping in our own rooms.

Once there, we dropped off our bags, cleaned up, then took a cab to a sports bar restaurant and grill Chad had discovered. When we got there, the TV was showing rugby games. I loved it because I got a crash course on the sport. I think I understand it now, not as well as NFL football, but at least I know what's going on.

After dinner we found a cab to take us back to the hotel. Of course, the driver dropped us somewhere else. At first, we thought it was our place, but it wasn't. Earlier, we'd left in such a hurry we forgot to get the address. So, there we were in the middle of somewhere not knowing which way to go. We had no Wi-Fi and it was close to midnight, so we walked the streets looking for our hotel. After about an hour and a half, we stumbled on an internet café and Chad looked up the address through his email account.

We hailed a cab. When we arrived, Chad looked furious—not at me but at the situation. I felt bad but, considering his mood, I was happy to be sleeping in my own room.

The next day, we checked out and took a cab from the airport to the Old Quarter. By the time we arrived at our hostel, I was ready to ditch my bags and take a shower. Chad had set up the reservation, so I let him do all the talking.

The desk agent said only one bed had been reserved—for Chad. I was livid. Was this happening again? To make it worse, the hostel was sold out for the next three days. I tried to connect to the Wi-Fi to look for other places to stay but it wasn't working so I decided that my best bet was to walk around and just find a place. I was so upset, I couldn't even look at Chad.

I wasn't sure if he'd done this on purpose and didn't want to hang with me anymore, or what. He'd been acting weird for a few days, but I thought it was because he'd been ill.

In a huff, I loaded my big green pack on to my sweaty back, stomped out into the thick, moist, hot air and turned left. Grumbling to myself, I walked straight, passing by local people and tourists alike without really noticing them. Cars are prohibited at night, so it was strictly a pedestrian city in the evening.

I followed a curve to the right and passed shops and restaurants. After passing a street performance that had drawn a crowd of about fifty people, I took the next left and walked straight into Blah Blah Hostel. After booking a room for the next few nights, I texted Chad and said I'd hurry back to meet him, but I was still flustered about the reservation mishap—and annoyed at his moodiness, so I took my time showering, making up my bed, and organizing my things for the evening.

I connected to the Wi-Fi and noticed a message from Jeremy, whom I'd met at Songkran about a month before. He said he and a friend were flying to Hanoi early in the morning and wanted to reconnect. This put a giant smile on my face, and I jotted a note:

> Hey Hun, I'm staying at Blah Blah
> Hostel. Meet me here when you get in.
> Let's explore Hanoi. Can't wait to see you.
>   XoXo, Tam

When I joined Chad and Fin (Chad's friend from California), he was in a much better mood. We bought some banh mi sandwiches from a corner shop, eating them while squeezed into the tiny chairs facing the street. People-watching is one of my favorite things and there were some characters out that night.

We drank 30-cent beers that a woman was serving out of an orange cooler and enjoyed each other's company. When our cups were empty, she would place them under the cooler spigot and say, "Best draft beer in Hanoi."

Chad and Fin talked with each other while I enjoyed the people show. There, on that black-bricked street, I watched the hustle and bustle of the Hanoi night life. Bicycles passed by with locals carrying odd sized objects that Westerners wouldn't dare attempt to carry on a bike.

The Old Quarter was amazing, and in spite of Chad's screw up, I was glad I'd made the journey. When I turned my attention back to the boys, they were getting cozy with a few ladies, so I decided to give them some man-time and go across the road to chat with a guy who had a huge bandage on his leg. He was also sitting and people watching.

I got up slowly, trying to be nonchalant about the toy chair that my butt had wedged into, and crossed the street. I sat down, said hello, and asked him how he'd hurt himself. He said it was a motorbike accident. I showed him my bandages and told my story of falling off a bicycle after an afternoon at the winery.

I stopped talking mid-sentence when I saw Gloria, whom I'd met during the Songkran festivities. I called to her. We greeted each other with surprise and excitement. She said she was staying at the Backpacker. I yelled across the road to Chad to let him know she was around. It was a mini reunion of New Year friends.

We were all primed for the bars and I invited my new bandaged friend, Brandon, to hang with us. We hit the dance floor first thing and showed off our moves. Soon after, Gloria joined us with an entourage of newly made guy friends/travel buddies. It was a blast.

Brandon and I really hit it off and he fit right in with our little crew. When *Gangsta's Paradise* came on, everyone on the dance floor lost their minds.

There was one annoying guy, though, who danced so hard he kept elbowing me in my back. Without even glancing at him, I decided to move away and find a more comfortable spot. But the rude dancer showed up again, bumping into me. We decided to move along to the next bar. When the guy showed up on *that* dance floor, I actually looked at him. HOLY shit! It was Chad, trying to get my attention. I had to laugh.

We continued bar hopping until the Vietnamese curfew kicked in and most of the bars and clubs closed. At this point I had lost track of Chad, but Brandon, Gloria, and her friends were still wanting to find the next party spot, so we kept on rollin', heading down the main street hoping to find an underground place.

Gloria spotted a bus that a bunch of people were boarding. It turned out to be heading to a late-night party. Brandon and I got on and—surprise! There sat Chad and Fin. Chad didn't seem very happy, so I went over, hoping to cheer him up. I sat in the seat across from him. Brandon took the seat in front of me. Before I could get a word in some guy sat next to me and said, "I know you." My immediate reply was "No you don't."

He said, "Yes I do. You're Madeline's friend from Songkran." My mouth dropped open. I knew Madeline and I had met up at Songkran, but I had no idea who this guy was. He introduced himself as Gus. I'm sure we chatted but I don't remember about what.

When we arrived at the party, I didn't see Brandon anywhere and still wasn't too sure about Madeline's friend, Gus. So, later, when Chad said he was going to head back to his hostel, I decided it was a good idea to go with him. He and Fin hopped in a four-door cab. I opened the door to join them and Chad said, "There's only room for two people." I was taken aback and confused but thought that he must be joking and said that there were four doors so I surely could fit. I got in. As we were about to take off, Gus hopped into the front seat. I could tell Chad wasn't pleased that he got in the cab, too, and the ride was long and silent.

When we arrived at the hostel, I pulled Chad aside and asked him what his problem was but he didn't answer. Giving up, I walked away feeling confused and defeated.

Gus came up and put his arm around me then walked me back to my hostel. He said, "I'm sorry your friend is being an asshole." I smiled, thanked him and said, "See ya tomorrow."

I walked into my dorm room and felt as if I been hit in the face with a bag of ice. I fumbled around for the thermostat but couldn't find it, so I put on the warmest outfit I could find, covered myself with the thin sheet the hostel had provided, then set my alarm and fell into a deep sleep.

BEEP, BEEP, BEEEEEP, went my alarm. I hit snooze a couple of times before I got up and I am sure my roommates loved me—not. I opened my eyes and noticed a slight crack of sunlight sneaking in through the partially covered window. It was 7 a.m. and Jeremy would arrive any minute. I checked Facebook Messenger to get word on his whereabouts and then readied myself for the day.

I figured Chad would talk to me when he was ready, so I decided to take the day for myself. Jeremy showed up with Jeff around 7:30.

When they walked in, I looked at Jeremy, with his curly hair and green shirt and I felt like I had known him forever.

It's so awesome how close we become to complete strangers when we step out of our comfort zone and travel alone. I was so happy to see him and remembered the good time we spent together in Chang Mai.

Jeff was cool, too. I invited my roommate, Darin, from Melbourne, to come along with us. We started with breakfast at a little coffee shop around the corner from our hostel and then proceeded to the streets of Hanoi. We walked to the famous church, visited Ho Chi Minh's memorial, the French Quarter— pretty much everywhere we could squeeze into one day.

While hanging out near the river, taking in the view, a local man approached. He was in good shape and commented to Jeremy that he liked his looks and asked about his workout habits. Jeremy said that he lifts regularly but hasn't in a while because of his world trip. Muscle man went on and on about how he tries to get big by working out twice a day, but he isn't satisfied with his results. As he was blathering about his workout, I noticed that he had skinny, chicken legs. I said, "It's clear you skip leg day!" He laughed and so did everyone else.

Jeremy, in true manly fashion said, "I don't skip leg day," and flexed his quads. That's when things turned really strange. Muscle man started talking about his penis size and how it was really small and how he was looking for ways to make it bigger.

That was more than I could stand, I excused myself and headed to the river. The guys followed soon after. The man, however, hadn't taken the hint and followed us, trying to show us his private parts. Finally, Jeff flat out said, "We have to go now. Bye!"

Hazard 80:

Flooded Hostel and Chad Still Bad

After a great day out, I went back to Blah Blah hostel to shower. Midway through, I heard a loud banging on the door and someone yelling, "Turn off the water!" I was all soapy, so I rinsed off quickly and got out. After drying off and dressing, I noticed water on the bathroom floor. When I opened the door, I saw water flowing down the steps and into the downstairs lobby. Not a tsunami, but it meant a cleanup job for someone. It was a good thing they didn't have carpet. It wasn't my fault they hadn't built a lip in the shower to prevent leakage, but the guy who had to mop it up was fuming-mad at me anyway. I couldn't figure out how anyone could take a shower there *without* that happening.

Refreshed, our group of travel friends went into the Old Quarter for food. The streets were closed to motorbikes and cars, so we were free to roam about without getting run over.

As Jeremy pointed to a restaurant he wanted to try, I heard someone call my name. I looked over my shoulder and saw Shawn standing in an open door at the top of a flight of three steps. Shawn and I had explored the Kong Lo Caves together. I was beside myself and ran over to give him a big hug. When he saw I was with others, he invited us all in to say hi to Sage.

Jeremy, Jeff, Darin, and I marched inside and joined Shawn and Sage for dinner. The food was good but the company was even better. Sage would be flying back to the States to start school. Shawn and his brother would be continuing on to Burma after their time in Hanoi.

What a great reunion!

After eating, we all went over to the main street and sat in tiny blue and red chairs at an equally tiny table for beers and to just enjoy the view. Shawn and Sage only stayed for one drink because Sage had to get ready for an early flight, but we got a group photo before they left.

I spent the remainder of the evening enjoying myself with Jeremy and my new friends.

Chad showed up and I thought for sure he would stop to say hi, if not to me, at least to Jeremy. But no, he stopped and stared for a bit and then left.

Jeremy thought that was super weird. So did I. We had traveled together for a long time and I wondered, what was going on with him. I was completely puzzled.

I spilled my guts about how Chad and I had been best buds, then told him the whole Arizona story. Jeremy looked at me like I was a dunce or something and said, "He likes you but didn't have the guts to tell you that he was jealous about you hanging out with someone else."

Jaw dropper! How could I have been so oblivious? I assumed we were just homies. *Anyway,* I fumed to myself, *what a fucking baby. If you like someone, tell them. It's pretty easy. The person either feels the same way or they don't. It's not the end of the world. Ughh.*

Jeff mentioned he was heading to Sapa the following day and I decided that it was time for me to start a new chapter, so later that night I bought a bus ticket for the following evening with plans to meet Jeff.

Unfortunately, Jeremy couldn't join us. He had to go home to Virginia. I was glad that he'd had a day's layover in Hanoi before his flight. Talk about a meant-to-see-each-other scene. What are the odds?

I had been in Vietnam for *one* day and we'd met up. I gave him the biggest hug—as if I'd never see him again. We promised to keep in touch, then he was off. I turned my attention to my two new friends, and we enjoyed the rest of the evening.

Around 9 a.m. I packed and had an intentionally short shower. No flood this time. After checking out of the hostel, they let me store my bags there while I explored the town before I had to leave.

Soon, I met up with Gloria. She filled me in on her love life and her newly formed travel posse—five attractive men—two from Australia, one from Ireland, another from England, and one from Spain. She showed me a photo of her special guy—the tallest of the bunch—and gorgeous with dark hair, hazel eyes, and muscles that could have challenged "The Rock."

We ate lunch at Tho. I ordered a vegetable soup pho and beer. We picked this restaurant just so we could sit in the air conditioning and, fortunately, the food turned out to be delicious as well. I filled Gloria in on the Chad drama. She was shocked and thought that was a strange and messed up thing for him to do.

I agreed.

Sweating profusely, we strolled around the city. I was wearing white and orange shorts and a turquoise Bintang tank top. Gloria was wearing a Chang Mai cut-off tee with elephant pants. Comfy, but honestly, anything but buck-naked was too hot.

Women and men stood outside their shops hawking at us to come in, each shouting that they had the best prices. There was something special about shopping in local markets or street-side vendors. I was really enjoying the atmosphere and hoping

I would find something I liked. It had been at least six months since I'd bought anything new to wear and I was so tired of all my clothes. I didn't want to buy too much, though because that would mean I'd have to carry it on my travels. My bag was already 23kg and exceeding that weight limit would get very expensive.

After we shopped ourselves into a near coma, we walked through the bustling Old Quarter to Gloria's hostel. Upstairs in her dorm I was greeted with hugs and cheek kisses from her travel buds. The smile on my face was so big my cheeks hurt. The room had eight single beds all occupied. Two of the people not with her group weren't in the room.

I liked the cream-colored walls of the triangular-shaped room with a large bay window that opened onto a balcony facing the busy street. It was a great people-watching spot.

Gloria's friends had a thousand questions for me. I introduced myself as Mat Backwards. Of course, as there often was, one person had trouble spelling M-A-T backwards, and his mates made fun of him.

I answered all their questions—California...San Diego...I've been traveling for six months...very single...not sure when I'm going home...not sure where I'm off to next.

Danny, from Ireland, asked me to join the group but I politely declined since I already had plans to meet Jeff in Sapa in the morning. He said they were heading that way in a few days and suggested I join them there.

He told me he wouldn't take no for an answer, so I said *Nein*.

He laughed and asked, "Can I at least have a maybe?"

I said, "Yes."

Then he said. "Ha! You said yes."

Then I said, "No, I said yes to maybe."

We all had a great laugh at our word roulette then played a couple of games of Rummy before it was time for them to head to the bus stop for their trip North.

I walked with them and carried one of Gloria's bags. We

hugged and promised to keep in touch.

Danny, as expected, came over for his hug and said, "See you in a few days."

I just shook my head, smiled, and said, "Maybe!"

After their send-off I walked back to my hostel to check email. Since I hadn't heard from Chad, and his actions the night before were so weird, I decided to be the bigger person. I'd sent him a message earlier that day that read:

> "Hey Chad, I am heading to Sapa tonight, I had a great time traveling with you, I didn't anticipate our travel together ending so abruptly. It seemed to me that you were having a great time as well.
>
> I'm not sure what happened, but I'm sorry for hurting your feelings, or whatever it was I did to make you so annoyed with me.
>
> My bus is scheduled to leave at 8:30 tonight and I wanted to say goodbye. Do you want to meet up before I leave?"

I was surprised to see that he'd answered.

> Really? Yes, I'll meet up with you before your bus leaves. I'll message you when I return to my hostel.

I replied, "OK," and thought about his message. Weird that he asked, "Really?" Like he wasn't surprised that I wasn't going to travel with him anymore.

He's something else. I walked over to the banh mi sandwich place that Chad and I had eaten at the first night, and bought two sandwiches—one for now and one to go. I stopped at a small corner shop on my way back to Blah Blah and picked up some other goodies for the ride.

As I entered the lobby, my phone automatically connected to the Wi-Fi and a message from Chad popped up. It read,

"Hey. I'm not going to make it back in time to see you off. Sorry. Safe Travels."

What an asshole! His dismissive message upset me, but by the time I boarded the bus, all was forgotten. I focused on my new adventure. I figured I'd run into him again at some point. Then, maybe we could be friends again.

ESCAPADE 81:

ESCAPE AND

A SMELLY BUS RIDE FROM HELL

The night bus had bed-like seats and the aisles were lined with blue party-lights. All the seats had numbers, but in my previous experience, they didn't count for anything. I picked a seat that wasn't directly under a light and with no A.C. blowing on me then stowed my small bag between me and the window and settled in.

After about an hour the driver walked around checking tickets and, to my surprise, seat numbers. I pretended to be asleep so I wouldn't have to move.

After about two hours we picked up more guests and the driver called me out on my "pretend asleep." He said I had to go to my assigned seat. Of course, it turned out to be the worst possible location—between two questionable-looking guys. There was no way in hell I was sleeping there. I looked at the bus driver and pointed out the situation.

He nodded in agreement and found me a new spot. I thought that was the end of it, but no. The arrivals on the bus were a smelly bunch. Someone had a rotten cheese stench radiating from his feet. It made me want to vomit.

The ride was long, bumpy, and near torturous. I didn't get much sleep. Just after midnight, and against my better judgment, I walked barefoot to the water closet. When I opened the door, the tiny room looked like a set from the *Texas Chainsaw Massacre*. Black mold covered the walls. The green-colored toilet sloshed with a continuous flow of water splashing out of the bowl and onto the floor. Black grates covered a dirty, sandy-colored slab underneath.

There was no way I was walking in there without shoes, so I went back to my seat to get them. I even thought twice about attempting to use the bathroom, but I still had a six-hour ride so there was no other option. I held my breath, trying not to touch anything while doing my business and hoped I wouldn't contract some rare tropical disease.

At 6 a.m. we finally arrived at Sapa. I gladly left the bus from hell. It was still dark, and the town was quiet. After asking a few taxi drivers for directions to the Green Inn, I discovered it wasn't far, so I decided to walk.

Sapa is in the mountains, so the temperature was just right. The smell of pine trees and the crisp air kissing my face was such a relief. I was tired of the hot, sticky climate that covered most of Southeast Asia.

When I arrived at the Inn, I booked a room for that night and asked if I could sleep on the couch until Jeff found me.

The Inn was a large log cabin with a big fireplace, a restaurant, and a good library. The dark-green couch had some white symbols or images on it that I couldn't make out. It sat in front of a large window facing the main street and overlooked the hillside below. I remember staring hard trying to determine what the images were but eventually drifted off to sleep.

"Tam," a voice softly whispered. I rolled over, squinting and feeling slightly disoriented. When I realized it was Jeff, I smiled and asked him if it took a while to wake me up because I was a pretty heavy sleeper.

He said it didn't and introduced me to Tessa. Jeff and Tessa met during their travels and just kept bumping into each other, something that extended travelers in that part of the world often do.

We grabbed a bite to eat at the Inn restaurant. I ordered my usual, fried eggs, a roll, and a coffee. During our breakfast, Jeff saw two others he'd met months ago in Thailand, Sarah and Doug. It's such a small world, but in Southeast Asia, it's even smaller.

Hazard 82:

Lost in Paradise

Jeff, Tessa, and I hiked all over the place even down to a tiny village, dwarfed by the famous mountain, Fansipan—the highest peak in Indochina. The mountain takes two or three days to hike and is over 10,000 feet high. At its summit, there's a metal pyramid installed by the Soviets to commemorate the defeat of Nazi Germany.

The 80°F temperature was comfortably dry and filled with a lovely breeze. The trail we followed took us deep into a lush, green valley where the sounds of town vanished and, except for our footsteps, silence was the main event.

The deeper we went, the cooler the temperature became and the more the canopy engulfed us. At that point, I didn't know we were lost but I was aware that we'd gone off the beaten path.

Jeff led the way and Tessa and I followed the ever-dwindling path until there was nothing but tall grass and a crumbling mountain range that loomed before us. I got the feeling that none of us wanted to turn around and head back, so we pushed on.

For hours, we walked and climbed, only occasionally glancing back to catch a glimpse of the road less traveled and the beauty that encompassed it. The rocky way wasn't as steep as our initial ascent tricked us into believing. The decomposed granite made our footing a little uneven, and as we rose out of the valley up through the canopy the temperature began to rise. My shirt became soaked with sweat where my backpack pressed against my skin.

When we reached a large outcrop, everyone agreed it was a great time to stop for lunch. We sat, saying little and enjoyed the spectacular view as we ate rolls and fruit.

The incessant honking and yelling and stinky streets had taken its toll on my senses, so the fragrance of trees and dirt and the sound of whispering wind was a treat. I laid down, resting my head on my pack and soaked in the wonderfulness of it all.

My watch beeped. When I looked at it, I realized two hours had passed. I'd been asleep. Jeff and Tessa had also dozed off. Jeff was stretched out on his back, hat covering his face, hands on his stomach. Tessa was curled up in a ball with her curly long hair mopping the smooth, rocky surface. It would have been so nice to camp there but we only brought day packs and it would get extremely cold at night.

After a few minutes, I woke them up and we continued the path of least resistance that eventually led us to rice terraces—a good sign we were heading into a village or small town. The emerald terraces were magnificent. In my travels, every time I saw them, I was amazed by their beauty and age. We walked across the ledges of the terraces as if on a tight rope, quietly concentrating on not falling off.

There wasn't another soul in sight, but we could smell smoke billowing from a small house in the distance and headed there to ask for directions. We knocked on the door, but no one was home, so we turned away and followed a nearby faint trail that eventually led us into town just as the sun began to set.

What a perfect ending to an unplanned day.

Later, we met up with Doug and Sarah for dinner and they told us about a "homestay" they went on and how amazing it was. It sounded like fun, so Jeff called and set it up for the next day. We enjoyed a few beers at a local restaurant then came back to our hostel, hung out by the fire, and played games.

I stepped outside for a bit. The cold, crisp air was so delicious. I gazed into the sky and stared, all dreamy-eyed, at the amazing, brilliant stars.

Jeff came out to tell me the next game was about to start.

I told him to look up.

He did and was just as mesmerized as I was.

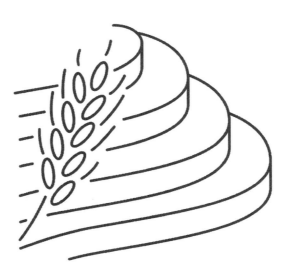

Escapade 83:

Homestay with Momma G

The next morning, I packed my large bag and added some extras to my day pack for our homestay then stowed it in the hostel storage room. I joined the others for breakfast then we headed into the town center to explore and shop while waiting for our host "mom" to meet us.

The morning was cool, and few people were out and about. A couple of little girls were selling bracelets, but mostly the town was quiet.

Our host mom showed up, introduced herself as Momma G and gave us each a lanyard for our wrists that she'd made using the colors of her village.

Our journey would take approximately seven to eight hours of hiking. We were all more than up for it.

The trek started downhill. We passed by our hostel/inn and the road we'd taken the day before then continued left along the paved, curved street. The road eventually leveled and transitioned into dirt.

As we began the uphill hike, we reached a farm. It wasn't like any I'd ever seen. The crops were planted on the hillside. I found it fascinating. I'd always thought of farmland as flat. I saw cabbage, potatoes, onions, spinach, and all kinds of other plants growing there.

We took lots of pictures and got to know Momma G.

As we continued, the path grew narrower and steeper. Large green trees blanketed the lower hillside. Long grasses dotted with boulders covered the upper hillside.

When we approached the next village, five tiny girls selling bracelets greeted us. They kept repeating in unison, "Do you want to buy one from me? Do you want to buy one from me?" in the sweetest monotoned voices. This reminded me of the seagulls repeating "Mine" in the film *Finding Nemo*. They were so cute, but we resisted the urge to buy their bracelets and traveled on.

Shortly, the road narrowed, a sure sign that we were heading into open country again. Up the mountain we went, trading off trail partners every so often when one of us had to tie a shoe, capture a moment with a camera, scale the cliff for a bathroom spot, or simply take a rest.

The four of us got to know each other as we tried to keep up with Momma G. She walked this trail often and was in great shape. I was convinced she could go a lot faster by herself. Us rookies slowed her down.

The next village had puppies running around. I was delighted. All it takes to distract me from anything I'm doing is to show me a puppy. I suspect that's probably true for most people. We stopped and played with them for a while.

I followed one down a small path less than a foot wide. The puppy led me to a little wooden shack with a locked door then stuck its head underneath. I peeked in through a crevice between the wood and saw about ten pigs. On the other side of the structure there was a door held slightly ajar by the corner of a wagon. Seconds later, a man appeared. The puppy started whimpering and the pigs started to get riled up.

The man grabbed one pig, tied it up, or I guess I should say hogtied it, and loaded it into the wagon. The pig squealed bloody murder then the door slammed and was locked. The sound of squealing grew fainter as the truck moved farther away from us toward what I'm assuming was the butcher.

I picked up the little puppy who was clearly distraught by the whole thing, walked back to the others, and dropped him off with his siblings. As we started up the mountain, a few puppies followed us but as we moved on, they lost interest and headed back to their village.

After that, our hike was peaceful. At times we all fell silent and just enjoyed the view.

I was glad when we arrived at Momma G's two-level house. This was going to be a fun experience.

She brought us in through the kitchen door and I noted that her home had wooden walls, a bamboo roof, and a dirt floor. There was a firepit to our left and a small table to our right. A larger table and chairs stood in the adjacent room. Leaving our packs in the kitchen, we sat at the large table and opened the beers we'd bought at a local market about a quarter of a mile from the house.

I relaxed and glanced around then spotted a ladder in the corner that led to the second floor where we would be sleeping for the night. I really liked how the loft bedroom had a view into the kitchen/living area. Moments later, we were greeted by Sun—a medium-sized, yellow dog who showed us great affection and just hung out with us for a bit.

When Momma G began making dinner, we asked if we could help. She politely said no, so we drank our beers and played rummy, enjoying each other's company. When dinner was ready the three of us were super hungry and practically inhaled the soup.

A short time later Momma G's husband came home from

tending the farm and assisting his neighbors with a new construction project for repairing the roofs of all the village houses. He was kind and spoke very good English.

He explained that after working on the village roofs, he tends his own farm. He said his son usually helps with the work but was currently just hanging with his friends. He sounded like a typical teenager, to me.

The three of us volunteered to help him with the farm work the next day. He accepted our offer and said it would be an early day, starting about 4 a.m. The work would be strenuous, but he could use the help.

We were definitely in.

After dinner, we played a few more card games before climbing the ladder. It almost felt like we would be sleeping in a treehouse. Our beds were on the floor and padded with thick blankets for cushioning and a wool blanket for cover.

I was warm enough and comfortable. Of course, though, after I got all snuggled into my bed, I had to use the bathroom. Reluctantly, I climbed down and headed to the outhouse. It was a creepy little shack with a hole in the ground and spider webs everywhere. *Sigh!*

The next morning Momma G. woke us up for a breakfast of fried eggs, papaya, bread, and coffee or tea. Papa G greeted us after our meal, gave us gloves and baskets, and told us we were on weed duty.

I laughed to myself then looked at Jeff and asked if we would be trimming marijuana.

He looked at me with wide eyes and asked, "You really think so?"

I smiled and shook my head as we followed Papa G into the field and got to work—on real field weeds.

After a few days of homestay in the small village, Momma G walked us back to town and thanked us for our visit.

We gave her a large tip, thanked her for her hospitality, and said we would be recommending her to any friends interested in a homestay.

It felt good to be back in Sapa. That small mountain town, though remote and quiet, had some big city perks, like running water and Wi-Fi.

We were all hungry after our long trek, so we cleaned up and met with Doug, Sarah, and Darin, from Australia, for dinner.

From there we would all go our separate ways. Doug and Sarah were heading to Taiwan. Darin had just arrived in Sapa, so he wanted to check it out a little longer and hike Fansipan. Jeff and I were on the night bus that evening back to Hanoi.

Hazard 84:

Drunk Driver and

Gross-Out Food

I don't understand how the bus schedules in Asia can be so inaccurate. I was supposed to arrive back in Hanoi around 6 a.m. but we arrived just before 2 a.m.

The bus station had two taxis waiting to take people to their destinations. I was approached by a driver who offered to take me to my hostel. We agreed on a price and he loaded my bag into the white cab.

One of the girls on the bus came up to me, introduced herself as Victoria, and told me that the taxi driver was drunk. Earlier, she had seen him drive over the curb and stumble out of his cab. She invited me to walk into town with her and some of the other bus passengers.

Victoria was my guardian angel in the flesh. She distracted my would-be driver while I snuck my bag from the trunk. He saw me snatch it and asked where I was going.

Victoria scolded with, "You're drunk and shouldn't be driving people around. This girl is no longer riding with you."

Victoria, me, and four other girls all walked to town. We split up when we neared our hostels. I forgot where mine was and searched for what seemed like forever. Later I realized that I'd passed it several times but didn't recognize it because the hostel was closed up by big warehouse metal doors. *Ughhhh!* Fortunately, the night watchman let me in.

The next day I met up with Jeff, toured the French Quarter, and went on a coffee crawl. Jeff was a coffee fanatic and knew that Vietnam had some of the world's best beans. So, we went to five of the top coffee shops discussed in the *Lonely Planet*. Boy, were we all excited.

My favorite place was the Labyrinth Coffee House. It has secret rooms and beautiful exotic plants everywhere. We wandered through the place trying to unlock the clues to get us through a secret passage that led to a rooftop sitting area. It took a while, but we made it.

We sat there enjoying our coffee yogurt, which was delicious. Who would have thought that yogurt and coffee made such a tasty combination?

For lunch we headed back to the French Quarter. While there we walked the alleys, passed by yummy smelling street carts, and even visited the opera house. As we came to a typical food cart, Jeff noticed something strange and did a double take. Instead of seeing a roasted pig on a stick, it was a roasted dog—tail and all.

We were shocked. I knew they ate dog in this part of Asia, but I'd never actually seen one cooking. I was so grossed out. I see dogs as pets, not food. I was even more disgusted when I learned that the dogs are beaten to death. Suddenly the gloss had worn off of the fun afternoon. I had to put those images out of my mind and move on. I was no crusader and couldn't really do anything to change their traditions.

Feeling better, I focused on enjoying the French Quarter. One of the most memorable events I witnessed were the fire drills. Jeff and I watched as a hotel manager set a fire outside the hotel and showed his employees how to put it out. There were flammable objects everywhere, the building itself, trees, plants, and shrubs. He kept repeating this and allowed everyone to practice putting the fire out.

We continued exploring, immersing ourselves in the city. Soon we smelled a heavenly scent and followed it to a narrow side street. It led us to a tiny restaurant, filled with locals. Luckily, we found the last open table and squeezed in.

The guy next to us was eating pho with seafood. It looked amazing, so when the server arrived, we both pointed to his dish.

We were not disappointed. The food was heavenly.

After lunch we got lost in the city. Wandering around, we found a park. The entry fee was only 5 Vietnamese Dong, about $.0002 US.

The park is massive, with lots of eucalyptus trees towering over various playing fields. School kids played badminton in their orange and tan uniforms. Young people performed skateboard tricks off the steps. Older men exercised on the stationary equipment. The park is well manicured and filled with activity. We stopped and watched a soccer match but were more entertained by elderly men playing badminton with their feet. They invited us to join them, but it was more fun watching them show off their skills.

Finally, Jeff and I walked back to the Old Quarter in the dark and said our goodbyes because he was heading to the states.

The next day Darin and I gathered our belongings and took a bus to Cat Ba. It was a beautiful and thankfully, short bus ride. We exited at the town square and left our bags on a nearby bench while we ran to the bay to take in the view.

The karsts that littered the bay were breathtaking. Karsts are land formations formed when softer rock, like limestone, or gypsum, dissolves from wind and rain and leaves harder stone untouched. It was like looking at a modern art sculpture. That and the partly cloudy sky created an eerie, alien-like reflection on the water. In the square, Vietnamese flags blew in the winds atop 25-foot posts.

After our mini exploration of the town square, we retrieved our bags and started the search for a place to sleep. We took the first left and followed the road up the hill, looking for a hostel.

When our way turned rural, we went right at the next intersection but still had no luck. We were beginning to think we wouldn't find a place to stay that night but shortly after, we found two on the same street. Darin checked one and I checked the other.

The place I investigated, the Made House hostel, was cheaper, so we stayed there. We settled in then walked around town all afternoon, enjoying a nearby beach and the cool water on the hot humid day. An occasional boat sailed by and reminded me that I'd heard Halong Bay cruises were great. I suggested we book one and everyone agreed.

Later, after showering, we walked to a three-level bar called the Cathouse. The food was typical bar fare, so I ordered fries and wings and a Vietnamese beer.

We chatted with some of the backpackers and played a few games of pool. Some people were going on a Halong Bay cruise and they gave us the information on how to sign up.

When we were back at the Made House, we inquired about the cruise and Darin and I signed up.

ESCAPADE 85:

CRUISE HALONG BAY

The next morning, we followed instructions to go to the dock and wait for Jim. As we walked, I started thinking the directions they gave us were a bit shady.

It reminded me that this kind of strange direction-giving was common in Asia. Sometimes they were outright weird, like:

"Walk down the nameless street until you reach a blue trashcan. Turn right at the blue trashcan and go down the dirty, dog-ridden street. Once you get to the dead end, go into the dilapidated building and your guide will meet you there."

Those kinds of directions sound like a set-up where Michael Myers would be waiting for me with his mask and knife.

But the crazy part was, I had followed several of those weird directions during my travels and all ended well.

Our directions to the Bay Cruise were equally odd but we found it. Jim showed up and took us to a large houseboat and told us to get comfy while he went to fetch the other guests. Jim soon returned with ten more people. His assistant loaded the boat with food and booze and we set sail. As we left the dock behind, the trash-filled water became clean and clear.

Darin befriended two guys from Scotland, Ainsley and Bruce. They were a ton of fun and enjoying Vietnam for a two-week work break.

The pointed limestone pillars covered in lush green plants made it look like we were cruising through a fairyland. I gazed at the surroundings and was overwhelmed by its beauty. Our wooden boat dodged in and out of the rock formations, some as tall as me, and others barely peeking up out of the water.

Captain Jim found a nice cove for us to anchor.

After lunch, we jumped into the water. Before I leapt off the top of the wheelhouse, I told a woman that I was excited to be in salt water again because I was more buoyant in it and could float a lot easier than in freshwater. I dove in and joined Ainsley and Bruce, who were snorkeling by a nearby arch.

As we watched the tropical fish and jellies suspended in the photic zone, our idyllic moment was interrupted by screams coming from near the boat. A woman shouted while frantically slapping her arms as if she was drowning.

We were far out but swam to her as fast as we could. Fortunately, before we even made it halfway, Jim jumped in from the deck and rescued her. I felt responsible because I had told her how thrilled I was to float easier in the salt water. I think she took it literally and thought she could do it without knowing how to swim. I was really glad she was okay.

After we all boarded again, Jim took us to a few scenic spots—some with limestone pillars, others with caves.

Close to sunset, we arrived at a group of tiny, uninhabited islands that looked heavenly and serene in the setting sun. Darin, Ainsley, Bruce and I sat on top of the wheelhouse and enjoyed the amazing view.

Escapade 86:

Motorbike Ride through Jurassic Park

I mentioned to Darin that I couldn't ride a motorbike, so he was hell-bent on teaching me how. We had planned to take a ride through the jungle and find a well-marked hiking trail. It had to be well marked so we wouldn't run the risk of being blown up by unexploded ordinances.

Darin picked up the scooter and I had the directions, so we headed into the jungle. When we were out of the city limits, he pulled over and told me to get off. He secured the bike then climbed off and gave me an instructional tour of the bike, showing me the brakes, the gas, and how to start the scooter. Then he stepped back and said, "Give it a try."

A nervous wreck, I straddled the seat, turned the key, then unintentionally sped off lightning fast. It scared me half to death. My heart raced and I could hear it pounding in my chest. As I got used to the gas handle, I calmed down a bit and slowed to a comfortable speed. I circled back to where Darin was watching me.

When I came to a stop, he climbed onto the seat behind and let me lead the tour. I thought the jungle was beautiful with its tall, thick trees surrounding us. It reminded me of the setting for the movie *Jurassic Park.*

As we continued along the road, I felt more comfortable and sped up until the trees became a green blur. Our first stop was a small, marked cave we thought was worth checking out. Nice, but not spectacular.

The next stop was when we reached water too deep for the motorbike. We looked for a bridge or another way across, but it was only by ferry and the next one wasn't due for two hours. With no other option but to wait, we had lunch in a local restaurant. I ordered a banh mi and water.

After lunch, we headed back through the jungle and stopped at the Cat Ba Hospital Cave. Darin parked the bike and we paid 40,000 dong ($1.75 US) and entered. The cave served as a secret hospital that had been hidden from the Vietcong leaders and the explosives during the American-Vietnamese War. It was built in 1963 by the Vietnamese with assistance from China and never discovered by the Americans.

This natural cave had been converted into seventeen rooms and wards. The limestone walls were covered with block walls, so it looks more like a prison now. The top floor still has remnants of the natural cave. Looking at the ceiling under the dim lighting I saw rock formations and eroding limestone. The history alone made that place worth seeing.

After we arrived back in Cat Ba, Darin turned in the bike and we walked to the beach. It was so nice we decided that the next day would be strictly beach.

Rising early, we headed to the sand. The beach we'd visited the day before was just below a resort. As the first ones to arrive, we took advantage of having the place all to ourselves and picked the best towel spot then frolicked in the water.

We swam for about an hour until the sky grew cloudy and buckets of rain poured from the sky. We scrambled to the sand, grabbed our belongings, and dashed to shelter on the resort patio where we watched as the storm grew progressively worse. The waves became massive and started pounding the wall we were sitting above. Rain splashed on us, but the spectacular show was worth it. When lightning stabbed into the water a few times, parts of the resort lost power. It was mind-blowing!

Hungry, we went inside. The lunch buffet was ready, so we filled our plates then went back to the patio to witness more of the incredible acts of Mother Nature.

When the rain finally let up, we hoofed it down to the beach to check out a horseshoe crab that had been washed onto shore. We poked at it but when it didn't move, Darin pushed it back into the sea.

We thought the break in the storm might be our only opportunity to get back to our hostel without being soaked, so we grabbed our belongings and walked back, dodging the massive puddles the storm had left behind. At Made House hostel we packed and waited for the bus bound for Dong Hoi.

Escapade 87:

Like an Old Western Movie

On the bus to Dong Hoi Darin and I talked about how we were looking forward to visiting the Phong Nha caves and the Phong Nha Ke Bang National Park.

When we arrived we stayed in Son Trach village. It felt like stepping into an old western movie. The shining sun illuminated all the dust particles on the dirt road. Few people were out because of the extreme heat and the wooden buildings were age-worn.

Our hostel turned out to be an old mansion converted into the perfect living space. I checked in and was taken on a tour around the grounds. The house is a colonial style home with beautiful big shutters and a spiral staircase.

This house has five levels. My dorm was on the second floor—four beds, two bunk beds, and a bathroom shared with the room next door. There is a pool in back and a bar/restaurant attached. The common area is huge and has several couches, a cabinet full of board games, beer pong, and a pool table. This place is a backpacker's dream and I was happy to be staying there for the next few days.

After we settled in, Darin and I headed for the common room where we met Paul and Edward, from Canada to talk about where to eat. In the end we decided to just go out and find something that looked good.

Without a definite plan we walked down the street and found an unnamed place that looked interesting. I ordered beef pho. It was tasty but not as good as the place that Jeff and I had eaten at in Hanoi's French Quarter.

Paul and Edward asked if we wanted to rent motorbikes and ride out to the Phong Nha caves. We accepted the invitation and decided to head out first thing in the morning.

Escapade 88:

The Most Remarkable Caves in the World.

Darin, Paul, Edward, and I parked our bikes and hopped on the ferry heading to the Paradise Caves. The sun was blazing so it felt nice to be on the water and I was stoked to be visiting one of the most beautiful caves in the world.

Inside, the inky-darkness made walking a little difficult, so we carefully followed the boardwalk with wooden railings. Soon the darkness was punctuated by glistening stalagmites.

The walls looked like melted candle wax oozing toward the ground. This cave is huge, and I thought the ceiling looked like it rose deep into space.

The air was cool and grew even cooler the deeper we went. After about twenty minutes we reached a dead end. The walls in this alcove are like sunshine reflecting off of a cracked mirror. Blue, purple, and gray hues cover the cave, giving it a tranquil feeling.

We took a group photo then hiked back to the entrance and to the ferry that took us to the car park. We rode our motorbikes to some nearby smaller caves and explored them until the sun set behind the trees.

When we arrived back in the small town, it was a lot livelier than it had been earlier. I really liked this place. It was simple and nestled amongst a massive ancient green rock garden of karst outcrops and pillars. I stood on the roof and gazed up at the stars, lost in their spectacular beauty.

Escapade 89:

Something Special in the Dark Cave.... and Goodbye.

In the morning, we loaded our bikes and made our way into Phong Nha National Park to visit the infamous Dark Cave. It's an obvious name for a cave but it was reputed to be incredible.

Our group of twelve was more than ready for a day of exploring. We drove out of town and into another jungle that resembled *Jurassic Park*.

The road meandered around giant karsts and cut through a large canopy. We passed small creeks with quick-running water and enjoyed the birds that filled the sky.

Without warning, Darin pulled over. The rest of us followed, thinking something was wrong. But it was something right, instead. He'd spotted a small lake and thought it would be good to jump in and cool off.

We all agreed it was a fantastic idea and took off our helmets, locked up our bikes, and hiked down the rugged hillside through the dense vegetation to the edge of the lake. We left our belongings on a massive boulder outcrop and jumped in.

Minnows swam alongside larger fish in the crystal-clear water. The minnows congregated around my legs and nibbled on my skin. It tickled so I wriggled them off.

I reminded everyone not to pee in the water because I'd read about a parasite that can swim up the urethra and attach itself inside with razor-sharp teeth, causing great pain. Dahlia from Germany thanked me for that reminder.

We stayed a while enjoying the cool water then laid on the rocks and dried off before continuing through the jungle toward the cave.

By the time we arrived, we were all hungry and ate at the only restaurant around before going to Dark Cave. From there, we had a great view of other visitors ziplining across a beautiful, turquoise lake to the limestone mountain and the entrance to Dark Cave.

After we were done eating, we put our belongings in a locker and waited for our guide to take us to the zipline.

When it was my turn to zip, I ran, jumped off the platform, and zoomed across the pristine water heading to the green shrubs at the base of the mountain. At the end, I let go and dropped into the water, screaming from the sheer joy of it all until the ice-cold water shocked me. I swam up to the surface as fast as I could. I had expected the lake to be warm because the air was. Surprise!

After everyone reached the other side, the guide gave us all headlamps and we began our journey inside the cave. It was pitch dark. No natural light penetrated the inside. Some of the caves I'd previously visited had fractures in the ceilings, which let in light.

The dark cave's beauty was different from any of the others I'd visited. We entered chamber after chamber that had toe-deep, thick mud. The final chamber was full of deep, thick mud.

The guide pushed Darin into the mud pool and he just floated on top. It was so buoyant, you could take a nap on top of it and not sink.

This was remarkable, so we all jumped in and played. We even had a mud fight. I hadn't realized that mud could be so buoyant. The guide told us that it was good for the skin and had healing properties.

We stayed here for a while tossing mud at each other and floating and laughing. It was almost like quicksand except you floated instead of sank.

When we'd had enough of mud play, we backtracked out. Just outside the entrance our guide took photos of us covered in the thick, smooth, gray mud and looking like we'd just walked off the set of a scary movie.

We followed the jagged rocks to the lake's edge, jumped in to rinse off, then climbed into kayaks moored on the rocks and paddled across the lake to the start of the zipline.

Securing the kayaks to the docks, we headed to the smaller zipline that ran straight across the lake toward the mountain. This was only a third of the distance the large zipline covered by spanning diagonally across the lake to Dark Cave entrance.

Everyone lined up on the wooden steps that curved around a treehouse and waited for our turn to sprint through the air and do a sort of trick or flip before slamming into the brisk water. Some swam around and played on the floating lake-toys and others continued jumping off the zipline.

It was a great afternoon.

We dried off, gathered our belongings then headed toward town, stopping in a beautiful meadow to watch the sunset. The sun morphed into pinks and purples as it slowly subsided below the green rolling hills.

Back at the hostel we joined other backpackers in the pool. We swam and relaxed. The pool was refreshing but also seemed to have a more pungent chlorine smell than usual. When I exited after being in for a while, I was surprised that my purple, sparkly-heart two-piece swimsuit was now a dull white color. There was way too much chlorine in there and I immediately went to shower.

Later, I rejoined my pals and played a round of trivia, followed by a few games of Irish Snap, then made plans to go exploring neighboring towns and cities the next day.

I was exhausted and went to bed earlier than the others. I left my cards, though, for those who were still playing Irish Snap. They said they'd return them to me in the morning.

Refreshed after a good night's sleep, I hopped out of bed, showered, readied my things, and headed down the wide spiral staircase for the free breakfast. I ordered my usual—two fried eggs, fruit, toast, and a cup of coffee.

Sitting down with Paul and Jeff, I asked them where the cards had gone. They didn't have a clue but agreed to help me locate them.

I'd carried those cards around for almost five months. They'd been to so many countries, and I'd made so many friends while using them, I didn't want to lose them. Sadly, though, they were never found.

I'd been in this town a little less than a week before deciding to join Paul, Jeff, Dahlia, and Darin on an unplanned journey.

We caught a local bus heading south to see where it would take us. Hours later, we ended up in a little town where no one spoke English. We got around by pointing at pictures and making hand gestures. Pretty effective, too. We managed to find a hostel which had just opened a week before. It was right on the beach—prime real estate for only $8 US per night. When I walked out of the dorm, all I saw was the big blue ocean.

I was happy to learn that the hostel had a beach bar that served dinner. There was relaxing music, foozeball, and a variety of other games. Beanbag chairs and couches were scattered about for lounging and enjoying the view. But the best part was that locals would come and hang out with us. It was great.

On our first night there we swam in the ocean and admired the bioluminescent plankton. With little light pollution, the stars were brilliant. I was in a tiny town on a big beach with nothing surrounding it.

We swam for what seemed like hours in the warm ocean. This was the closest to heaven I could get.

The next morning, we borrowed the hostel bicycles and traveled to the war caves. Afterward, we shopped at a market where fresh fruits, veggies, and all sorts of yummy-looking spices and foods were being sold.

Around the corner from this market, we stopped to eat in a little restaurant. The place had a picture-menu—perfect for us. We ordered several types of meat and made our own spring rolls. We dipped the rice wrapper in water to soften it, then added mint leaves cilantro, meat, and veggies, rolled them up, and dipped them into a secret sauce. They were delicious. I don't remember how many we rolled up and ate, but we finished everything on our plates. That restaurant was so good, we vowed to go back before we continued south.

No one in the whole town spoke English—except the guy who ran the hostel.

There were no resorts or big buildings blocking the ocean view, making it a perfect place and a nice stop before my journey south to Hoi An for the Lantern Festival. There, the town turned off all the electric bulbs and signs and lit hundreds, if not thousands, of lanterns.

Before I left for Hoi An, I met Debra from the UK. She was just beginning her travels through SEA and asked for some tips. Since I was just wrapping up my journey, I took one last flip through my *Lonely Planet Guide* then gave it to her as a gift. I said, "I hope this helps you as much as it has helped me. Safe travels."

I finished gathering my things and went to the front desk to ask about the taxi they had ordered for me. Chen said it would be there in an hour. *An hour?* I told him, "I had scheduled it to arrive right now. I have to get to the airport for a flight."

Oliver, one of my dorm mates, overheard and said he would take me. Relieved, I thanked the hostel for a great time and left.

Oliver led me to his motorcycle. *What?* I looked at him like he was crazy. I had my fully-loaded, green backpack that was big enough to fit a four-year-old in and still had the statues I'd been carrying around for months. There was no way we were going to fit me and all my stuff on that bike.

Oliver said, "Have you been paying attention at all? Literally just yesterday, I watched a man driving a motorbike with a huge desk on it, so surely your backpack and statues can fit."

I thought a moment, and said, "Good point. I *have* seen the strangest most awkward objects being toted around on motorcycles." I was still not completely convinced, though. I knew that if I shifted my weight or lost my balance with the 23-kilo bag on my back I was a goner.

Oliver knew that too and said to hang on tight and to follow his lead—when he leaned I leaned.

I arrived in Hoi An without incident, looking forward to the Lantern Festival. When I discovered that the place was also famous for making high-quality custom clothing, I had three dresses and some sandals made especially for the festival.

I also hiked with two Canadians, met up with Paul and some friends, who had rented a six-level Airbnb, and played hide-n-seek.

I knew that the Lantern Festival was my last experience in Southeast Asia. It felt like it was time to say goodbye to this strange and wonderful land. I thought back on all the friends I'd made; all the caves, temples, tourist sites, bicycle rides, hikes, parks, beaches, and villages I'd experienced; the breathtaking sunsets, starry skies, and landscapes that filled my senses; villages, people, food, parties, karaoke, and booze buzzes all slipped into my mental photo album to be treasured forever, along with the mishaps, misunderstandings, crazy bus rides, tuk tuks, jeepneys, hazards, close-calls, and dangers.

It was time to leave—but not for home—not back to my normal life of job, family, friends, and routine. I was ready for a change, but not willing to give up my solo adventures. There was so much more world to explore. I'd been forging my own path for over six months—way longer than I'd originally planned, but the thought of going back home felt like a brick wall of "NO!"

I mused that *I might return to Asia someday, but I'd had enough for the time being.*

I'd tasted real freedom and wanted more.

Look For Tamara's Next Adventure—Europe!

....I wasn't going to let the rift with Chad spoil my Shangri-La. I was going to Spain. This was a now-or-never opportunity and I was living in the now. So, I bought a one-way ticket to Barcelona with my sky miles. The cost totaled a whopping $5.00 US. Thank you, Delta. I've always believed in kismet—when we are meant to do something, it has a way of working out. This felt like kismet in capital letters.

Remembering that the year before, my friend, Rocko had run with the bulls at the San Fermin Festival in Pamplona, I thought, *Now, that would be the adventure of a lifetime....*

Available soon on Amazon.com
Keep an eye out for the audiobook coming soon.

DIRECTORY OF RECOMMENDED BUSINESS
AND SERVICE PROVIDERS

John C. Lovio
Wildlife Biologist – Ecologist
4460 Cleveland Ave #4, San Diego, CA
619/990 6632
jlovio@cox.net

Saldana Fitness
Dan Saldana – NASM – Certified Personal Trainer
Online Coaching for a Busy Lifestyle
IG:@saldanaFitness
Saldanafitness.com
Saldana.fitness@gmail.com

Dapper Godz
Dexter E. Bryant II—Owner & CEO
Power Tie, Power Mind, Power Man
dexter@dappergodz.com
Instagram: DeBryantjr
Shop: Dappergodz.com
Stay Neat, Gentlemen

Jennifer Selinger
TV Host, Producer, Photographer, Documentary Filmmaker,
Inspirational Speaker, Travelpreneur, Joyologist
"What makes time stand still for you? Find your flow. These are your gifts. Share them with the rest of the world."
514/349 3020
Jenniferselinger.tv@gmail.com
IG: jenniferselinger/travelvisualjournalist
T: @jenadvisor
FB: travelvisualjournalist

Earth Hatz
Zeph Friedman-Sowder Aka..."Zman"
El Capitan@Earth Hatz
503/701 3833
Earthhatz.com
Earth Friendly & locally designed

Jessica Mose
Realtor DRE#01882433
m 858 736 5668
jessica.mose@compass.com
San Diego, CA

AAT – All About Technology
A Service Based Computer Company
Dexter E Bryant
Technician Specialist
E-Waste – Commercial Pickup Starting at $55—Neighborhood Pickup
discount starting at $30
Computer Onsite services: Free Diagnostics—Computer repair &
upgrades
Setup new installations/Maintenance
Data transfer/Media transfer (VHS to Digital)
E-Waste pickup
626/351 3227 – office
626/390 2118 – mobile
Debryant4@yahoo.com

Jonathan Schlossberg
Co-founder- GUUD Marketing
480/999 4911
jonathan@whatsguud.co
whatsguud.co

Polished by Sparkle
Sparkle
Health/Beauty Licensed cosmetologist
Polished by Sparkle
Text or email for appointment
323/514 9695
polishedbysparkle@gmail.com
Instagram: PolishedbySparkle

Work Realty Advisors
Nicholas Alvarez Wing
Broker – CALDRE# 01950605
909/908 5859
nick@workrea.com
workrea.com
Pasadena, CA

Mic Reed
Inspire – Motivate – Create
818/921 0818
mickiraproductions@gmail.com
Instagram: 1NELifeOfficial

Zachary Hughes
V.P. Business Development
Mocentric - Mobile Evolved
zac@mocentric.com
866/756 8975 x703
bit.ly/ZacHughes@mocentric

Komodo Biological Services, LLC
Chris Taylor Wildlife Biologist
Owner/Independent Consultant
952/607-7824
KomodoBiological@gmail.com

Oceanside Candle Company
Suzanne & Taylor Carr
760/994 9041
oceansidecandlecompany.com
etsy.com/shop/oceansidecandleco
oceansidecandlecompany@gmail.com
IG: oceansidecandlecompany
FB: oceansidecandleco
T: osidecandleco

Lulu's Cookie Bar
"You Crave It, We Bake It"
Luluscookiebar@gmail.com
Luluscookiebar.com

Made in the USA
Las Vegas, NV
13 August 2021